AN ICE AXE, A CAMERA, AND A JAR OF PEANUT BUTTER

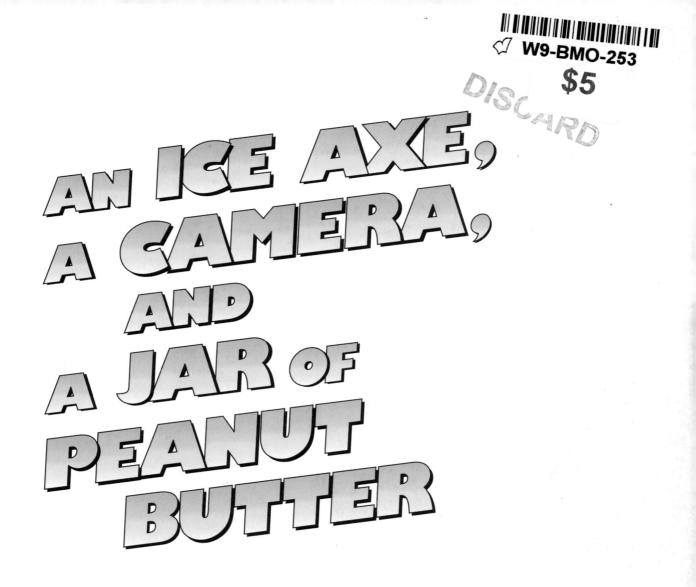

Ira Spring

A Photographer's Autobiography

THE
MOUNTAINEERS

Published by
The Mountaineers
1001 SW Klickitat Way, Suite 201
Seattle, WA 98134

First edition, 1998

Published simultaneously in Great Britain by Cordee, 3a DeMontfort Street, Leicester, England, LE1 7HD

Manufactured in the United States of America

Edited by Christine Clifton-Thornton
All photographs by Ira Spring
Cover design by Jennifer Shontz
Layout by Marge Mueller/Gray Mouse Graphics

Cover photographs: *Cowlitz Glacier, Mount Rainier Washington* by Bob and Ira Spring. *Peanut butter sandwich* by Tom Kirkendall
Frontispiece: *Air view of Scimitar Glacier on 13,177 foot Mount Waddington, highest peak in British Columbia. When first discovered in the 1920s, it was called "Mystery Mountain." This photograph was taken on an assignment illustrating glaciers for a textbook.*

Library of Congress Cataloging-in-Publication Data
Spring, Ira.
    An ice axe, a camera, and a jar of peanut butter : a photographer's autobiography / Ira Spring
       p. cm.
    ISBN 0-89886-520-4 (paper) — ISBN 0-89886-627-8 (cloth)
    1. Spring, Ira. 2. Photographers—United States—Biography.
3. Mountaineers—United States—Biography. 4. Naturalists—United
States—Biography. 5. Travel photography—Biography. I. Title.
TR140.S66A3 1988
770'.92—dc21
[B]

3 1252 01284 1615

98-23920
CIP

Printed on recycled paper

Contents

To Harvey Manning, who knows how to spell.
Without his help and encouragement, this
tale would never have been finished.

Foreword

by Jim Whittaker

In West Seattle, childhood home of us Whittakers, it not only was natural but also just about unavoidable that my twin brother, Lou, and I were adventuring in neighborhood forests and following Mother on paths down to the saltwater shore south of Lincoln Park. The gigantic "arroyo" (actually, an abandoned gravel pit) of Arroyo Beach was a terrific spot to jump and tumble and slide down precipices of sand.

Our folks loved to fish, and it was on family trips to the wilderness edge that Lou and I were permanently "greened." Scouting confirmed our green-bonding. Troop 272 took us beyond the edge into the depths of the wilderness, pack on back, sleeping bag on the ground, the great darkness of night all around. Some Tenderfeet were scared of it. From the beginning we loved camping in the wilderness and continued through the ranks to Explorer Scouts.

This photograph is typical of my modeling for Ira. First he made certain I was going to be safely belayed, and then he was lowered into a crevasse in the Cowlitz Glacier, so deep I could barely hear him. When Ira had his big camera ready, I jumped the crevasse once. Ira yelled up, "Do it once more. Your ice axe was in front of your face." Keeping my ice axe lower, I jumped a second time. "Sorry," he yelled. "I forgot to cock the shutter," so I jumped a third time. Ira called, "That was great, but just to be certain, try it once more." After the fourth jump and what I thought was the last, he yelled, "That was great, so now let's do it in color." As Ira wanted three exposures in color, I jumped that crevasse a total of seven times.

From there to climbing was a short step. Our first mentors were Tom Campbell, a legend for his one-armed climbs in the Bugaboos, having lost the other in the war, and Lloyd Anderson, for years the leading spirit of the Climbing Course of The Mountaineers. We learned balance climbing on Monitor (now Schurman) Rock, handy to our home in West Seattle, attained the summit of our first big peak (Si, of course), climbed The Tooth, and in 1945 sortied into the white above the green, the glaciers of Mount Olympus.

Soon thereafter the Whittaker and Spring paths crossed—and never since then have the twain got very far apart. As hero-worshipping teenagers we were awed to be invited to climb with such famous mountaineers, the Bob and Ira Spring whose byline and photos were featured in what seemed like almost every Sunday *Times*. I couldn't count the number of ice walls we climbed and crevasses we leaped for Ira's Speed Graphic.

There were, of course, the "perks" of modeling—the meals he served us, sandwiches of peanut butter spread on soda crackers and one-pot suppers of dehydrated vegetables that never rehydrated.

For me, the green-bonding that is Ira's theme in this book has more to it than color. For a person who through high school and college was constantly bumping his head on the roof of the bus and stooping to get through doorways, the freedom of the hills—of the out-of-doors—meant being able to stand up straight, no apologies for being six feet, five inches tall.

And felt more deeply than that was the sound of silence, hearing therein the Great Architect.

However, getting back to color . . . A sort of antigravity pulls a climber higher and higher into the nongreen of snow and ice, of rock, of the sky. Yet yielding at last to gravity, returning from the crystalline mineral to timberline, fills us with the warm glow of homecoming. No wildland experience is more vividly poignant in my memory than the descent from nearly three months in the sterile zone of the Himalaya when I spotted a blade of grass. Then a miracle! My nose caught a whiff of dirt. Never since have I been able to use the word "dirty" except as praise.

Said Thoreau, "In wildness is the preservation of the world." To which may be added, "In dirt is the beauty of our planet." Ira's tales of his life of green-bonding here in the dirty world help us know what life is—or should be, and in the end *must* be—about.

Preface

or
Adventure is Where
You Find It

My parents' love of adventure and awareness of wild places they reached by foot or canoe was the inspiration that led me into a life of outdoor adventure. In turn I taught my children the love of mountain meadows and glaciers.

Former Justice of the United States Supreme Court, William O. Douglas, wrote in his book *Of Men and Mountains:*

I learned early that the richness of life is found in adventure. Adventure calls on all the faculties of mind and spirit. It develops self-reliance and independence. Life then teems with excitement. But man is not ready for adventure unless he is rid of fear. For fear confines him and limits his scope. He stays tethered by strings of doubt and indecision and has only a small and narrow world to explore.

Discovery is adventure. There is an eagerness, touched at times with tenseness, as man moves into the unknown. Walking the wilderness is indeed life living. The horizon drops away, bringing new sights, sounds, and smells from the earth. When one moves through the forest, his sense of discovery is quickened. Man is back in the environment from which he emerged to build factories, churches, and schools. He is primitive again, matching his wits against the earth and sky. He is free of the restraints of society and free of its safeguards too.

Adventure has taken the Whittaker twins, Jim and Lou, to the top of Mount Everest, Henry David

Bob's 1948 picture of me working on a newspaper story next to a serac in the Emmons Glacier, Mount Rainier National Park. Like rapids in a river bed, seracs appear above deformities in the slow-moving river of ice.

Thoreau to Walden Pond, and bird watchers who hike jungle trails to add to their life list. But adventure can be found at home—some people find it watching insects in their own backyard. Here in the Northwest thousands of hikers find adventure on mountain trails or while whitewater rafting. Justice Douglas found adventure in the hills outside his home in Yakima.

During my teenage years my heroes were either photographers or adventurers. Edward Weston, founder of the f-64 Club, produced pictures so sharp and clear you could almost reach out and touch the distant mountains. The mountain pictures of Asahel Curtis are still works of art. His eye for composition was great, usually framing the mountains with a picturesque tree. His reputation left something to be desired. The manager at Mount Rainier claimed that when Asahel Curtis finished, he cut down the tree that framed his picture so no one else could duplicate his work.

In 1932 I was glued to the radio listening to the weekly broadcasts of Lowell Thomas, the radio commentator who made his broadcasts from remote parts of the world, and Admiral Byrd at the South Pole. I read everything I could about the adventures of Ome Daiber, Bradford Washburn, Roy Chapman Andrews finding dinosaur eggs in the Gobi Desert, and William Beebe, a distant cousin of ours, descending to depths of the ocean farther than anyone else had ever gone.

Richard Halaburton opened my eyes to the world with his book *Royal Road to Romance,* about his around-the-world adventures. I had a copy with me during the war and must have read it a dozen times.

Among my contemporaries, Dee Molenaar and Maynard Miller became famous in their fields, Dee for his maps and Maynard for glacier research. Of the teenage models I took on photo trips back in the 1950s, some made names for themselves in the mountaineering world: Jim and Lou Whittaker, Pete Schoening, and Fred Beckey for their climbs, and Harvey Manning for his writing skills. Others, like Gary Rose, the Marston sisters, Joan and Carol, and my own children, John and Vicky, are not yet famous, but they are living adventuresome lives to be envied.

I hope that telling the story of my adventures will help young people find their own, whatever those may be in the twenty-first century, just as William O. Douglas helped my generation find adventure during the last century.

CHAPTER I

Mountains, Cameras, and World of Wonder

or
Is Adventure Inherited?

A 1914 picture of our parents in front of their home. Mother as a "Bloomer Girl" was dressed in the height of fashion. Dad always wore a tie while canoeing.

Which came first for me, the camera or adventuring? Did the one cause the other? If so, which was the one and which was the other?

Photography must have been a family inheritance because I remember Dad taking pictures of all kinds of landmarks and risking the dangerous flash powder at indoor family gatherings. One Christmas he hung up a sheet and made clever silhouettes of us.

But at the same time I also inherited from my parents the quest for adventure that was in the hearts of both Mother and Dad. Maybe the biggest influence my folks had on me was "Dare to be Different." They certainly were.

In 1911, at the age of twenty, our father, Elliot Beebe Spring, left his home in Jamestown, New York,

Twinflower, one of Mother's favorite flowers that grew at her doorstep in Olympia.

and moved west to Olympia, Washington, where he met our mother, Allena Loomis. In his words:

On the final advice of my mother upon leaving my Jamestown home, I attended the Congregational Church the first Sunday I reached Olympia, where I met your mother and soon I was seeing her once or twice a week at church meetings. Somehow we got to walking home up on Sherman Avenue together and then her folks invited me to dinner. Now mother Loomis was a fine cook and her pies were out of this world, so all I needed was an invitation for dinner and we saw more and more of one another. Then I had the Peterborough canoe, and when your mother says it was the pies that attracted me to her home, it's just possible it was the canoe that really brought us together.

Mother and Dad were married September 4, 1913. They lived on the beach three miles from Dad's job in Olympia. Depending on the weather and tides, he either walked the beach to work or paddled a canoe. The

A 1914 snapshot of Dad and his Peterborough canoe at Tumwater Falls. At high tide a canoe could be paddled from Budd Inlet up the Deschutes River to the falls.

family album has a photo of him in the canoe wearing a suit, white shirt, and tie.

There were plenty of wilderness trails when our parents were married. Getting to them, though, could be an expedition. The Model T was only four years old, and most roads were built for wagons and horses, not machines. However, at their porch was Budd Inlet and miles of uninhabited beach to explore. My folks used a canoe both for transportation and, on holidays, for canoe camping. They lived off the land or, to be more accurate, off the beach.

In 1913 the civilized way to enjoy Puget Sound was to take a vessel of the mosquito fleet to resorts scattered around Puget Sound. My folks dared to be different and explored Puget Sound by canoe, paddling from beach to beach, up calm waters of finger inlets and across windswept reaches of open waters.

Dad kept a diary of his canoe trips. A sample entry:

On the late afternoon of June 14, 1916, we packed our duffle, consisting of ground cloth, blankets, dishes, the "black crow" [made from a ten-pound coffee can blackened by many campfires], *and food in our canoe and took off for Shelton. We stopped at Silver Spit, a pretty little sandy beach about half way between Olympia and Mud Bay Spit, ate supper, and continued on. We proceeded around Mud Bay Spit where Allena pulled in a nice two-pound trout on her line trailing the canoe. It was getting dark so no more fishing, but we soon ran into the greatest school of salmon we ever encountered. The fish were so thick some were jumping out of the water. We kept hitting them with our paddles and they kept bumping our boat. We hoped one would jump in the canoe, but no luck. Then a full moon came up casting a trail of light behind us, and our paddles broke the water with a phosphorescent glow. To climax the dramatic evening, the Indians on Squaxin Island started a fire on the beach and their chanting reached us clear across the quiet water as we went around Hope Island and past Steamboat Island. We pulled up on Arcadia Point, which was entirely vacant in those days, and laid out our blankets on the soft grass and vines. The only thing that disturbed us was one or two curious rabbits nosing around our camp.*

From Arcadia Point they entered what was then called the "Big Skookum" and paddled through the narrow channel around the "Golden Horn" to Shelton. There, Mother's brother-in-law loaded the canoe on his horse-drawn wagon to carry them to his homestead in the Skokomish Valley, where they launched the canoe in the Skokomish River and let the current carry them to Hood Canal. On the canal the waves were high and a strong wind blew them to the opposite shore where they used the canoe as shelter from the rain.

When the weather moderated, they paddled into Lilliwaup Bay, camped by Lilliwaup Falls, and spent a day hiking. From there they went to the end of Hood Canal at Belfair, where they paid a farmer to portage them to Allyn on North Bay at the end of Puget Sound. They paddled south through Pickering Passage past Arcadia Point and back to Olympia.

When my twin brother, Bob, and I were born on December 24, 1918, it didn't stop my parents. Except for trying to keep my brother and me from tipping over the canoe, our arrival did not change their love of paddling. My best childhood memories are of camping and canoeing. Ordering us to "sit still," our folks took us along. I remember a two-week trip in 1932. Miles of uninhabited beaches were, then, truly wilderness. To camp we had only to pull ashore in any cove. Driftwood was abundant and so well seasoned that a little kindling and a match would start a fire. The water from the streams was drinkable, the delightful little Olympia oysters lay there for the picking, and a shovelful of beach turned up a meal of clams. Mother always had a fishing line hanging over the side of the canoe and what she called saltwater trout were generally on the breakfast menu.

In 1929 the family spent a week in a cabin camp at Rialto Beach near La Push. On the way home we side tripped to Sol Duc Hot Springs, where Mother and our sister Kay stayed while Dad took Bob and me on our first overnight hike—to High Divide. The trail started near the resort on "Lovers' Lane" and climbed to Deer Lake, where we camped in the three-sided shelter cabin. Next morning we boys were awed to find ice in our water bucket. Ice in July! On the crest of High Divide we looked down on Hoh Lake, farther down to the Hoh River, and across to the glaciers on Mount Olympus. The scenery impressed us less than Dad pushing a big rock off the middle of the trail, setting it rolling down the hill. A marmot in its path started running just a leap ahead of the rock, at the last second making a sharp-angle turn to escape.

I still have fond memories of canoeing, but after High Divide mountain trails became so important to Bob and me that hiking boots replaced paddles.

Looking back to that first overnighter in 1929 and all the way to 1945, I can see how school, my hobby, a hike, a war, my parents "daring us to be different," and a free camera shaped my future desire for adventure. The most benign was my hobby of stamp collecting, which opened my imagination to faraway countries of the world. In school I was fascinated with textbooks that told about the Seven Wonders of the World, the giant rock statues on Easter Island, stone money on Yap,

Air view of the Golden Horn (officially Cape Horn) and Hammersley's Inlet where my parents canoed in 1916. The turmoil of waters at the change of the tides makes for rough canoeing.

Mount Fujiyama, Mount Everest, and the strangeness of foreign cultures. Maybe the greatest factor of all that ultimately set me on a course of a world traveler was World War II!

The High Divide hike was the beginning of seventy years of the mountain adventure that became the central theme of my work. Then, in 1930, Eastman Kodak celebrated its fiftieth anniversary by giving a Box Brownie camera to every twelve-year-old boy and girl in the United States. The Kodak dealer in Shelton was a bit perplexed about giving two cameras to one family. But when it was explained that Bob and I were twins, with due ceremony he presented a camera and a free roll of film to each of us. The Box Brownie was a very simple early version of a modern "point-and-shoot" camera—no "f" stops, shutter speeds, or focusing to bother with. The single-element lens was about the equivalent of f.8 and the shutter speed was roughly

⅟₂₅ of a second, give or take 100 percent. But considering the latitude of the old black-and-white film the camera worked fine. Fine, that is, if the subject had strong lines, such as a mountain, and the lighting came from a 45-degree angle. Before 1930, it was uncommon for children to have a camera of any kind. The Brownie was an arrow pointing us toward our later life, as it did a number of other twelve-year-old children that year. The gift must have been a good investment for Kodak, selling a lot of film. It has been a long time and a lot of film since then, but I think I used that first free roll to take pictures of Mother's flower garden. The fact that the black-and-white pictures didn't show any color was disappointing, but this didn't dampen my enthusiasm.

Bob and I are fraternal twins and have never felt the

High Divide, where Dad took Bob and me on our first backpack in 1929. I could not find Dad's 1929 photograph taken at this same place with his folding Kodak.

attachment that identical twins are said to have. We just felt like regular brothers. We quarreled like brothers and had our own interests. During college years, Bob dated girls and I arranged skiing and hiking trips with someone who had a car. Bob generally had a heavy weekend date, but more than one girl was left in the lurch when, at the last minute, he changed his mind and went off with my group.

If I have little to say about family life during my teenage years, it is because I lived for hiking and photography. I spent too much time looking out the window and daydreaming at school to do well and I lacked the coordination for athletics. I did ride a bicycle to school and prided myself on pedaling up our steep hills in Shelton. Bob had other interests, such as girlfriends, drawing, and bicycling. One summer, instead of going to Scout camp, he and a friend bicycled around the Olympic Loop, quite a feat back when the road had only been open a few months and over half the distance was loose dirt.

My first mountain picture, Upper Lena Lake, taken with my free Box Brownie in 1931. I was very proud of this photograph. Considering the cheap lens and erratic shutter it wasn't bad.

With my Box Brownie I had taken several photos of Upper Lena Lake that were praised by friends, and one even said they looked professional, so my life course was set. With photo magazines and some older hiking friends who were into photography, I gradually learned what I was doing. I took pictures for the high school annual—but not very good ones—the Box Brownie had its limits. Encouraged by Dad, in my senior year I bought a 6X9-centimeter view camera and set up a darkroom in a basement closet, not an easy thing to do back then. The photography book said the darkroom must be dark, so I painted the closet walls black. The main ingredients of the developer were elon and hydroquinone. They deteriorated rapidly when mixed or exposed to air and had to be mixed each day. A scale was essential for the mixture—two grams of this, three grams of that, and another gram of this and that. Premixed developer wasn't available until World War II was half over, and then it was so expensive that for another ten years many photographers continued mixing their own.

CHAPTER 2

My Mountains

or
My Love Affair with the
Olympic Mountains

1940 winter trip to Mount Gladys.

It was hiking trips in the Olympic Mountains that Dad took Bob and me on, and the Boy Scout leaders from Camp Cleland, that set me on mountain adventures.

I can only remember scraps of a song the Boy Scouts sang around the campfire in the Olympic Mountains—"Hiking over the trails we will climb the slopes of snow and shale." From there it went, "Lake of the Angels nestled in the cloud." It is surprising how often those two little bits come back to me. There has to be more to that song, just as there is a lot more to the Olympic Mountains than snow, shale, and Lake of the Angels. There are moss-covered rain forests, rivers that run clear, ridges that rise above timberline, meadows, glacier-covered peaks, and ice-cold lakes for a quick skinny-dip on a hot day. As mountain ranges go, the Olympics are not very high, but they're close enough to the ocean that they get the full blast of Pacific storms.

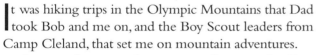

Bob's picture of Puget Sound country and Mount Rainier, taken in 1937 on one of our many ascents of Mount Ellinor when it was a climb of 4,840 feet.

Ten feet of rain falls each year on the Hoh Rain Forest. Even though Mount Olympus is less than 8,000 feet high, it has three major glaciers. Flowers are everywhere, some rare and endemic to the Olympics. Deer, elk, bear, and marmots are common along with squirrels, chipmunks, and little mice that find your food supply at night.

When Bob and I were eight years old, Dad's work took us to Shelton, a logging town in the foothills of the Olympic Mountains. From our hilltop house, the Olympics were just beyond the living room window. Every morning we looked to see if "the mountains were out." Mount Ellinor, Mount Washington, and The Brothers dominated the skyline, along with bits and pieces of other peaks we eventually identified and climbed.

Although it was the 1929 backpack to High Divide that set my future love of the mountains, our first venture was in 1928, when Dad took Bob and me for a climb of Mount Ellinor. Lake Cushman road ended at a resort near the dam, where Dad rented a boat and rowed four or five miles to the trailhead at the other end of the lake. Rowing was tough going, as half the

Morning flag-raising at Camp Cleland. "A Boy Scout is Loyal."

was a long, dusty ride past Hoodsport and Lilliwaup to Eldon, at the mouth of the Hamma Hamma River. There we transferred to the railroad tracks of the Hamma Hamma Logging Company, riding a workers' speeder eight miles to the Lena Creek trailhead. The first half-mile of trail was being clear-cut, so we had to climb straight up the fireline. The hill was steep, the sun was hot, and the leaders charged ahead at a pace that nearly killed us Tenderfeet, overloaded as we were with all the extra clothing and blankets our mothers were sure we needed, or might possibly need, to survive beyond reach of their apron strings. (Can't blame it all on Mother—our Box Brownies were also in the pack. The pictures in the forest did not turn out very well, but we got some nice mountain shots.) Pooped out and left far in the rear, somehow we staggered the rest of the two miles to Lena Lake, site of Camp Cleland, consisting of

lake (or reservoir really) was covered by great drifts of logging slash, trees, and other debris that moved with the wind. Not until the 1950s was Tacoma finally required to clean up its mess.

After rowing across the lake, we landed under Mount Ellinor and found the Staircase trail. Dad tried to locate the Mount Ellinor trail but evidently went the wrong way. I remember passing lovely Cushman Falls, plunging through a fern-covered slot. The cliff with the beautiful slot was eventually blasted away to make room for a logging road.

Instead of Mount Ellinor, we found the Mount Rose trail and changed plans. As it still does, the trail dead-ended before we had a view. On the way down, first Dad stepped on a yellowjacket nest, then I did, but it was Bob bringing up the rear who got stung nine times.

In 1930 we joined the Boy Scouts and went for ten days to the Tumwater Area Council's summer camp on Lena Lake. Our Troop 25 rode from Shelton in the back of a truck. Pavement ended at the city limit, so it

a large cookhouse, a canvas-roofed, open-air "mess hall," ten large army tents, each with space to sleep five to six boys, two buildings for staff, an eight-hole outhouse, and eight rowboats that had been carried up the trail. There was a dock to swim off of—no swim suits needed. Girls and mothers were nowhere to be seen or to see. The cook was an old woman (maybe thirty), so she didn't count.

We did our duty at earning a few (as possible) merit badges, but the camp director had a higher priority: He wanted every boy to appreciate the rare gift of the great out-of-doors. Instead of boasting about merit badges earned he had the boys boasting about the animals and plants they had seen, and we even had little rubber stamps to paste on each Scout's camp achievement certificate. Hiking was another priority. We Tenderfeet took a number of day trips and one three-day backpack to Upper Lena Lake, where we climbed "Old Baldy" (now named Mount Lena).

By today's standards our backpacking equipment

was pretty crude. Bob and I each made our own packboards from patterns we found in *Boy's Life*, the Scouting magazine. Bob's was a simple lightweight frame; mine was a much heavier frame with a curved back that I spent hours making, steaming a piece of wood to bend the right way. The first year we carried a Boy Scout bedroll made of two heavy wool blankets. The first blanket was folded lengthwise three ways; the second was wrapped around the first, making a tight cocoon for a small boy. Later, Mother made us warm

(but much too heavy) sleeping bags from down quilts, and with her help we made pup tents that were waterproof—except when it rained.

In the mountains one can use a homemade packboard and a bedroll made of old blankets, put up a tarp when it rains, and wear a torn coat and ragged pants, but shoes must fit with soles that will grip wherever one walks. In the Boy Scouts we were happy with smooth rubber soles for our tenderfoot hikes. As I progressed to advanced hikes, though, I needed something better. The next step was hobnails, little steel tacks nailed into leather soles. Coming from a logging town, I also added sharp caulks in the instep that helped when walking on logs. It wasn't until years later when I entered The Mountaineer's Climbing Course that I

"A Boy Scout is Brave, Clean and Reverent." Sunday service on Chapel Rock at Camp Cleland. Although the camp is gone, the memories are still there.

heard about the tricouni-nailed boot, seen now only in museums. Imported from Europe, tricounis are three (the "tri-" of tricouni) sharp points on a small steel bar nailed to a thick leather sole, twenty or more to a boot. Tricounis did very well on everything but smooth rock but, with the thick soles and the metal, the boots were heavy. After a long hike with a heavy pack, one would feel each of the twenty tricounis grinding into the sole of each foot. It was during World War II that the Vibram sole was developed, commonly referred to as waffle-stompers because of the pattern they left in snow or mud. The first models didn't do well on steep heather slopes, so I was years behind in making the switch.

Bob and I were thoroughly hooked on Camp Cleland and returned for the next three or four summers. We saved all winter from our allowance and

Bob and me with typical Tenderfoot packs on our way to Camp Cleland in 1931. Boy Scouts of the day never forgot their hatchets and on their belts always carried their Boy Scout knives.

paper route to be able to afford not one but two of the ten-day sessions, and we graduated to progressively more difficult hikes, some as long as five days. Simply being in camp was a reward itself, and in addition to the regular periods I signed up for "work periods." One year we carried twenty-foot lengths of pipe and installed a water system. Another year, helped by loggers donated by Simpson Logging Company, we replaced the sleeping tents with six patrol cabins, each with bunks for eight boys.

In 1932 the Hamma Hamma Logging Company ran out of trees on private land where it had cutting rights and pulled up the rails. The railroad grade became a one-lane road just passable for the truck to haul us to the trailhead. It was a rough ride, bouncing over the ties, and viewed from the back of the truck the high-trestle crossings were harrowing.

The second year the trestles were bypassed, the road began to be improved, and the camp went downhill. Visiting mothers were bad enough, but sisters put the camp in an uproar, and suddenly the hated swim suits were essential. Then came the vandals who moved in each fall when camp was closed. The rowboats stored in the cookhouse were borrowed and not returned. The first winter three of the eight boats were ruined by being left on the lake. The next year two more were crushed. We hid the remaining boats in caves a long way from camp, but still they were found. The third year, after the road was open, the boats were all gone. The buildings became firewood. By 1941 the Scouts gave up and moved to a lowland lake where buildings could be looked after. Camp Cleland became a memory. Last time I was there, the only trace I could find was some of the water pipes.

CAMP CLELAND

The lake, the mountains, and the remoteness were the essence of Camp Cleland. The camp director, Tom Martin, was one of the greatest people I've ever known. A schoolteacher, he went into politics, was Washington State treasurer for eight years, and then became head of Washington State Parks.

Tom had a special gift for storytelling that kept the boys at the evening campfire, hanging on every word. One almost believable story was the time on the slopes of Mount Baldy he came upon a Sidehill Gallynipper, an animal who on steep hillsides had a big advantage over other animals in that its left legs were longer than its right legs, allowing it to walk easily on the steep slopes of the Olympics. Tom said he was watching one grazing on the lupine and blue huckleberries on the side of Old Baldy when it was distracted by a bear that walked by, and passed up an especially good patch of huckleberries. When the Gallynipper realized its mistake, it could not go back and had to walk all the way around the mountain. A spooky campfire story that may have been true, or nearly so, was of the two prospectors who died mysteriously in the East Fork of Lena Creek. I don't remember the story, but even now it is called "The Valley of Silent Men."

A certainly true story was the tragedy of Carl Putvin, a young trapper. Around 1911 or 1912 he built his cabin at the head of the Hamma Hamma valley, some twelve miles from the nearest road. One winter, while tending his traplines somewhere between Mount Stone and Upper Lena Lake, he had an appendicitis attack and died before he could get back to his cabin. His family must have looked after the cabin for years afterward. In 1936 the cabin and grave were neatly kept up. Remains of a small cabin at Milk Lake were assumed also to be Putvin's.

There were other stories, songs only a Boy Scout would sing, and bad jokes not worth repeating— and other great leaders. When Tom Martin became State Treasurer, Tom Hardy became camp director. Of the assistant leaders, the most outstanding were Norm Bright, a marathon runner in the 1932 Olympic Games, and Chet Ullin, a mountain climber and schoolteacher.

My most memorable trip was in 1936, led by Chet. We hiked the

Above right: *Ski trail to Mount Gladys above the Flapjack Lakes cabin.* **Right:** *Cornices on Mount Baldy (USGS Mount Lena) photographed on an early summer hike.*

I titled this picture, taken in 1939, "The Wizard of Oz." This is one of the few arty pictures I have taken and it got an award at the Puyallup Fair.

dropping to Lake of the Angels, surrounded by glacier-polished rock. For the first time I saw the "Lake of the Angels nestled in the clouds." Fortunately the day was clear and we could see forever. Before Camp Cleland was founded, Chet, as a Boy Scout from the Seattle Area Council's Camp Parsons on Hood Canal, had been this far and had a part in giving such a fitting name to the lake. From here on Chet pioneered a new route across mountain passes and through miles of heather and huckleberries. On the side of Mount Henderson we accidentally stampeded a herd of fifty or more elk. They came thundering down the mountainside a hundred feet in front of us, raising such a cloud of dust we could hardly see them.

From Lake of the Angels we dropped to Carl Putvin's cabin in the upper Hamma Hamma valley. Solving routefinding problems on the way, we camped the third night at Mildred Lakes. On the fourth day Chet led us under the sharp spires of the Sawtooth Range and past Mount Washington to a final camp on Jefferson Lake. The last day we found a trail leading to Elk Lake and a logging road.

YEARS LATER

After all those years the hazards have faded from my memory. What I remember are the adventures. The highlight was Saint Peter's Gate. Dad took Bob and me through the same route to Lake of the Angels several times.

The Hamma Hamma valley has long since been logged, destroying Putvin's cabin. Evidently Putvin's grave is now lost in brush, and only a Forest Service sign at the foot of the Putvin trail remains, saying the grave is nearby and giving his birth date as September

first day to Upper Lena Lake, amid alpine meadows and steep mountains. The next day we left the trail and climbed over Mount Baldy (now on the U.S.G.S. maps as Mount Lena), traversed miles of meadows, and ended the day climbing over Saint Peter's Gate, a 6,000-foot pass near the top of Mount Stone, and

1892 and his death as January 10, 1913. Young as Putvin was, he must have had children, for in 1991 I received a letter from a young girl, Vicki Fitzgerald, who wanted information about her grandfather, Carl Putvin.

Although I have not been over Saint Peter's Gate since World War II, forty-five years after my first trip I revisited Lake of the Angels and marveled at how the leaders ever herded a bunch of boys in smooth-soled shoes across the rough terrain.

We aren't the only ones to have enjoyed the traverse. In his foreword to the book *Alpine Lakes*, then-Governor Dan Evans wrote about a cold skinny-dip followed by sunbathing on glacier-polished rock beside Lake of the Angels.

From the size of the trees you would never know the first half-mile to Lena Lake had ever been clear-cut. The two-mile-long trail was a good grade for hiking. However, in the 1960s it was regraded for motorcycles and became three and a half miles. Fortunately a new district ranger saw the fallacy of mixing a large number of hikers with motorcycles and the motors were banned. From Lena Lake to Upper Lena Lake, the first two miles was a good trail in 1930, the next two miles a boot-beaten path up cliffs. About 1935 the Civilian Conservation Corps (CCC) extended formal trail to the upper lake, but the steep hillsides are not stable and the tread has always had troubles.

Cushman Dam, Mount Ellinor, left, and Mount Washington, right. The dam flooded the North Fork trail to Staircase, which had to be rerouted.

STAIRCASE

Scouting in the Olympic Mountains was important to us, but there was more. With the opening of the road around Lake Cushman in 1933 we were able to drive to Staircase in a few hours. It's hard to visualize what Dad saw on his first visit to Lake Cushman in 1914. It was then a natural lake some two miles long, site of the rustic Antlers Hotel. He remembered a camping trip with his friend, Harry Cleese, and their wives. The two couples drove from Olympia through Shelton to Hoodsport and then up the hill to Lake Cushman, passing a farmhouse near the lake. It was a long day's drive on the narrow, twisty road. The way had recently been paved as far as Shelton, but beyond that was dirt.

The natural Lake Cushman discovered in 1852 was homesteaded in 1885. In 1890 Lieutenant O'Neil used it as a jumping-off place for his expedition across the Olympics. The reports from the O'Neil party in 1890 brought trappers, prospectors, and tourists. Later that year a road was opened from Hoodsport allowing easy access to the heart of the Olympics, and several hotels were built on the lakeshore.

Apparently, the first trail into the Olympics was built by the O'Neil party, starting at the lake and following the south side of the Skokomish River. Most of the way was easy valley bottom. At Staircase, though, the river butted up against the 400-foot cliff of Fisher's Bluff. During low-water periods O'Neil would have been able to wade the river, but during high water the

Photo of cloud-filled Jefferson Creek from Mount Ellinor, taken in 1940.

travelers had to find a route over the cliff, which was first named Devils Staircase and later became simply Staircase. Beyond Staircase the valley flattened again and a small cabin camp was built to accommodate prospectors exploring the area. Eventually a trail was blasted around the base of Fisher's Bluff and, though the Staircase trail up and over the cliff was no longer used, the name stuck.

In 1926 Tacoma built Cushman Dam, drowning the Antlers Hotel, the homesteads, and much of the valley bottom. The reservoir wiped out the trail to Staircase and a new trail was built around the north side of the lake. A suspension bridge, sturdy enough for a pack train, was constructed across the river to the Staircase cabin camp on the south side of the river. A ranger station was built on the north side.

In 1933 the CCC widened the trail to a one-lane road around the lake past the Mount Ellinor trailhead to Staircase. The suspension bridge built for pack trains was just wide enough for a Model A Ford.

A year after the road was opened, Dad drove us to the Mount Ellinor trailhead and Bob and I reached the top of our first real mountain. It became our favorite day hike from Shelton. The trail started at lake level and gained 4,840 feet to the summit, enough of a chug that during many climbs of Mounts Ellinor and Washington during our school years we never met anyone. Nowadays logging roads have shortened the trail and cut the elevation gain to only 2,100 feet and the way is crowded. Until 1989 the trail ended at the 4,500-foot level, leaving a steep rock scramble to the top. The elevation gain when we were young weeded out the inexperienced; the shortening of the trail attracted crowds, many on their first hike, ignorant of the danger of falling on slippery slopes and falling rock. In 1990 three eighty-year-old volunteers eliminated the hazard by building a trail all the way to the top.

When the road was open, our family spent many weekends at Staircase. It was quite a sight to watch the suspension bridge, built for packhorses, sag as a car crossed. I once spent a month at Staircase with my Uncle Arthur. I have always had trouble with allergies, both food and hay fever. Spring and summer were especially bad, and it was discovered I was much better in the mountains. One spring when I was so bad I couldn't go to school and Uncle Arthur was out of work, my folks rented a cabin at Staircase for the two of us. The dozen cedar cabins had been built before the road, so the flooring and windows came from the outside by packtrain. The rest was from split logs. Primitive by today's standards, they were comfortable. The arrangement suited Uncle Arthur because he could spend his days fishing (and escape from his very religious wife), and it was fine with me because I could explore nearby trails. Some days we hiked miles up the river to fishing holes. I even found the old Staircase trail over the cliff. Behind our cabin I had a close-up view of a "selective logging," a new concept at the time. Huge trees that were too heavy to drag out with a small bulldozer were left standing, and only the medium size trees were cut. The Shady Lane trail passes this area and it is hard now to find where the logging took place.

My allergies probably account for my parents encouraging me to head for the hills, go to Scout camp, and take hiking trips and spring ski tours. I thoroughly enjoyed the "medical treatment." I don't suppose it did my schoolwork any good.

FLAPJACK LAKES

One of the other places of special meaning to me was wintertime at Flapjack Lakes, a few miles beyond the Staircase road end.

Before World War II, ski developments were in their infancy. A few rope tows were at the passes, one in the Olympics at Deer Park, two at Paradise, and maybe one at Mount Baker. From Shelton, where I lived, all these were long drives on slow roads. The Bremerton Ski Cruisers sought a handier ski area. An aerial survey spotted great open slopes somewhere near Mount Lincoln. Somewhere—but where, exactly? Finding good

skiing from the air was the easy part. Now came the hard part. New Year's Day, 1938, the Cruisers tied skis to feet, climbed 3,000 feet and floundered in deep snow near Wagon Wheel Lake, but found only cliffs on the side of Mount Lincoln. Three months later they again skied to the lake, crossed the Sawtooth Range, skied down to Mildred Lakes, and bushwhacked to the Hamma Hamma River road, but still no ski slopes.

In April the Cruisers, joined by the Shelton Ridge Runners, tried again, this time by way of Flapjack Lakes. Six feet of snow made good going up Mount Gladys, and at last they found the great open snow slopes photographed from the air.

In the winter of 1939–40, the Shelton and Bremerton ski clubs each raised $500 for a cabin. The Forest Service gave approval and even indicated it would build a road to Flapjack Lakes from the road under construction between Staircase and Lake Quinault, which already had reached the Flapjack Lakes trailhead, the right-of-way cleared another half-mile toward Big Log.

The summer was spent designing the cabin and

Flapjack Lakes ski cabin, which I helped build in 1939.

Lower Flapjack Lake and Sawtooth Ridge.

choosing the site on Upper Flapjack Lake. Work started in September. In 1940, $1,000 was a lot of money. Besides the hardware, it paid a month's wages to two unemployed loggers and the services of a packer with two mules for ten days.

Volunteers plunged enthusiastically into the work. Several men timed their vacations to help the loggers, and the rest of us spent every weekend at Flapjack Lakes through the fall until the road was closed by slides. The Bremerton bunch drove to the trailhead early Saturday morning, but one or two carloads of Shelton skiers left Friday evening after work and hiked in by flashlight. Until the new cabin had a roof, we stayed in the three-sided Forest Service shelter between the two lakes.

Generally when we arrived at the trailhead it was raining, and as we climbed higher the rain would turn to sleet. Most of the fellows brought their wives or girl-

friends, who hiked slower than me. I was the youngest of the Shelton Ski Club members and was also unencumbered by a girl. I and a similarly free companion would shoulder our packs and take off while the others were still getting ready. We would hike ten minutes and stop, strip to our underpants, and put our somewhat dry clothes in our packs. Free of wet clothing and urged on by cold rain or snow flakes on bare skin, we hiked the four and a half miles to the shelter in record time, put our dry clothes back on, and started a fire. When the others arrived cold, wet, and tired an hour or so later, they marveled at how fast our clothes had dried.

The packer was able to carry everything up to the site—hardware, flooring, windows, stoves, and even the chemical toilet—in the allotted time. We did have an accident with the fuel for our Coleman lanterns. The ten gallons we ordered came in two five-gallon cans in a wooden crate. Assembling the crate, some workman had driven a nail into one of the cans and all its fuel was

Skiing on Mount Gladys above the Flapjack Lakes cabin in 1940.

gone. The replacement had to be carried in on our backs.

Weekdays the two hired loggers axed and sawed trees to proper size. Weekends the volunteers dragged the logs in and helped nail them together. A few inches of snow made the quarter-mile of log-dragging relatively easy.

The cabin was habitable in November. A separate room for the chemical toilet was named by one volunteer, a banker by trade, "the bank." In midwinter, when the cold became more intense, he reported the bank had frozen assets.

I once set a record of sorts. At home after a weekend at the cabin I discovered I had left my camera in the cabin. My pack was so heavy I hadn't noticed it was eight pounds lighter. I didn't dare leave it there for fear the road might be closed for the winter and I wouldn't see it until spring. After work the next night I drove the family car to the trailhead. I dashed by flashlight the four and a half miles up to the cabin

in fifty-eight minutes, grabbed my camera, and returned in fifty-six minutes.

In the winter the road was often blocked by slides along Lake Cushman and washouts beyond Staircase, at Slate Creek. When we were able to drive to the trailhead, heavy snow on the trail made reaching the cabin difficult. In April and May the road was open and spring ski tours were great. However, we soon became aware of the frequent avalanches and the limited amount of safe terrain. These, added to the road problems, clearly meant that Mount Gladys was never going to make a good ski area.

We enjoyed the cabin during the spring, summer, and fall of 1941. In December came Pearl Harbor. Military service and gas rationing orphaned the cabin. Sometime during the war a tree fell across the roof and broke the rafters. When Flapjack Lakes became part of Olympic National Park, the rangers tore down the remains, along with the three-sided shelter. No trace of either can now be found.

Due to the regular washouts at Slate Creek, the road from Staircase to the trailhead was turned into a pleasant three-and-a-half-mile trail. The conversion was so tastefully done that many hikers do not realize they are walking a road. (The trail, like the old road, is frequently washed out at Slate Creek.) And hardly anybody can believe that roads were intended—and actually under construction—to penetrate the innermost vastness of the Olympics.

WILDERNESS IN THE MAKING

Today's hikers have little notion of how much "civilization" there used to be in the Olympic wilderness. In the 1920s and 1930s dozens of three-sided shelters and peak-top lookouts were scattered throughout the mountains, all hooked together by miles of telephone wire. I remember using shelters up the North Fork Skokomish River at Big Log, Camp Pleasant, Nine Stream, and Flapjack Lakes, and a couple of years ago I found a schoolmate's name with a 1936 date carved on a shelter that is still standing on the South Fork Skokomish River.

The Antlers Hotel was destroyed when a dam flooded Lake Cushman. A small resort with fifteen to twenty cabins was located at Staircase. A two-story building was located across the river from Eight Stream, probably a dormitory for miners. (There turned out to

be no ore to mine, just stock to sell.) A resort and large swimming pool were at Olympic Hot Springs, and the historic two-story Enchanted Valley Chalet, thirteen miles from the nearest road, is still a marvel. Up the Hamma Hamma valley was the Putvin Cabin. Besides the nine buildings at Camp Cleland, Lena Lake had a three-sided hiker's shelter and Conway's Cabin, built by a prospector of that name. A tiny cabin stood at Milk Lake, a short distance from Upper Lena Lake. I understand there were buildings at the Black and White Mine near Smith Lake, reached from the Flapjack Lakes trail. Up the Dungeness River valley trail fourteen miles from the nearest road was the camp town of Tubal Cain Mine, another hole in the ground producing nothing but sweat. Deer Park had a pair of shelters built before construction of the road. The road allowed Deer Park to become a ski area of sorts, with a warming hut, bunkhouse, and rope tow.

Many big ideas were puffed up for ways to give automobiles the "freedom of the hills." During the Depression, promoters, using Work Progress Administration (WPA) and CCC workers, made great plans to crisscross the Olympics with roads. The roads to Deer Park and Hurricane Ridge were the two ends of a planned ridge-top meadow drive. The location stakes still could be found after World War II. The first two miles of trail to the Enchanted Valley are on the abandoned grade of the proposed across-the-Olympics highway to Hood Canal. The first three and a half miles of the North Fork Skokomish River trail are on the abandoned road that was in-

Above left: *Home Sweet Home shelter on an early summer hike. This is the standard Forest Service model once found throughout the mountains. Few still stand.* **Left:** *Mount Steel from Home Sweet Home shelter on a spring ski tour.*

Cloud-filled Quinault Valley and Mount Anderson.

tended to go over Home Sweet Home to Lake Quinault. Fortunately, the road stopped at the Flap-jack Lakes trail-head, but not before trees were cut in the next mile.

We can thank the "radical environmentalists" of that period who understood the value of wilderness and were able to stop the roads before they permanently changed the character of the Olympic Mountains. We now have a network of wilderness trails instead of a network of roads. While the post–World War II victory of the wilderness concept halted the most grandiose schemes, the Forest Service kept extending logging roads until it ran out of forest. The old trail shelters have been made obsolete by modern lightweight tents and sleeping bags—not to mention the overcrowding of the shelters by the backcountry population explosion. Most other buildings have been removed or lost in the

jungle. No trace remains of the two-story ski hut I helped build at Flapjack Lakes in 1939–40.

Since 1958, when Pat and I bought our present home on a hillside north of Edmonds, Washington, the Olympics have again been just beyond the living room window. Mounts Jupiter, Constance, and Townsend now dominate my skyline. Although I have to look harder, my favorite childhood peaks south to Ellinor are still in the picture.

There are more spectacular mountains in the North Cascades, larger flower fields at Mount Rainier, bigger lakes in the Alpine Lakes Wilderness, and quaint villages in the European Alps, but "there is no place like home." Upper Lena Lake has special memories, the more poignant the longer I live. It is where I spent my youth, and where Pat and I spent our honeymoon. We returned there on our twenty-fifth anniversary and wonder if we will be able to return for our fiftieth, only a few years away.

• CHAPTER 3 •

Is There Life After the Olympic Mountains?

or
How about Mount Rainier?

Avalanche lilies, taken in 1938 with my 6x9-inch view camera.

Living in the Puget Sound region, one is very aware of 14,410-foot Mount Rainier sticking up like a sore thumb high above the surrounding foothills. From a distance all one sees is barren rock and ice with no indication there are lakes, forest, and huge flower-covered meadows enriched by layers of pumice from past eruptions. Close up the barren-looking rocks and glaciers take on a dramatic life.

While the Olympic Mountains were—and still are—"home," by climbing the roof of our house in Shelton I could see Mount Rainier over the tree tops

Mount Rainier, photographed in 1937 from my dormitory window with the free Box Brownie camera. Late afternoon sunshine highlighted the snow texture. The picture won a five dollar prize in the Tacoma News Tribune, *my first income from photography. It was such easy money I just naturally had to do it for a living.*

and it beckoned me. I graduated from high school with the class of 1937. To help with my college fees, I applied for a summer job at Paradise Inn and was hired as a lobby porter—really a glorified janitor—a job I held two summers, working eight hours a day, hiking and taking pictures twelve hours a day, and sleeping when the weather was bad.

Dad had taken our family to Mount Rainier two or three times, but always in cloudy weather, so the day I arrived at Paradise Inn was the first time I had seen The Mountain close up. To say it mildly, I was overwhelmed and ready to explore each and every flower-covered meadow and the exciting glaciers. My job was around-the-clock; three of us alternated on eight-hour shifts. Having initially been assigned to the 4:00 P.M. to midnight shift, my first day was left free. Before breakfast I took off uphill. I knew I wasn't supposed to go far, so I stopped short of the climber cabin at 10,000-foot Camp Muir and visited the watchman at the fire lookout on 9,500-foot Anvil Rock. He gave me some tea—the first I'd ever tasted. It must have been sitting around

Top: *Cornice on the Muir Glacier, Anvil Rock Lookout beyond. Taken with my Box Brownie in 1937, the first day I worked at Paradise Inn. Bottom: Avalanche lilies pushing up through the edge of last winter's snowfield, a phenomenon that fascinated me then and still does.*

Paradise Ice Caves, the popular destination for tourists, and the top money-maker for the Park Company photo shop.

a few days for it was awful, and it took me years to develop a taste for it. With my Box Brownie I took some interesting pictures of snow cornices near the lookout and I was back to Paradise for lunch. The next morning I ran the three miles over to Pinnacle Peak and gasped at the spectacular view of Rainier. This looked like it was going to be a great summer.

That evening at a staff meeting the hotel manager listed the employee rules. No boys in the girls' dorm (so what), be on time for meals or go hungry, and a bunch of other things that didn't worry me. Then the boom dropped—the hiking rules. We could not go more than one mile in any direction and could not set foot on the glacier. What a blow! I'm sure, looking back, that without those rules there would have been a few broken bones, if not necks. As it was, one boy did hike farther than the specified mile, was caught in a fog, and became lost. Rangers and guides spent all night searching for him, and when he was found he was fired. Disappointed though I was, I found plenty of hiking and exploring could be done within the rules.

I was enchanted by the flowers. When I first arrived at the end of June the meadows around the inn were still white with three feet of snow. A week later just a few patches were left and the ground was white with avalanche lilies. Another week and the meadows turned blue with lupine, and by midsummer they were a rioting rainbow. I was especially fascinated by the avalanche lilies that pushed up through the edges of snow patches, obviously in a hurry to bloom.

Afraid of damaging my new 6X9-centimeter view camera, the first year at Paradise I used my Box Brownie, but the second year I was more confident with my new camera and was able to take close-ups of flowers. My favorite is an avalanche lily poking up through the previous year's snow.

My dorm room had a great view of The Mountain. I literally could take pictures from my bed, which I did when the sun was low and the snow showed every contour. A bed-view photo won me a five-dollar prize in a snapshot contest. Not bad for my Box Brownie. Another picture, taken that first day of Anvil Rock Lookout, was used years later in one of our lookout books—and it's in this book, too.

When I worked at night, during the day I sometimes took a blanket and tried to sleep in a secluded nook overlooking the Nisqually Glacier. It didn't work.

I was much too fascinated and distracted by rocks falling off the cliffs on the far side of the glacier, seracs breaking, and the occasional major avalanche in the icefall.

Although I didn't get the sleep I needed, I did begin to understand the slow-moving river of ice we call the Nisqually Glacier. Moving only an inch or two a day, it is much too slow to see, but a time-lapse movie taken over three months definitely shows movement. Like a river of water, the glacier moves over bumps and, like a river, there is a ripple above every bump, which on a glacier is where the crevasses open. If the bump is wide, the crevasse may reach across the glacier or, depending on the shape of the bottom, it may be crisscrossed with crevasses leaving towers of ice called seracs. If the glacier goes over a cliff, it is called an icefall, as big chunks of ice break off and crash below to reform the glacier.

Snow accumulates at high elevations where more snow falls in the winter than can melt in the summer. On Mount Rainier the snow may reach a depth of several hundred feet. Its own weight compresses the snow into ice and, like water, starts a downward movement until it reaches lower elevations where it eventually melts faster than it accumulates.

OFF TO COLLEGE

The inn closed on Labor Day, as did Bob's summer job. We enrolled at Central Washington College of Education, in Ellensburg, which then offered the state's only photography classes. The instructor, Glen Hogue, encouraged us to turn professional. He was a stickler for darkroom work and insisted on quality prints, for which I have always been grateful.

While I excelled in photograph-related subjects such as chemistry, English was my bugaboo. I was dumped into English 101, which was usually referred to as dumbbell English. At the end of the term the professor called me in and said my spelling and sentence structure were atrocious and he needed to flunk me; however, the adventures I wrote about were so fascinating he just had to pass me.

Bob's picture of his wife, Norma. Mount Rainier and Klapatche Lake before World War II, when the water was considered safe to drink.

A photo taken while piloting "Mount Piper," a great viewpoint for photographing crevasses on the Emmons Glacier as well as for grasping the awesome size of Mount Rainier's crater, where I had been standing the week before.

In two years I completed the entire photography curriculum and some extra work and then dropped out without graduating from college. I did graduate to a full-size professional camera, a 4x5 Speed Graphic.

Upon leaving college I moved back home to Shelton and got a job in the research lab of Rayonier's pulp mill washing test tubes for the chemists. My free time went into taking pictures and improving darkroom techniques. For five months I even quit my paying job to work for free in Shelton's only photo studio.

During the summers of 1939 and 1940, I divided my free weekends between going back to my favorite Olympics and exploring trails around Mount Rainier: Klapatche Park, with the reflection of Tokaloo Rock in a small lake; a hike up Burroughs Mountain, where I could look down into the crevasses on the Emmons Glacier; the Carbon River trail to Moraine Park, under the towering 5,000-foot cliff of the Willis Wall; Spray Park, with its acres of avalanche lilies; and

Indian Henry's Hunting Ground, where I found Asahel Curtis's famous picture of Mount Rainier reflected in Mirror Lake, a picture that was used on a 1934 postage stamp.

The summer of 1940 I made my first climb of Mount Rainier with a couple of friends. Although we had ice axes, rope, and crampons for safe travel and emergencies, fortunately none of us fell into a crevasse, as only one of us had any knowledge of self-rescue. I took pictures of a giant ice cliff on the way up but was too exhausted at the crater to get out my camera.

In the winter, I joined the Shelton Ridge Runners. When snow closed roads into the Olympics we spent our weekends at Mount Rainier. Paradise Valley was the most popular ski area in the region, referred to as the Valley of the Ten Thousand Sitzmarks. The public could only drive as far as Narada; however, Paradise Inn was open during the winter months, so a one-way road was kept open from Narada to Paradise. From Narada, we either walked thirty minutes up the snow trail to Paradise or for ten cents took the shuttle bus operated by the Park Company. Don't laugh, we often walked, for ten cents was a significant sum in 1939, when the minimum wage was twenty-five cents an hour. There was a rope tow on Alta Vista, but it, too, cost ten cents a ride. Most of the skiers spent their day yo-yoing up and down the rope tow on Alta Vista. I seldom wanted to spend my money on a lift ticket, and never would waste a clear day on a tow hill. A bunch of us Sheltonites would ski over the top of Panorama Point for a 1,500-foot drop down the wide-open, untracked slopes to Edith Creek Basin. If there was time, we would do it twice. If the weather was impossible, we skied in the timber on the Devil's Dip Trail from Paradise to Narada and rode back up on the ski bus to do it all over again. Devil's Dip was notorious, a narrow, steep trail dropping 1,100 feet in a scant mile. When the trail was busy it became terribly icy and generally pockmarked with sitzmarks. I wonder if one of the skiers I dodged was my future wife, who made the same loop over Panorama Point and skied Devil's Dip with her friends. If so I wasn't impressed.

In the summer of 1941 I applied for a photographer's job at Paradise Inn. So many boys had been drafted, the Park Company must have been desperate, for they made me the manager of the photo shop, overseeing an assistant photographer and two salesgirls.

The photo shop was squeezed between the Paradise Ranger Station and the guide house. The ground level was the store and darkroom, with sleeping quarters in the daylight basement. Our job was to accompany the twice-daily guided foot trips to the Ice Caves and take pictures at four different places along the way, at the same time getting pictures of the horse trips. We were given three 5X7 studio cameras that were never meant for the out-of-doors. The focusing was done on a ground glass, and every picture had to be taken on a tripod. The 5X7-inch film came in sheets that had to be loaded in the darkroom in holders. All told, the camera weighed around forty pounds.

We were young and strong, so the weight of the camera wasn't the problem—it was the time needed to set up the camera on the tripod and focus on the ground glass at each photo spot. Fortunately the tourists were slow and the guides would stop and talk to their party and give us time to put the camera away and let us run ahead to the next location. After the last picture, we hastily folded our camera and tripod, ran back to the photo shop, developed the film, and made 8X10-inch prints, which would be on display when the horse and foot parties staggered in an hour later. In that pre-Polaroid era the tourists were amazed to see themselves in print so quickly and the salesgirls were waiting to take orders and the pictures were mailed out a day or two later. It was fun but hard work and long hours. Arriving home at the end of summer I slept thirty-six hours without waking. Mother was about to call the doctor when I finally stirred.

I had hoped to run the photo shop the next summer, but by then I was in the army. The photo shop went by the wayside during the war for lack of help and was never reopened. Even the building has disappeared.

I guess my path crossed Pat's that summer, for she was on one of the guided trips I photographed. I'd like to say I was deeply stirred by her presence. Who knows, maybe I was. However, I'm afraid that to me she was just another upside-down face on the ground glass. Besides, she was probably wearing braces.

Japanese ship beached on Guadalcanal. A few years later, during a violent storm, it slid into deeper water.

CHAPTER 4

Hip Two Three Four, About Face

or
World War II, The War to End All Wars

Troopship in the South Pacific. The first night out most of the boys were seasick. What a stinking mess!

Three and a half years in the army is a big chunk out of anyone's life—and it looked even bigger to me when I was only twenty-three years old. However, though you'd have had a hard time convincing me back then, being drafted had two compensations, eventually if not immediately.

For one, I was immensely lucky to be assigned to duties that (usually) were not particularly dangerous and certainly were not the boring routine suffered by so many of those behind the lines. Having been hooked on photography by the Box Brownie, having studied it in college, and having worked at it a summer at Paradise, the Army gave the added experience to become a professional.

For the other, childhood years of collecting stamps and studying the pictures in geography books of strange lands with strange languages, strange money, and strange people might be said to have given birth to a potential wanderlust—except in those years a person might dream all he wanted about the big round world and be certain he'd never get far from home. Foreign travel was time-consuming and expensive. None of my

family or friends had ever been abroad or had any real plans to go. Then the army came along and offered free trips and wouldn't take no for an answer.

To be honest, given a choice, I'd rather have been sent to better climates with fewer bugs. Still, simply being in a far corner of the planet reinforced the urges awakened by stamps, to see the world. The army days gave me time to find out that "seeing the world" is not enough, one must experience the world, one must get out of the tent and hike the trails and meet the people.

Many years later, when I returned to the scenes of my war years, friends were startled that I would twice in my life, the second time voluntarily, visit New Guinea. But besides the fascination with the country, for me it represented the Big Step from Shelton and my home hills to—well, the rest of the planet. So the trip to New Guinea was a revisit to my youth, as significant as, say, revisiting (as I often do) Mount Rainier. As with other members of my generation, the Big War was the Great Divide, and going back was a way, of sorts, of seeing where I came from, where I'd been fifty years before.

In 1940 Bob won a low number in the country's biggest lottery ever and knew that one day soon he'd receive "Greetings" from President Roosevelt. In the spring of 1941, his knowledge of photography got him assigned to an X-ray unit in a mobile hospital. His unit followed the battles through North Africa, to Sicily, and to Anzio beachhead a day or two after the first landing. Moving on through France, he was well into Germany on Victory in Europe Day.

I got a high number, but my hiking companions soon were all drafted. Less from patriotism than from having no one to go hiking with, I said farewell to boss and friends, took the bus to the big city, and volunteered. However, on the day of my medical examination the grasses were pollinating, making my eyes red and nose drip, and I was rejected. In the spring of 1942 the army no longer cared about hay fever and I was drafted.

At Bob's suggestion I showed a folder of my mountain photographs to the army interviewer along with a letter from Rainier National Park Company telling of my management of the photo shop. He was impressed, added a few extras to my accomplishments, and after boot camp I became an Army Air Corps (in 1946 the name was changed to Air Force) ground photographer and was assigned to a photo unit in the 13th Army Air Corps in the South Pacific, one of the smallest and most obscure Air Corps in the war and overshadowed by the larger and famous 5th Air Corps, also in the South Pacific. The next three months of my army life were spent training at Duncan Field near San Antonio, Texas, where we worked with a lot of photographic equipment—interesting stuff, completely unrelated to what we would eventually be doing. We were still subjected to an hour of drilling each day and a lot of work projects. For this we had a rotten corporal and sergeant who vied with one another to see who could be the rottenest. I did figure out that when they asked for volunteers for some "dirty job," it was always easier and more interesting than other jobs, so I ran contrary to army rules by volunteering regularly and thereby avoiding the miserable KP duty. In mid-October we were sent to the Bay Area to wait our turn to ship out.

Six months after being sworn in I boarded a troop ship in San Francisco bound for the South Seas. Having volunteered for something the day before we sailed, I missed KP duty that first night, and thank golly. Our ship was a freighter. The lower decks were solid-packed cargo. Our "stateroom" was in a hold with row after row of narrow bunks stacked three high. Open-air showers and four rows with thirty toilets each were housed in a specially built cabin on the deck.

Our ship was part of a large convoy zigzagging across the ocean. I spent hours on deck fascinated by the deep blue water. As we went south to warmer weather, we were able to sleep on the hatch covers. I used to lie there under a blanket, watching a ship's mast sway back and forth against a black star-studded sky. On my back, looking up, the mast appeared still and it was the stars that were swinging back and forth across the sky. The Southern Cross appeared. We went over the Equator accompanied by dolphins and flying fish.

I hadn't planned to keep a diary, but at Duncan Field I had written home daily and continued to do so on board the ship each day on a writing tablet. For the three weeks we zigzagged across the Pacific to New Caledonia, there was no opportunity to mail the letters, and it was another two weeks after we arrived before our post office was in operation. Then I found that my five weeks' worth of letters would not pass the censors and I had to rewrite them, leaving out place-names and what we were doing. Since the original letters couldn't be sent home, they became the start of a diary, and I just kept on with it, eventually filling seventeen writing tablets. Most entries are about nothing but the boredom of army life, but a number were detailed accounts of hikes to jungle villages on days off and the numerous bombing raids on our camp in Morotai.

The letters that turned into a diary were just a simple chronicle of things as they happened. At least half the time they were written on my lap in pencil, sitting on a bunk, in an airplane, or aboard a ship. The diary was written as if the entries were letters home, and similar letters *were* written home, but the diary "letters" included personal thoughts and activities that would not have passed the censors. Many days there were just brief notes, "Same as yesterday." Unfortunately, I didn't always say what I had been doing "yesterday." The diary said virtually nothing of what we were doing for the war effort.

When I got home the diary was forgotten until fifteen years later, when my folks discovered it while moving. It is from the diary that I have written the story that follows.

Beyond the Golden Gate Bridge we were met broadside by big waves and the ship began to roll. Soon half the soldiers were sick: the hardest hit were those on KP who had to dump a week's worth of rotten garbage. For six hours we paralleled the waves setting up a wild rocking motion, the sick going from bad to worse. The sleeping quarters was a stinking mess. When I needed a toilet, all 120 were busy with a GI sicker than a dog, sitting on the floor straddling a toilet, dirty water sloshing back and forth across the floor, not that they noticed. I felt a bit woozy but didn't lose anything. The ship eventually turned into the waves and quit rolling, and by the next day everyone was back on his feet. That is, all but the drill corporal, who spent the entire three weeks of the voyage in the infirmary and didn't recover until we landed and thereafter was a totally different person, never again barking at the boys.

A STRANGE LAND

Three weeks from San Francisco we arrived at Noumea, capital of New Caledonia. I volunteered to help unload the ship. That was a mistake. The hatches were opened and the bunks and floor removed, exposing thousands of boxes. We carried and wrestled big and little boxes to a net that was hoisted up and onto the dock. When the first floor was emptied, another floor was opened and emptied, and then another—for two weeks, twelve hours a day, seven days a week. So much for my volunteering to avoid dirty jobs! However, Noumea was a very French city, and after my twelve hours, I was able to wander around and buy tiny little ice-cream cones.

At last we were finished and driven twenty miles out in the country to our camp, located near Tontouta Airport. First up were prefabricated steel buildings to house the repair depot. Most of the metal pieces fit together pretty well, and those that didn't were bent until they did. After that was done, we assembled a wooden mess hall, officers' cabins, and finally our own quarters.

Sunday, December 7, 1942
Tontouta Air Base, New Caledonia

Rain again. Worked some more on the buildings. Sure was sore and stiff this morning. Only two little half-cooked pancakes for breakfast. Not much for lunch either, but dinner turned out fair.

Our photographic equipment finally arrived, six 4×5

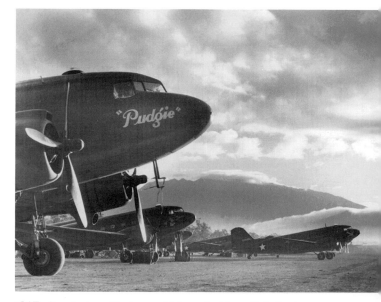

C47s lined up at Tontouta Airport in New Caledonia, where I was first stationed. The C47s were the workhorse of the South Pacific, carrying supplies from island to island. People too, but they had to sit on boxes.

Speed Graphics, dozens of film holders, a year's supply of black-and-white sheet film, cases of chemicals, printers, enlargers, and—best of all—my personal 120-size folding camera hidden amid the GI gear.

I was darn lucky; forbidden by censorship regulations, other cameras had been discovered in personal luggage and destroyed.

After all those months, for the first time we learned what was expected of us. An airplane is a complicated piece of machinery and during the war the planes were constantly being modified in the field to fit a specific situation. Every time a modification was made, it was carefully documented on blueprints and photographed. It was our job to record the work in progress and show how it look when finished. I spent many hours inside a plane taking pictures of some nut or bolt. Trying to focus a 4×5 view camera in a tight corner was a hassle. We worked out a guess-and-by-golly system by which we would guess the space and prefocus the camera, set it in place, and then hope by golly it was pointed in the right direction. I don't know if anyone ever looked at the pictures, but I loved the work and occasionally I got

Roc du Notre Dame on the west coast of New Caledonia, a distinctive landmark.

me take their picture, and thanks to the photographer for whom I'd worked in Shelton (for free) I always had film for my own camera.

Days off, most of the boys hitched a ride into Noumea for its two special treats, real French-style bars with ladies of the evening (they were there all day) and the Pink House, an army-operated place of pleasure. Any GI who entered the grounds was given a VD treatment whether he was there to be pleased or only looking. I once walked by the Pink House just to lay eyes on so famous a place. It was a large pink house alone in the middle of a block surrounded by a high stone wall that kept me from seeing the yard. A line of GIs waiting to get in extended from the gate in the middle of the block around the first corner and halfway to the next corner. It hardly seemed worthwhile to wait in line and get a VD treatment to see the yard.

to fly to photograph the modification in action.

The damp, hot tropical climate was tough on us, heat rashes being just one of our miseries. It was tough on cameras, too. Fungus grew on the lenses, the shutters corroded, and the flash connections just plain didn't work.

Now and then we got time off to see the island. The backbone of New Caledonia is very rugged hills 3,000 to 4,000 feet high. Dirt roads ran up each side of the island, connected by one tortuous over-the-mountain single-lane road. The river crossings were on man-powered ferryboats. The French colonists owned the farms and chrome mines. The natives farmed for themselves and wanted nothing to do with anyone else's work. The manual labor was mostly done by indentured Indonesian laborers, a very beautiful people, very homesick and very intelligent, some with a working knowledge of as many as seven different languages, including English. Everyone was happy to let

Wednesday, April 7, 1943
Tontouta Air Base, New Caledonia

*What a day! Crash! Crash! **CRASH!!!** This morning the New Zealanders wrecked three P-40s. While I was taking pictures of that, a Navy plane ran off the runway and sheared off both wings. While I was photographing that, another Navy plane ran off the runway into four other planes. It just touched the first three, but it cut the last one in two. What a mess, but no one was hurt.*

My diary recorded twenty-five wrecks during my stay on New Caledonia. Why so many? Part of the problem was that the pilots were young and hadn't been flying long. Second, the planes were all fast and hard to handle and, finally, there were a lot of careless factory workers back in the states. I just hoped there were enough planes to reach the front.

I got involved in a project to make wooden practice bombs, as real ones were always in short supply. To

Above: *A wooden practice bomb and the real thing dropping from a B-25 bomber. Photographed while lying over the open bomb bay, two crew members holding my legs. Above right: The same plane skip-bombing with a wooden practice bomb, taken from the ground.*

study the pattern the bombs made, I laid over the open bomb bay with two crew members holding my legs while I held tight to my 4X5 camera for pictures of the bombs falling. I did this with the wooden dummies and, later, with the real things on a bonafide bombing run over a Japanese airfield on the island of—New Britain.

I never felt particularly bad that my work was all behind (or above) the lines. To be honest, I felt very lucky not to be in combat. The first year the photo work was pretty demanding, but the second year the repair shops were doing the same modifications to several dozen bombers at a time and didn't need photographs of each. As the work dropped off, our crew spent more time developing pictures for the officers than doing war work. Therefore, when an opportunity came to transfer to public relations, I jumped and, after a year and a half on New Caledonia, moved northward to the Solomon Islands.

In public relations I got to see the world, or at least a large portion of the South Seas. I spent time on Guadalcanal, Treasury Island, the Admiralty Islands,

New Guinea, Morotai in Indonesia, and the Philippines. I was teamed up with a former newspaper reporter. Together we were flown to various islands where I would photograph all the GIs we could find at work while the writer interviewed them. The story and photograph of each boy was then sent to his hometown newspaper.

Sunday, April 16, 1944
Guadalcanal, Solomon Islands

Went for a walk back into the jungle this morning. It was just a tangled mess of dead limbs, trees, vines, bushes, and ferns. A lot of the bushes have nasty looking stickers on them. Noticed a lot of bugs, mostly spiders. Some are very pretty, bright green and orange. The birds seem to be having a field day with some of the most unearthly screams. Saw two birds about the size of an eagle. They sounded like dogs barking.

Most of the time I had one day off a week, which I spent hiking jungle trails to native villages. I talked to a headhunter in the Solomon Islands who showed me a picture of himself in *Life* magazine holding a Japanese general's head.

On one flight over the Solomon Islands we circled an active volcano on Bougainville. The volcano was shrouded in smoke so there really wasn't much to see. I spent a week on nearby Treasury Island, a coral island only slightly larger than the airstrip that covered it.

Wednesday, April 19, 1944
Sterling Field
Treasury Island, The Solomons

I don't know what more I can say about this island except that it is very pretty along the bay.

I have a lot to learn about living on a small island. There is no water on the island, so fresh water has to come by boat and we are rationed one canteen at a time. I saw the boys taking a shower during a cloudburst so next time it poured I grabbed my soap and went out too. The rain felt like a warm shower and I was soon all lathered up. Suddenly the rain stopped, just as if someone had turned off the faucet. There I was all covered with soap and no water.

Left: *A Solomon Islands family on a trail near my camp.*
Left bottom: *Village in the Guadalcanal jungle six or seven miles from my camp.* **Below:** *Natives walking the beach on Admiralty Islands.*

It was a no, no, but I had to use water out of my canteen.—Then I found out the boys first fill up their helmets with water running off the tents and when the rain stops they still have rinse water.

Sunday, April 23, 1944
Sterling Field
Treasury Island, The Solomons

Rained all night and all day so I couldn't take pictures. I spent the day writing letters and for the first time in weeks I am all caught up. This afternoon I developed and printed some of the pictures I have been taking. I am using a makeshift darkroom and the prints are very poor.

I thought there was something wrong with me the first night I was here. Several times I woke up feeling like my cot was rocking. It seemed weird so I didn't say anything for a couple of nights, but finally it was too much. Everyone's bed rocks. We are only 15–20 miles from the volcano on Bougainville and there are earthquakes day and night. During the day we are too busy to feel them but they are quite noticeable at night lying down. The boys have gotten so used to them they don't notice the rocking.

After the Solomons we spent six weeks in the Admiralty Islands. I made friends at a native village four or five miles from camp; I took pictures during my first visit and then returned with prints for them on my next visit. I bought a carving I named "Mary." It now sits at home on top of our TV set.

My experiences in the South Seas were to me like articles out of *National Geographic*, but out of 10,000 soldiers and sailors on these islands, only a handful were interested in the world outside their tent. The vast majority, on their days off, laid around camp or played poker. Not until they reached the Philippines were they interested in the natives or, to be more exact, the girls.

Monday, October 9, 1944
On board the *Robert C. Grier*
Morotai, Dutch East Indies

Morotai at last! We are anchored in the harbor. Hope we don't have to stay on the ship too long. The anchor was barely down when a little outrigger canoe came alongside with some boys. The fellows tossed some coins and the boys dived for them. The little boats look well constructed from handmade boards. They have outriggers on both sides and sails woven out of grass.

We are told there is an air raid every night.

Morotai was my first and only taste of enemy action. Ashore every night for two weeks we were bombed and strafed. The occupants of each tent built their own foxholes and at first alarm jumped in. Some

Admiralty Islands natives and "Mary," the wooden carving I bought. Termites were eating Mary when I sent her home. Mother preserved her in formaldehyde and Mary now occupies a place of honor atop the TV in our Edmonds living room.

Dutch East Indies island of Morotai. This scene was taken on a beach hike to the village of Dayo.

Thursday, November 22, 1944
Morotai

It was pretty bad last night. Fortunately, only two men were killed. One was in a foxhole that took a direct hit. The other was sitting on the edge of his foxhole only 15 feet from where the bomb landed. The rest of his tent mates were down in the hole and were not hurt.

I was working in the darkroom after dinner, and when the alarm sounded I crawled under the photo lab and hugged the ground. The bombs made a lot of noise coming down CHOOOOOOOOSSSE———BOOOOOM. I hope I don't hear that again. One bomb hit the other end of the building I was under but no one was hurt. I could tell a bomb had landed somewhere near my tent, so as soon as the planes had gone I ran towards my tent. However, before I could get there shrapnel started raining down from our AA guns. I stopped under a shed with a tin roof and listened to the ZING, ZING, PING as shrapnel hit the roof. The roof stopped the little stuff, but a couple of big pieces came right through.

I waited a few minutes under the tin roof and then ran on to my tent. The medics had ignored the shrapnel and were already there. I was just in time to help lift the boy who had been sitting outside his fox hole onto a stretcher, he didn't look too badly hurt, but he was.

My tent was only twenty feet from where the bomb had landed. It was still standing, but hanging in shreds. My bed and clothes were perforated. My helmet had a big hole in it, but my personal camera hanging next to it was untouched. Today is Thanksgiving, but I am not in the spirit. Should I be thankful fragments missed my camera by three inches, or should I be thankful I wasn't hit? It was impossible to be thankful when my next-door neighbor was killed.

of the boys slept with their clothes on. Most slept in their underwear, and a few even wore pajamas. I have always slept with nothing on and, when the alarm sounded, there was usually plenty of time to put on my pants and jump into my foxhole before the action started. One rainy night a plane snuck in low and was on us so fast we just dived for the ground, which was mud. When the raid was over the boys had to take a shower and wash mud off their clothes, but I only had to take a shower.

Not all attacks were that funny.

Morotai in the Dutch East Indies (now Indonesia) was my favorite, because of the people, whom I had first come to admire in New Caledonia.

Transportation on the island was by water or foot trails. Days off I hiked the beach five miles to Dayo Village, where I made friends and photographed the natives at home and work. If I was lucky I even hitched a ride on a patrol boat ten miles to Sangowo Village.

Morotai was one of those islands where we established only a perimeter and never went after the few Japanese hiding in the interior. No one worried about them and we walked the beach to the native villages with never a problem. *Hardly* ever. On one trip I got trapped on the return by a flooding river. Knee-deep water I had waded earlier was now over my head. I was finally able to cross about midnight but, much more worried about meeting up with an army patrol than the Japanese, I crawled under a tree and waited for daylight to make my way back to camp.

In Morotai, for a story on a rescue squad, I went on a search mission in an army Catalina flying boat. A B-25 was down off Mindanao. The approximate location was known and the crew members had been seen getting into a life raft. Allowing for drift during the night, sixteen square miles of water had to be searched. The

Sunday, December 2, 1944
Morotai

On the way back from Dayo I caught up with a man and two kids. When we came to the waist-deep river the tide was in and the water was now chest deep. I waded across carrying my camera, but one of the little boys insisted on carrying my shoes for me. Holding my shoes above his head, the water came up to his chin. It looked funny to see him going deeper and deeper with my shoes over his head. It looked as though he was going to go all the way under. I don't know what would have happened if the water had been any deeper for he was a very determined little kid.

On one of my visits to Sangowo Village, I noted the people were putting up decorations in preparation for something unusual. I was urged (by sign language) to return the following week. Sure enough, a festival was underway, the village street decorated with bamboo archways. The only outsiders were two Dutch officials, who must have been invited, and several GIs. I was to recall it all vividly, fifty years later, rereading my diary description of the festival of November 25, 1944. Instead of the usual topless wrap, women were dressed in finery and men wore shirts. The festival was in celebration of the defeat of the Japanese and started out with a mock battle and ended with dancing in the street.

Top: *Sangowo village celebration November 25, 1944, at Morotai, Dutch East Indies.* Bottom: *Seaplane rescue of a B-25 crew off Mindanao, Philippine Islands. To our eyes in the sky the life raft was a tiny dot in a very large ocean and took hours to find.*

Aboard an inter-island sailboat, called a banca, off the island of Leyte, Philippines. I spent the day on the boat talking with the crew and passengers as we sailed towards my camp.

picked up a ride on a banca, headed to Tacloban, a town near our camp. A banca is a sailboat with outriggers, and the one I rode on was medium sized and had two sails. The boat had come from Mindanao, and because of a poor wind, the trip had taken five days.

There was a crew of five, a half dozen passengers, three hogs (alive), a rooster, and a cargo of bananas in the hold. It was only about half loaded as it had already made several stops.

It was very pleasant sailing; however, the wind was poor and at times we were barely moving. At other times we went along at a good pace.

I enjoyed talking to Pedro Pepino, the owner of the boat, and the other people on board. I had a lot of questions to ask them and they, in turn, wanted to know all about my life. I showed them the family pictures which I always carry in my billfold.

A couple of the fellows had guitars and tenors, a small instrument that looked like a harp, to pass the time away. One fellow was lying in the end of the outrigger, and every time a wave came along he would get a free bath. Others just sat around and smoked. They didn't have matches so by rubbing two pieces of wood together, in a few minutes they made fire by friction. For a stove, they used a small, cut-down oil drum. They cooked rice and sweet potatoes. Boats like this travel four or five days, at night the passengers just stretched out on the tiny deck.

raft had bright-colored dyes and smoke flares, but it's a great big ocean and took more than two hours of searching to spot the tiny dot. The plane set down and took on the happy crew, then took off. Before returning to Morotai it landed at 6,000 feet to drop off supplies at a guerilla strip in the highlands of Mindanao.

As the war moved on toward Japan I was transferred from Morotai to the Island of Leyte in the Philippine Islands.

Thursday, June 21, 1945
Leyte, Philippines

I don't know when I have enjoyed myself as much as I did today. It was my day off, so bright and early I hitched a ride 10 miles down the beach and hired a young boy to paddle me out in his dugout canoe to one of the bancas. I

Another time I caught a ride on banca with a crew from Mindanao. It was a very restful ride and took about eight hours. This was a sailboat with sails made of reeds woven into cloth. The banca was headed toward our camp loaded with fresh produce—and girls. The boat wasn't very big but they held a dozen or more people along with a couple dozen chickens.

On the boat I had time to talk to the people about their customs. I found that when a man goes to another island for work, he leaves his family and adopts a temporary wife and kids near his new job. When he is finished, a month or a year later, he simply returns to his legal family. All kids were loved and it didn't really matter who the father was, a great arrangement for everyone. Anyway, there were lots of jobs for men around the army base and a great demand for girls from the GIs and natives. One mother wanted me to take her very attractive daughter as a temporary wife. I pulled out my picture of my sister, Kay, and her two kids, and explained I already had a family. She replied, "Oh! But she is so far away." She just couldn't understand my not wanting a temporary wife, especially as she would be there to look after the daughter. Some of the boys did take on temporary wives and a whole village of shacks grew at the edge of camp.

Village market near our camp on Leyte, Philippine Islands

Wednesday, August 15, 1945
Leyte, Philippines

Just another day at work, but the news is full of the A-bomb and how it may force the Japs to surrender. When the news of the A-bomb first came out last week, it sounded like just another super blockbuster.

I had no idea what "atom bomb" meant. We were used to 100-pound bombs, 1,000-pound bombs, and blockbusters, and assumed this was a new super blockbuster.

Terrible as the device proved to be, I have to admit we in the army felt relieved. The general belief in the ranks was the Japanese would never give up, and a half million of us and two million Japanese would be killed in the coming invasion.

The futility and stupidity of war became apparent ten years later when Russia, one of our allies, became our enemy, and the two countries we defeated, Germany and Japan, became our staunch allies. I certainly never dreamt a Japanese army officer would become a good friend or that he would tell me the atom bomb was a blessing as it gave the Japanese a "face-saving" surrender. Otherwise, he said, they would have had to fight to the last man.

In November of 1945, almost three years to the day, I arrived back in San Francisco. We docked about midnight and a group of sleepy army musicians, assigned to greet every shipload of returning soldiers, struck up the band—probably for about the thousandth time. We were serenaded for half an hour and then the band packed up. We were bused to an army camp and at four or five o'clock in the morning were served the army's compulsory steak dinner for returning soldiers, never mind that we would rather have been in bed asleep. A week later I was home. After three years in the tropics, I spent the first month at home sitting on top of the heater.

• CHAPTER 5 •

Life Begins at Thirty

or
How to Starve While Working

Lumberjack standing on a springboard cutting a large fir tree with an axe, working out of Camp Grisdale in the Olympic Mountains. Having first notched the Douglas fir to insert a springboard, he is swinging a double-bit axe to make an undercut. Undercut completed, he and his partner will move to the other side of the tree and pull on the misery whip (a two-man crosscut saw) until time to yell "TIMBER" and jump for their lives.

When I got out of the army, I had two things in mind, to become a freelance photographer and to find a wife. Getting started on freelancing was urgent; looking for the right girl could wait. Before the war, my dream was to work for *National Geographic* and roam the world taking pictures of natives in Africa and climbers in the Himalayas. Although three years in the South Pacific made my dream seem possible, instead of spending time traveling to distant places, I decided that for a start there was no place like the mountains at home.

While still overseas, Bob and I had agreed by mail to become partners. He beat me home by a few months, set up a darkroom, designed our logo (two photographers in alpine hats and a background of

Bob below a bergschrund on the Emmons Glacier, taken for a Seattle Times *assignment on The Mountaineers Summer Outing of 1946.*

mountains), and was already promoting what became our trade name, Bob and Ira Spring.

In 1946, the first summer after the war, Bob and I plunged full time into photography, accompanied by Bob's wife, Norma (a key member of our business—we took the pictures, she wrote the stories and neatly typed them). We photographed all aspects of our state: sawmills, logging, wheat-farming, cattle roundups, commercial fishing, Puget Sound freight boats (last survivors of the mosquito fleet), tugboats, and all kinds of recreation. Mountain stores got most of our attention. The *Seattle Times* gave us a jump start. If we could put together a group of pictures that made a story, the

Seattle Times would buy them for the Sunday Rotogravure. The paper was the stepping stone to magazines. Magazines led to books. Books opened the door to assignments from major accounts that paid for many pounds of hamburger and jars of peanut butter.

FIRST ASSIGNMENT

Chet Gibbons, the Sunday feature editor of the *Seattle Times*, was so enthusiastic about our work, he gave us our very first assignment photographing the 1946 Mountaineers Summer Outing around Mount Rainier, spending three weeks circling Rainier on the Wonderland Trail. Of course he only paid for one of us but, anticipating other sales, we both went along.

From the beginning, The Mountaineers have been a leader in protecting our mountains. However,

looking back, 100 people wearing hobnails and tricouni nails accompanied by twenty pack animals had a considerable impact on the mountain environment. But hikers were few and far between then, and the meadows had time to recover before the next boots

---

The Mountaineers 1946 Summer Outing at Indian Henry's Hunting Ground, Mount Rainier. This was our first Seattle Times *assignment, photographed by both Bob and me; Norma wrote the story. After the* Times *used the story, it was sold to the* Toronto Star. *Today hikers recognize the impact on the fragile terrain, but hikers were so few and far between then that meadows had a number of years to recover before the next camper came along.*

came along. When that became no longer true, The Mountaineers gave up their cherished Summer Outing.

Most members of the 1946 outing were from Puget Sound, but a few were from as far away as Boston. We gathered at Longmire Campground in preparation for an early start. In the morning our tents and sleeping bags were loaded on pack animals; with only cameras and a day's supply of film in our day packs we were off on a great adventure. Our first day was an eight-mile hike to the flower-covered meadows of Indian Henry's. The camp kitchen, under the direction of Nashie, was set up complete with tables, wood stoves, and enough pots to feed the hundred people. Horses dragged in dead trees and we cut them into firewood with crosscut saws. We had our own tents, either surplus army tents that, being totally waterproof, were always dripping inside even in clear weather, REI's Highender, designed by Lloyd Anderson, or a homemade tent of our own creation. There was no hanky-panky allowed with sleeping arrangements. Married couples' tents were in the center with single men to the far left and single women to the right.

For the next two days people broke into groups depending on their special interest, birders who roamed the meadows, scramblers who bagged Pyramid and Mount Ararat, and climbers who explored high on Success Cleaver. On the fourth day camp was again loaded on horses and moved seven miles to a one-night camp at Klapatche Park. Day five was spent moving to Golden Lakes. Part of the outing followed the Wonderland Trail eight miles to the lakes; the rest of us took a very strenuous high route, climbing above 7,675-foot Tokaloo Rock, contouring across the Puyallup Glacier, crossing the rocky slopes under the Colonnade cliffs to the Colonnade fire lookout trail, and descending to camp near the Golden Lakes patrol cabin. The day was very grueling and some people had to be helped. By the time we reached camp it was dark. Day six, camp was moved six miles to Mowich Lake, where a truckload of fresh food awaited us.

The next move was an easy three miles to Spray Park for two days of exploring Mother Mountain, Knapsack Pass, and Echo and Observation Peaks. Day eleven we moved another six miles, dropping below the snout of the Carbon Glacier and climbing to Mystic Lake. I remember the last two miles well. The group started out together but everyone hiked at their own speed, so eventually three of us gung-ho guys were hiking together. Two miles from the lake we caught up with Eleanor Buswell, who kept going faster and faster. We couldn't let someone at least five years older, especially a mere woman, outpace us. At the pass above Moraine Park all four of us collapsed in agony. When we asked Eleanor why she was going so fast, she said it was we who were going fast, and she didn't want to hold us back.

At Mystic Lake we had time to explore Vernal Park, Elysian Fields, and Old Desolate and climb high alongside the Willis Wall. Our next move was dramatic. From the lake, as the pack string followed the trail over Skyscraper Pass, we on foot crossed the Winthrop Glacier, climbed over St. Elmo Pass, and slid down the Inter Glacier to a camp in Glacier Basin. It was a difficult and thrilling adventure for those of the party who had never been on a glacier before.

We spent the next morning exploring the deserted Starbo Mine buildings, and then fifty of us trudged up to Steamboat Prow to a high camp for the next day's climb of Mount Rainier. After twelve days on the trail we were in great shape and everyone who started made the summit. Of course, the mountain then was only 14,408 feet high, not to reach its lofty height of 14,410 feet until a new survey in the 1970s or its 1989 grandeur, measured by satellite, of 14,411.1 feet.

The story was a great success. The Seattle Times gave it an eight-page spread, and then the story was printed by six other newspapers, including the Toronto Star, and was used by a car magazine.

Next, Bob and I spent two weeks that busy summer at Camp Grisdale, a logging camp near Shelton. Bob and I were lucky to have seen and photographed the transition from cutting trees by brute strength to the machine age, from the crosscut to the chainsaw, and from railroad logging to trucks, to helicopter and balloon logging. It was a joy that summer to photograph the proud men pulling on eight- or ten-foot crosscut saws, called "misery whips." The lumberjacks took great pride in their skills and strength. If the partner on the other end of the saw goofed off, the saw would move just as fast and no complaint, but the next day the goof-off was run out of camp. Making undercuts with double-bladed axes, they sent chips flying like a flock of birds. That year was the beginning of the end of an

Top: *Tree-topping at Camp Grisdale, 1946. This was the most glamorous job in the woods, strictly for star loggers. In the 1960s, portable spar poles came into use. We lost a great photo opportunity, however the job became much safer for loggers.* Bottom: *Clearwater log drive, Idaho.*

era. The first power saw was a big, heavy contraption that took two hefty men to hold. I remember a logger saying that with improvement the power saw might work on level ground but never would be practical on hillsides.

OFF TO THE BIG CITY

As soon as the first summer was over, I hopped a train for New York and enrolled in the School of Modern Photography, one of the many schools that opened with the advent of grants provided to vets by the GI Bill. Bob joined me three months later.

The school concentrated on commercial studio work, photographing silverware, glass, jewelry, mechanical objects, and even professional models. The school had nothing to do with out-of-door photography and at first it seemed a waste of time. In the classroom the camera sat on a big tripod and wasn't moved. The instructor drilled into us the importance of highlights and shadows. By moving the lights around (easy to do in a studio) he showed us how a round shape could change from a feeling of roundness when lighted from the side to a flat surface when the light was directly over the photographer's shoulder. It was slow coming to me that these same techniques also applied to the out-of-doors. One may not be able to move the sun but the sun moves across the sky so it is a matter of timing the photo when the sun is in the right place. The south side of Mount Rainier is a great classroom example of this, as early morning and late afternoon sunlight that angles across the mountain highlights every contour and ridge, giving the mountain a rounded appearance; however, at midday when the sun is over one's shoulder the mountain looks like a flat curtain. We could move our models at school for a pleasing composition but, unlike the sun and studio lights, the mountain does not move. However, we can move the camera to find the most pleasing composition before even setting up the tripod. Textbook photography is one thing, but mountain photography is at best a compromise. A compromise between what the eye sees and what the film is capable of recording. A compromise between the best lighting for the mountain and best lighting for the flower field in the foreground. Rules be darned, the photographer is really on his own.

We may not have learned a heck of a lot about photography in a six-month course, but we did gain confidence and learned how to sell pictures. During our school time, New York was the center of half the country's publications. With the encouragement of our teachers we contacted ad agencies and book publishers and sold some mountain stories to magazine editors. We also met Selma Brackman of the Freelance Photographers Guild, a photo agency that for fifty years has sold many of our photographs.

While I was waiting for Bob to finish school in New York, the photo editor at the *Seattle Times* asked me to fill in for a photographer who was hospitalized. That was in 1947. At the end of that job, I received my very last pay check—*ever.*

We questioned our ability to make a living—that is, *two* livings—from mountain pictures and bought into a child portrait studio on Seattle's lower Queen Anne hill as our bread and butter while freelancing on the side. Much to our surprise, the outdoor pictures were selling, so when our four-year lease was up we dropped the studio.

The first five years we lived hand to mouth. To build a stock file we had to invest in a car, pay travel expenses, and buy film. That, and starting a studio, quickly used up our savings, so notice of a sale was a triumph. Actually being paid (a few months later) for the picture was a second triumph, permitting us to pay the rent and buy another pound of hamburger. At the most critical period we had help from a provision in the GI Bill that aided self-employed veterans by giving us each a grant of $1,000. Our leading competitor, Ray Atkeson, was generous with good advice, but the loyalty of Chet Gibbons was the crucial factor in our eventual success.

Starting with nothing had one big advantage. In 1946 credit did not come easy; no bank in its right mind would lend someone with no steady income money to buy a refrigerator or a car. Therefore, we

Above right: *The play of light and shadows on the Blue Glacier.* Right: *The play of light and shadows on an early summer snowfield on Mount Gladys. The instructor in the New York photo school had no idea that 2,500 miles away two of his students would use his studio lighting lesson to show texture on mountain and glacier photographs.*

Above: *Bob's picture of Glacier Creek from the Mount Olympus trail. My pack was heavy and I went blindly charging past this view, but Bob, bringing up the rear, called me back. While waiting for me to return, Norma had taken off her heavy pack—good thinking.* Opposite: *Bob and Norma on the Blue Glacier on Mount Olympus in 1946. This was one of the stories we did purely on speculation. The gamble paid off—the Seattle Times bought the story and several eastern newspapers picked it up.*

were forced to save our money and pay cash. We found dozens of ways to hang onto pennies that eventually added up to dollars. For the first two years we made do with just one car between us. This meant only one of us at a time could be out taking pictures, so we bought a second car as soon as we had the money. Those first years were tough and we didn't know whether to celebrate or cry when after five years we finally made enough to start paying income tax.

By perseverance, our name was becoming known. When selecting pictures, art directors don't care who took the picture. They pick the one that fits their layout, but at least when they sent out a request for pictures, they remembered to ask us, too.

The logging pictures at Camp Grisdale are a good example of how our freelance work goes. Thanks to our good relations with the *Seattle Times*, we sold a couple of small stories that within a month, paid our

out-of-pocket expenses. During the next few years we sold individual pictures to *Encyclopedia Britannica*, *World Book*, and several textbooks, and one picture was used as a full-page ad in the *Saturday Evening Post*, so five years later the two weeks spent taking logging pictures provided a tidy profit.

CHAPTER 6

Girls! Girls!! Girls!!!

or
Pat on a Collision Course with Ira

Pat rappelling from Pinnacle Peak, with Mount Rainier in the background. She had come a long way in three years from the day in 1947 when her knees shook on Monitor Rock.

I didn't have a date until I was in college. I was afraid of girls, too scared of rejection to ask for a date, and tongue-tied when I was around them. I caught a real nice girlfriend of Bob's on the rebound. She was into photography and liked the out-of-doors and I thought it was true love, but she switched her affections to someone else. All through the war I wrote to a wonderful friend of Norma's I had met a week before I was drafted. However, we had little in common when I got

My "Esquire Girl" photograph of Pat rapelling was used twice by Esquire *magazine, which in 1948 was the most risqué magazine on the newsstands. The picture of Pat and our trip leader, John Klos, was taken in the Hourglass on the Mount Shuksan climb where we were benighted above the Fisher Chimneys. The Spring reputation survived the scandal of the night on the ledge. Anyone who thinks it is romantic to spend a night stranded on a cliff above a glacier, even with a pretty girl, is urged to try it.*

back and she wasn't romantically interested in me.

After the war I was definitely interested in girls, but not just any girl. I had seen too many boys take a girlfriend, who would appear to love the out-of-doors, for an easy hike or two but, once married, they never went hiking again. My girl had to love hiking, mountain climbing, and skiing. If she passed those tests, all she had to do was pose for pictures on the lip of a crevasse, back to the camera, or wear red to add color to a scenic photo.

In The Mountaineers I met a lot of girls on weekends at the ski lodges. Having gotten over my fear of asking for a date, I went out with a dozen girls over a two-year period. Some were wonderful, but I seldom asked a second time. If they liked skiing, they didn't like mountain climbing, or if hiking not skiing. I was looking for something very special.

Fisher Chimneys, the series of connecting ledges and gullies which provides a "highway" to the high glaciers of Mount Shuksan. They are a dangerous highway at night, so we bivouacked at the top rather than descend in the dark.

Pat Willgress was something special. Maybe it was the similarities of our backgrounds that made her that way. One set of her grandparents carved a farm out of a Vancouver Island wilderness. The other homesteaded in the Saddle Mountains of Eastern Washington and built a vacation log cabin on the Dungeness River, miles from the nearest road.

As a teenager, her father did the usual farm chores but was also expected to help keep the family's larder full by hunting deer (the limit then was two deer a day) and fishing, of course. When he moved to Seattle,

where Pat and her brother were born, weekends were spent fishing (for recreation), farming (for the love of it), and vacationing at the wilderness cabin on the Dungeness River. Pat enjoyed sharing her parents' activities, but they were mainly interested in rivers and lakes. She began to wonder what was on the hilltops. Her winter horizons were expanded by skiing at Mount Rainier, Mount Baker, and the Canadian Rockies, Fortunately for me, to expand her summer adventures she took The Mountaineers' Climbing Course in 1947, the same year I did.

I had my eyes on her at the clubroom lectures and wondered if she wasn't the one, but she was always surrounded by boys and it didn't look like I had a chance. The first field trip was a practice session on Monitor Rock (Schurman Rock), designed in the 1930s by Clark Schurman for climbing practice and constructed by the WPA in Seattle's Camp Long. *At last I had my chance!* I told her I was taking pictures for the *Seattle Times* (my best line) and asked her to pose rappelling off the rock. She had never leaned back in space before, trusting the rope to keep her alive, and her knees were shaking so badly I had to shoot at a very fast speed to get anything but a spunky girl quivering in midair. Afterward I asked her to go along, the next day, on a ski trip to Mount Baker and, on the way home from there, asked for a date to the movies. On that first date I told her I was going to marry her. She laughed, little realizing that was not just another of my lines. I was dead serious.

It's a wonder Pat kept going with me. On our first ski trip I crashed into her. I wasn't hurt, but she got some nasty bruises, as her father observed the first time I met him. On the second Mountaineer Climbing Course practice trip, a backpack, I pointed out a nice soft hollow for her sleeping bag. The rains came, and her hollow became a pond. Several other times I took her home soaking wet. With a group of five we set out to climb Mount Shuksan, and to ensure enough time for a good picture story we carried food for five days. The first three days were stormy, confining us to tents at Lake Anne. The fourth day started bad but at about eight in the morning the mountain cleared. It was much too late but we took off anyway. The late start, a wrong turn, and extra time taking pictures resulted in our enjoying a gorgeous sunset on the summit of Mount Shuksan. We descended the glacier to the rock ledges above the Fisher Chimneys, where the daylight gave out. We didn't dare tackle the cliffs by flashlight so the five of us huddled against a large boulder to keep warm. No, it was not a romantic bundling. We spent the night looking up to a sky full of brilliant stars and down 4,000 feet to the twinkling lights of Baker Lodge, thinking about the fire roaring in the lodge's huge fireplace. The picture story of that climb appeared in the *Seattle Times, Ford Times*, and the old *Esquire* magazine, and one of the pictures won an award in *Popular Photography*.

In the summer of 1948 Pat signed up for The Mountaineers' ascent of Mount Rainier. So many bachelors were on the trip roster that in defense I went along, too. The route was the Kautz Glacier which, after the popular Gibralter Ledge route slid out in the 1930s, was considered the best way up from Paradise. In clear weather we carried our heavy packs to Camp Hazard, 11,500 feet, at the base of an ice cliff on the Kautz Icefall.

Thunderheads in the night staged a spectacular light show over Mount Adams, spattered our sleeping bags with hail, and swirled menacingly over the ice cliff. At dawn, however, the cloudcap melted away in the sunshine. A sea of clouds drowned the lowlands from horizon to horizon. By the time we had climbed to the top and returned to our high camp, the cloud had risen nearly to camp.

It was so beautiful above the clouds Pat and I chose to stay with the rear guard for a few more pictures and we were last to leave Camp Hazard. The clouds were lapping at our feet when we started our descent to Paradise and we were immediately in the soup. It was

Kautz Icefall from Camp Hazard, near where Pat lost her sleeping bag on our 1948 Mount Rainier climb.

assumed the cloud layer below us was, at most, only a few hundred feet thick and in the absence of crevasse or the danger of a storm, no one was concerned about a little fog—how wrong could we be.

We hadn't gone far when Pat's sleeping bag slipped out of her pack and rolled toward the Nisqually Glacier. Fortunately, through a break in the fog we were

The second week of our honeymoon was spent climbing Glacier Peak with sixty Mountaineers. The climb from high camp was easy, giving us time to explore the Chocolate Glacier after reaching the summit.

man I thought I knew everything about weather. I expected to break out below the clouds at any minute, but the clouds below us didn't quit as expected. Instead the fog got thicker and thicker. But the tracks were so many and so clear a person couldn't get lost, could he?

Yes, he could. A whole lot of persons got lost. Some lost the trail in the first quarter-mile and ended up miles away in Indian Henry's Hunting Ground. But the major blunder was when the correct route dropped off the ridge into the Nisqually Snow Finger, the only safe way leading down through the cliffs to the Nisqually Glacier. Pat and I were late and I was hurrying to catch up and would have followed the wrong tracks. Pat saved the two of us from that error when she recognized a big rock where the route leaves Kautz Ridge and descends the snowfinger. We followed the correct route down to the glacier but the tracks soon disappeared on the hard ice. From memory, Pat and I groped our way across the glacier and up to what, in the fog, appeared to be the side of Alta Vista. The area was all snowfield, crisscrossed with tracks in every direction. No problem; I had spent three summers here, so I headed for where I knew Paradise was, but in the dense fog I ended up in Edith Creek Basin. From there the trail was unmistakable. We had spent so much time wandering in the fog I was sure we were hours late. Expecting to be reprimanded I sheepishly checked in at the Paradise Ranger Station. We found that we were nearly the first ones back! Driving home in what turned from fog to drizzle to downpour, we encountered bits and pieces of the party here and

able to watch the bag bounce a thousand feet and stop just above a cliff. Pat and I glissaded down, fetched the bag, and climbed the thousand feet back to the tracks that forty pairs of feet had made, and again headed down toward Paradise. Being an experienced mountain

there, including a forlorn bunch at the Nisqually River bridge trying to thumb a ride up to their cars parked at Paradise.

TRUE LOVE GROWS SLOWLY

I knew on our first date—or at least suspected—Pat was the one for me, but true love doesn't really start at first sight. It grows slowly. Despite the *rigors* of our *rugged* courtship, Pat accepted my proposal, and after more well-chaperoned hikes and climbs we were married July 30, 1949. Pat was a mere twenty-six and I was thirty. Obviously it was my money she married me for. After paying the minister I still had a fortune in the bank—ten dollars.

Our honeymoon was in two parts: a week by ourselves at Upper Lena Lake, then two weeks photographing a Mountaineers Summer Outing in the Glacier Peak area. Our first day of marriage we made camp halfway between Lena Lake and Upper Lena Lake. Bough beds are a "no, no" nowadays, but when we were young it was a woodsman's art. I spent an hour cutting soft boughs and weaving them into a super-soft, bouncy, and aromatic mattress and as a final touch, covered the boughs with a layer of ferns. The finished mattress was over a foot thick—as fine as any honeymoon bed in the world's best hotel. We crowded into our sleeping bag, but the wedding day had been too much for Pat; she threw up all over the mattress and we had to move to the hard ground. The next day I got sick on the trail. Neither of us was very healthy when we finally reached Upper Lena Lake.

I thought we would have the lake to ourselves, but it was noisy with a Boy Scout troop. Worse luck, I was recognized, and we were surrounded by eager boys who wanted to talk about cameras. Under other circumstances I'd have enjoyed this reunion with myself as a Boy Scout. However, under the circumstance we went on. The alpine meadows above the lake cured our ills and invigorated us. In another mile or two we came to a small lake I had discovered years ago. At last we had a lovely little lake all to ourselves.

The second part of our honeymoon was photographing eighty-six Mountaineers climbing Glacier Peak for a possible magazine story. Our camping gear was loaded on a horse and all we had to carry in our "light" day packs was my heavy camera, film, changing bag, tripod, and flashbulbs. Pat's pack was even bigger than mine, and the other hikers were appalled that I made her carry so much. Little did they know that it was full of lightweight flash bulbs.

The highlight of the outing was climbing Glacier Peak by way of the Chocolate Glacier, the most remote, most beautiful, and least-used route on the mountain. Our high camp was at timberline and while we had dinner we watched a herd of over sixty mountain goats grazing on a nearby ridge. In the morning the lowlands were covered by a sea of clouds that gave one the wonderful feeling of being separated from the rest of the world. From our high camp the climb was short and we spent most of the day exploring the crevasses and ice cliffs on the glacier.

At a camp near Image Lake we were hit by a violent windstorm that shook loose a line holding up the tent pole. I got out in the pitch-dark and tied it up. At dawn the weather cleared beautifully; Pat and I hurried to get dressed and out for sunrise pictures. However, Pat couldn't find one of her unmentionables. We tore the tent apart looking for it, so I urged her to go without. After all, who would know what she wasn't wearing under a flannel shirt, a sweater, and a parka? But she said nothing doing. The sunrise wasn't waiting so I had to leave her. As I stepped out of the tent, there waving in the breeze like twin flags was her missing underwear, apparently having tangled in the rope when I retied the tent during the night.

At least that is my theory. Pat has other ideas.

• CHAPTER 7 •

Family Life

or
The More the Merrier

Go! Go! John in a car seat attached to his mother's Trapper Nelson packboard.

The first year of marriage didn't change our lifestyle. With photography income being insufficient to both eat and pay thirty dollars a month rent, Pat kept her secretarial job. However, by the next summer we decided to either sink or swim and Pat gave up her (our) paycheck.

We rented an apartment near our child portrait studio. Our apartment was in an old house that had been divided into four units. Our side windows were only a foot or two from a brick wall; our back windows looked out on the storage yard for a roofing company. Each morning the workers would start up their smelly tar heaters and let them run a smelly hour before hauling them to construction sites. One friendly little touch was the morning glories that found their way into our bedroom through a crack in the window sill. We lived there when our son, John Elliot, was born in 1950. Soon after, Bob and I gave up the studio and built a small duplex on Queen Anne hill with apartments for

Campers' eyebrows lifted when Pat gave Vicky her daily bath in the old Paradise Campground.

Bob's family and ours, with a darkroom and office in the basement. Finally we were fully committed freelancers. In 1953 Victoria Ann was added to our Queen Anne household.

Children were bound to slow us down, but they added a new dimension to mountain photography, to say nothing about new challenges and different kinds of adventure.

The summer of 1950 Pat was pregnant and it slowed her hiking—a little. When we did a story on The Mountaineers' Mount Robson Summer Outing in the Canadian Rockies, Pat was five months along. The outing leader, an older bachelor, worried about her "delicate condition" and required her to take it easy and hike with the elderly people who would be taking two days to cover the twelve miles to Berg Lake. It was good someone younger was with them for some of the older folks needed her help. Though she was a bit lopsided she waded the raging streams, holding their hands while they kept their feet dry crossing on narrow logs. On

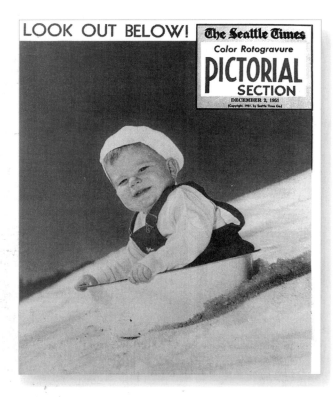

LOOK OUT BELOW!

The Seattle Times
Color Rotogravure

PICTORIAL
SECTION

DECEMBER 2, 1951
[Copyright, 1951, by Seattle Times Co.]

"Look out below!" John on the cover of the Seattle
Times *Pictorial Section, 1951.*

the way out Pat put her foot down and hiked the twelve miles in a single day. A couple of strong men replaced her as helpers.

John was born December 3, 1950. The next summer Pat was still carrying John, but on her back. The other way had been easier and faster.

The summer of 1952 we were back again in the Canadian Rockies, on a Campcrafter Outing with other Mountaineer couples who had young children. Because Pat had been on Mount Athabaska in 1946 and had not reached the top, I stayed in camp with John while she climbed.

One evening we drove to the garbage dump for bear-watching. Feeding the bears used to be one of the standard tourist entertainments, but doing it by hand has always been a "no, no." We were watching other people feed them out their car window, and I wasn't paying attention when a bear approached from the rear of the car, stood up, and put his paws on the window next to me— only the window was open for pictures, so he put his

paw on my face. At campfire that night I was asked about the scratches and told the truth, "a bear hit me," and laughed. No one believed me. They thought Pat and I had quarreled and I got the worst of it.

Vicky was born April 17, 1953. It was pretty obvious she had been conceived on the Canadian Rockies trip, and we liked to believe it was while we were camped below beautiful Mount Victoria, and thus her name. At three months she started saying words, and at six months was saying whole sentences and paragraphs, though she was the only one who knew what she was saying. When she finally did start talking our language, she never stopped talking except when she had a book in hand. She read in the car and she read on airplanes. When we stopped to rest on a hike, out would come a book. Her favorites, such as *Heidi*, were read dozens of times. We made her turn off her lights at eight o'clock in the evening, but she'd turn them on at five o'clock in the morning and read for an hour before we called her to get up.

For virtually 100 percent of our photography travels we camped. On the go as we were all spring, summer, fall, and winter, our basement was always full of drying tents, in winter sometimes still snowy and icy. The exception was when taking winter pictures of Mount Baker, where we appreciated staying weekends at a Mountaineer cabin—no wet tent to take home.

John and Vicky took to camping and hiking like they were born to it. As long as they were warm and fed, it didn't matter where they were. Two kids were no more trouble than one, especially since John always looked after his sister. When Vicky was only four months old we took her on a three-day backpack to Cascade Pass for a story. There she produced her first tooth for us to admire.

The kids never knew any life other than mountains.

A 1959 photograph of Mount Adams from Takhlakh Lake. I set my camera on a tripod and used a string to pull the trigger. This was made when few people braved the thirty-five miles of dirt road and lake water was safe to drink. Takhlakh Lake is still as beautiful, but a good road and a formal campground attract a lot of people and we can no longer set up our tent on the lake shore.

My work kept me there, and I kept Pat there, too, so they had no choice. When I was single I could eat breakfast, break camp, and be on my way in a half-hour. Add Pat, and getting going took one hour. Add John, and we were lucky to be on our way in two hours. When Vicky joined up I stopped looking at my watch. While the kids slowed down my photographic work, being with them in the wilds was the quintessence of "quality time." Besides, as models for magazine stories, they worked cheap. Between Bob's stories and mine, in the 1950s and 60s the Spring kids must have been the most publicized children in the country, appearing in *Saturday Evening Post, Friends* magazine, *Good Housekeeping,* and local and national magazines.

Giving three-month-old Vicky a bath within sight of glaciers at Mount Rainier, camping at Cascade Pass with three-year-old John and sixth-month-old Vicky, and snow camping raised eyebrows and a few pointed comments from passing strangers. This was the first stage of installing the self-reliance one gets from adventuring into a mountain wilderness.

We, like all parents, worried about our children's safety. Unlike most parents, we used our knowledge to train them to cope with hazards. Given a lead, children discover strength and general inventive solutions that will serve them well in their adult lives.

CAMPING WITH CHILDREN

Carrying a small child is easy, but there comes an awkward age, around two or three years, when he or she is too heavy to carry and too small to walk very far. Parents who fail to adjust destinations only make themselves and their children unhappy. During this period getting our whole family to Cascade Pass gave us the same sense of accomplishment and adventure we had felt a few years earlier climbing Mount Rainier.

Children haven't changed, but equipment for their backpacking has. We had to improvise a packseat for children, cut down sleeping bags to their size, and make our own tents, not so much to keep out the rain as to make life livable in mosquito season. Nowadays a person can buy child-carriers, pint-sized sleeping bags, and tents that weigh a third of the ones we made. Cutting limbs for bough beds is now forbidden, but the modern lightweight sleeping pads are more

Small pool at Cascade Pass when hikers were few.

comfortable and solve the problem of a bough-end sticking in one's back. Freeze-dried, easy-to-prepare meals permit the novice to easily feed the family. When no longer a novice, though, one may well follow our example and buy supermarket food, which doesn't have the "freeze-dried" taste and costs a lot less.

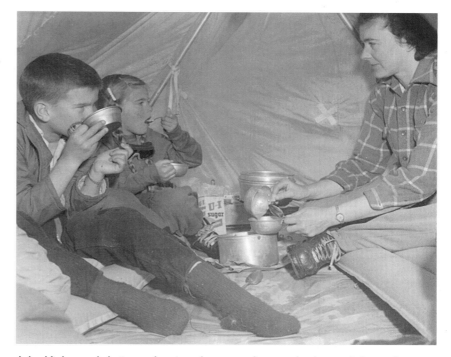

John, Vicky, and their mother in a homemade tent that stayed dry as long as it did not rain.

We used to tell the kids they had to be good or they couldn't go with us. Empty threat. We couldn't have left them home. Hiking is work, especially for short legs, and kids would rather play with pebbles or a puddle than keep moving. Our strategy was to point to a spot a good distance up the trail and say when got there we'd stop for an energy break—that is, for trail candy. Since we never let them have candy at home, this bribe really worked and, who knows, the extra energy may really have helped. One evening at the Longmire Campground in Mount Rainier National Park, I had set the sleeping bags and food boxes on the ground while I reached for the tent. Pat and I were busy setting up the tent, when four-year-old Johnny started screaming. We looked around in time to see a raccoon running off with our plastic bag of trail candy. We chased it up a tree and out on a limb. There, to John's consternation, it calmly proceeded to eat our candy and let the shredded wrappers drift down for us to pick up. Hiking the next day, John kept complaining about his lack of energy.

On a camping trip in Idaho we stopped at a wet, soggy campground on the Salmon River. Year-old Vicky was napping in the car. Without waking her, Pat and I proceeded to set up the tent. John suddenly screamed, we jumped, and found him pointing to a huge rattlesnake a few feet away. The snake was wet so there was no sound from its rattles. Pat, never having seen a rattlesnake, thought the tail had a poisoned stinger like a bee and offered to grab its head while I cut off the tail. I explained the facts of life to her, took a stick, and threw the critter as far as I could. The in-cident so unnerved us we spent the night in a motel. It is worth remembering that rattlesnakes don't always rattle.

When Vicky was five and John seven, we did a three-day ski tour to the crest of the Tatoosh Range. That was the plan, anyway. The weather was fine when we left Seattle but deteriorated as we skied the two miles to Reflection Lakes. In the face of such weather, we camped near the first lake, had dinner, and settled down. Snow began to fall, turning to rain. I was experimenting with a tent fly of the latest sensational "miracle fabric." Some miracle. The rain slowed down a little but kept right on going through, soaking our sleeping bags and creeping into our shoes. During the night the rain stopped, the temperature dropped to ten degrees, and by morning the tent and everything in it was one big cake of ice.

Not quite everything; the four us were warm enough to have breakfast. While I rolled up the sleeping bags, Pat held the frozen shoes over the stove, not in the hopes of drying them, but at least to get them warm, wet, and flexible enough to slide our feet in.

THE TALE OF A FORMER KID

In her foreword to *Best Hikes with Children in Western Washington & the Cascades*, by Joan Burton, photos by Bob and Ira Spring, published in 1988, Vicky wrote:

When I heard my father was doing the photographs for a children's hiking guide, I was thrilled. I consider my father and my mother to be bona fide experts on the subject. They took me on my first hike when I was five months old, taught me to hike the same day I learned to walk, kept me interested when I was a teenager, and encouraged me to set out on my own as an adult.

It has been quite a few years since I was a little child, trailing along after my parents, walking through rainstorms and crying because I was promised two nights out in the snow and only got one. However, I still remember my feelings when I had short legs and everybody else had long ones.

Hiking was fun because my parents told me it was fun, and I was a very trusting child. And my parents worked to make it fun for me. First, we always had a destination. I knew when my feet hit the trail how far I had to go, and woe and misfortune to anyone who suggested that we should turn back before reaching some wonderful lake; the tiptop of a real, but probably quite small mountain; or, best of all, an old lookout site that was sure to be strewn with treasures.

Second, I always had the company of my older brother, and maybe a cousin or a friend. This was very clever of my parents because we competed with each other to see who could go the fastest the longest. By myself, with just my two parents for company, I would have gotten bored and quickly become exhausted.

Third, my parents always carried incredible treats whenever we hiked. At home we never were given big chunks of chocolate, or any kind of candy at all, that I can remember. However, on the trail they carried "energy food" and, believe me, my brother and I fell for that trick quite happily. "Five more switchbacks

and we take an energy stop" would have us running up the trail as fast as we could.

There are a lot of unpleasant things about hiking that bother little children. My parents took care to make sure that these things did not ruin our experience. They wanted us to want to go hiking again, so we were not asked to become macho woodsmen overnight. I can remember being carried on my father's shoulders through nettle patches, being lifted over logs, being taught to make slapping mosquitos a game, and being fed dinner in a warm tent when it was raining.

As soon as we were old enough, my parents liberated my brother and me. We were allowed to go ahead as long as we stuck together and stayed on the trail. This was the best. Together we never had time to be tired. Our first aim was to get as far ahead of our parents as possible. Then we proceeded to have a great time, playing at being motorcycles, trucks, or race cars as we zoomed up the switchbacks.

Looking back, I would say that my parents' most effective ploy was to have only one day pack for my brother and me. When my brother realized that he was to have the pack and I wasn't, he was very proud and I was green with jealousy. They dumped pounds of stuff in that pack and still my brother carried it, just because he knew how badly I wanted to. And can you believe this? As soon as my parents let us go ahead, he would let me carry it for miles as long as I promised not to tell! It wasn't until I was nine and had read Tom Sawyer that I finally caught on, and my parents had to buy me a pack of my very own to get me to carry anything.

Maybe the most important thing my parents did was never to complain in my hearing. If the trail was bad, if they were cold, tired, or just out of sorts, we never knew it. My parents were excellent role models on the trail. I really didn't know it was okay to complain when things were really bad. After all I had never heard them complain.

One day my mother nearly got sick when she saw me pull off my socks, bloodstained almost to the ankles from bleeding blisters. This was really unfortunate, because the best thing about hiking was that it got my brother and me out of doing our mandatory four hours of work around the house before we were set free to play. So you can understand that I was devastated when my mother decided that I would have to stay home until the blisters on my feet healed to her satisfaction. I got blisters on my hands from working in the garden before I was allowed back on the trail with new boots.

Now that I am grown up, carry a heavier pack than my parents, and sometimes slow down enough to hike with them, I'm not sure if being given a taste for the outdoors was a good thing. By the time I was a teenager I was hooked on the outdoors; now I'm addicted. My house is filled with tents, skis, hiking boots, climbing ropes, and bicycles. And holding a steady job is not to my taste at all. Rather than sit at some old desk, I would much rather tighten my belt, load up the pack, and head for the outdoors whenever I want. It's all my parents' fault. . . .

—Vicky Spring
Former Kid

Five-year-old Vicky and seven-year-old John help their mother tie down our tent on the Tatoosh Range. The weather had been awful the first attempt at a ski tour, but two weeks later everything was perfect.

Mine came first so I could crawl out and start packing. Then John's and Vicky's shoes. She had just held one of her own over the fire when the stove ran out of gas, leaving her shoes frozen in the wrong shape! My laughter didn't improve her disposition.

The return to the car was only two miles, but bucking a cold wind was miserable. Vicky started crying. Pat and I were afraid we would never get her hiking and skiing again. But no, the five year old was wailing because we had promised two nights out and we were going home after only one.

Three weeks later in perfect weather we skied from Reflection Lakes to the ridge top just east of the Castle (peak) and made camp. In one direction was a spectacular view of Mount Rainier, in the other Mount Adams, Mount Hood, and Mount St. Helens. Sunrise? Well, it was one of those events a photographer would die for.

MORE ROOM FOR A GROWING BUSINESS AND GROWING CHILDREN

In 1957 the Bob and Ira Spring families, having scraped together enough money from savings and partnership funds, moved from the duplex on Queen Anne hill to side-by-side houses in Edmonds, each with office space and the darkroom and fireproof film vault in Bob's basement. The Edmonds branch of the National Bank of Commerce chanced to be remodeling and for the price of scrap metal, the door to the bank vault became the door to the film vault. There is no hoard of gold in there to steal, so if anyone doesn't believe us the combination is written on a nearby wall.

Bob and Norma's three children, Terry, Jacquie, and Tracy, were close enough to the ages of our children to be like brothers and sisters. I used to tell Jacquie and Tracy I hated girls, and they felt very sorry for Vicky. One time Jacquie asked me, "If you hate girls, how come you married Aunt Pat?" I told her Pat never confessed she was a girl until after we were married. Jacqui felt very sorry for me.

We never felt the need or desire to get away from the kids. When possible, I planned trips to include the family. For more rugged ventures, Pat and the children would stay with her parents or go off with them on a fishing trip. Even when busy writing, I was able to tune out the noise and confusion of two active children at my feet, leaving the coping to Pat.

As time passed the kids carried more of their weight on hikes, and I looked forward to when they would start carrying part of mine. No luck with John. In high school, John spent three summers in the Student Conservation Association's (SCA) program doing volunteer work under Jack Dolstad in Olympic National Park. His first summer in the SCA he helped build a patrol cabin twelve miles up the Elwha River trail; the next year he worked on the ocean beach trail and the third summer photographing the various SCA projects in Colorado, California, and here in Washington. During his university years he was a summer ranger at Mount Rainier.

Back around 1970, bargain flights to Hawaii looked so good to my thrifty eye that for three years we loaded our tent on the airplane to spend the week following Christmas Day photographing Hawaii. One year John so liked his Christmas present, a down vest, he wore it on the plane and was still wearing it when we landed in blazing sunshine. At our camp the first night at 5,000

John, the Eagle Scout.

feet, the thermometer plunged. The rest of us were dressed for the tropics. John had the last laugh.

John did great in high school and took pictures for the annual. He attended Edmonds School District Ski School and could soon out-ski his parents. He joined Boy Scout Troop 312 under the leadership of Cliff Shaw and with the help of his mother passed from Tenderfoot to Second Class to First Class ranks. All on his own he proceeded to Eagle Scout, thus out-Scouting his father. In 1970 John enrolled in the recreation program of the College of Forest Resources at the University of Washington, spent two summers as ranger at Mount Rainier National Park, and graduated with a B.S. degree in 1974.

During John's final two years at the university, his Grandfather Willgress urged him to work summers at Cascade Machinery. He started in the repair shop, mucking

Vicky, a friend, and Tom in Jackson Hole, Wyoming.

out motors (mucking is a very messy, dirty job of burning and chemically cleaning motors). When he graduated, with further grandfather nudging, he agreed to work at Cascade Machinery one year to see if he enjoyed it enough to make it a career. He did and advanced to sales, then management, and finally ownership. John still hikes, climbs, and skis, but he also loves the water.

Whatever Vicky does is done with enthusiasm and energy. Her high-school grades were excellent. At Edmonds Ski School she was on the cross-country and racing teams and, when snow wasn't handy, played on the volleyball team. Lacking John's opportunities for summer work, during vacations she helped with my guidebooks, patiently dogging my footsteps, carrying more than her share of camera equipment, perfectly content to read her books while I set up my tripod and fiddled with my cameras.

Her last year at the University of Washington she

spent the summer working with a research team on the Blue Glacier of Mount Olympus. Her "work" there included serving as unofficial alpine guide, hauling visiting scientists and dignitaries to the top of the mountain. Finally deciding that in spite of her father's bad example she wanted a career in freelance photography, in 1979 she enrolled in a two-year course at Brooks Institute, a photography school in Santa Barbara. She was disgusted by her fellow students, interested only in flashy, high-paying photo assignments and much too sophisticated to ride bicycles to school or go hiking. The one exception was Tom Kirkendall, content to eat macaroni and cheese instead of sirloin steak and, to the consternation of school staff, riding his bicycle to class. Tom and Vicky were married September 20, 1981, and set out on the same path I chose in 1946.

Our children have grown up and left home, but they, and their families, are still the most important part of our lives.

• CHAPTER 8 •

Climbing Stories

or
Our World Has Its
Ups and Downs

My first glacier picture, on the Nisqually Glacier in 1938, taken with my 6x9-inch view camera.

B y its very nature, mountain climbing is dangerous and "old" climbers are probably the cautious ones who have taken great pains to minimize the risks. The others made headlines. Being cautious and being easily frightened has served me well. The physical and mental challenge of a summit climb has its rewards, but old climbers know their limitations and are willing to turn back when the weather turns bad. Just being in the mountains has its own rewards.

When I went to work at Mount Rainier in 1937, employees, even janitors, were entitled to one free guided trip. It could be a horse trip to Reflection Lakes, a foot trip to the Ice Caves, or, as I chose, a tour of the

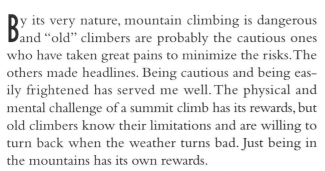

A large crevasse on the Emmons Glacier of Mount Rainier. Taken on the 1946 Seattle Times assignment. Eastman Kodak bought this photograph for a display in camera stores.

Nisqually Glacier. The free trip included all necessary equipment, which meant hobnailed boots, wool clothing, and "iron pants" with a reinforced seat for sliding. The guide had an ice axe and the clients were given alpenstocks, stout steel-tipped poles five to seven feet long. At the glacier's edge the guide tied six of us to a manila rope and led us safely beside crevasses. I was fascinated by the color of the ice, the beautiful shapes, and the interesting lighting on the formations. However, the guide didn't dare lead his inexperienced tourists to photogenic places. I was frustrated to see spectacular crevasses and be unable to get to the best viewpoint to photograph them. Right then I was determined to own an ice axe and learn to climb.

In 1940 I found my way to the Co-op (now called Recreational Equipment Inc.—or, REI) and bought my ice axe. Learning to climb was more complicated. I joined The Mountaineers in 1940 but lived too far from Seattle to take the Climbing Course the club had been presenting since 1935. Several fellows working in

I spent hours searching the Nisqually Glacier to find this wonderful block of ice with just the right sunlight highlighting the details. This photograph was purchased by the Seattle Art Museum and used in Argosy magazine.

Boy Scouts, and the 7/16-inch manila rope standard for climbing was available at any hardware store. When hiking I carried my ice axe and whenever near a patch of snow I did ice-axe self-arrest until I became pretty good. However the stumbling block to glacier climbing was I had nobody to team up with. My break came in 1946 when I moved to Seattle and was able to enroll in the Climbing Course. I got double my money's worth, for it was there I met the girl I was determined to marry. My first birthday present to her was a pair of crampons.

While learning to climb, I also had to learn to take glacier pictures. My first few trips garnered some interesting black-and-white shots despite badly exposed negatives. Photo books said nothing about glaciers but did say that exposure readings on snow should be taken off a gray card. The surface of glaciers is mostly snow, so for my next glacier ventures I took a gray card. It worked fine until I set it down on the snow and got it wet. I then discovered the same reading was given by using my own dirty hands. What the manual failed to say was that the real secret on snow or ice is crosslighting, the same principle taught in photo school for use in a studio. If the sun is beating straight down, the snow turns out as a big white blah in the picture. However, if the rays of the sun are skimming the snow or ice, such as along the edge of a tilted serac or a slope or a hillside in late afternoon, every contour and crystal shows as shadows and highlights, bringing a snowfield or an ice formation to vivid life. Colorful as the deep blue in a crevasse can be, my first choice is the stark beauty captured in black and white.

Shelton had been guides at Mount Rainier and Mount Baker during their college years, and I conned them into taking me on the Nisqually Glacier for my introduction to mountaineering photography.

I knew how to tie a bowline-on-a-bight from the

No matter what the photo books say, filters are seldom, if ever, useful for black and white pictures on snow, especially if one expects them to darken the sky. Even without a filter the sky often photographs unreasonably black. I have tried a Polaroid filter to help with snow texture, but any improvement is too slight to be noticed.

The biggest bugaboo for a mountain photographer is dust stirred up in the pack by the motion of hiking. A few ruined pictures (and lost sales) taught me the seriousness of the problem and the simple solution of keeping the camera wrapped in a plastic bag.

It is remarkable the difficult places where Bob and I carried our cumbersome 4x5 view cameras and even more remarkable the photographs we were able to make. Maybe it was the time it took getting the camera set up that instead of shooting rolls of film to maybe get one good picture, we spent hours looking for the perfect picture before getting the camera out of our packs. The blessings of modern times is that magazines and newspapers no longer require 4x5-inch color films. The heavy Speed Graphic view camera can be left at home on climbing trips, replaced by the 35mm. The saving isn't only in weight, nice though that is, but the hassle of reloading color film in holders during a climb. The 4x5-inch film comes only in sheets, and without a handy darkroom the film has to be loaded in a changing bag. There's a limit to the number of film holders a packsack will accommodate, so I sometimes had to change film two or three times a day. I might have to stop in the middle of a glacier or halfway up a rock cliff and find a flat place where I could lay my changing bag.

Emmons Glacier. Note how in both this picture and the one opposite the sun is skimming the snow, bringing life to an otherwise flat surface.

Under the best conditions the process was a pain. Conditions never were the best. It was either too hot, too cold, or too buggy, and always took too much time. With the 35mm I can just slide in a new cartridge.

Our first attempt at selling climbing stories was

such a resounding success I did as many as I could. National magazines regularly carried stories of expeditions in the Himalayas, Alaska, and the Andes, but Bob and I were the only ones covering our own Pacific Northwest mountains. At first, when we had only one car, Bob came on all the climbs, but a story doesn't take two photographers, so after three or four years he left climbing assignments to me.

AT HOME ON A GLACIER

I have always felt more at home on glaciers. I am prepared at all times for a hidden crevasse. One time I spent five days camping at 11,000 feet on the Ingraham Glacier. When my companions and I reached the camping area, it was one big white expanse of snow. There had to be crevasses hidden under the snow, so before the tents were set up, I carefully probed the snow and figured out where the crevasses were. I wouldn't allow anyone to leave the tent unroped even to fill the snow bucket. The days were cloudless and the snow softened under the hot sun. What had been a wide expanse of snow was now crossed by large crevasses and the tent, just as I had predicted, was on a 20-foot-wide area between two crevasses.

As climbers soon find out, mountains that stand alone like Mount Rainier make their own

Little man what now? Fred Beckey in the Stuart Range. Used in Sports Afield *and featured in* Encyclopedia Britannica's *Picture-of-the-Year Book.*

weather. Guests in shirt-sleeves sipping an ice-cream soda at Paradise Inn may gaze at the mountain and note a picturesque cloudcap like a hat perched on top, but in that cloudcap climbers may be battling a snowstorm driven by an eighty-mile-an-hour wind. Other days guests at Paradise Inn may be driven indoors by rain and fog while climbers find themselves in shirt-sleeves in the sun above a sea of clouds that covers all of Western Washington.

The glaciers on Mount Rainier are natural for climbing pictures. For special assignments I have driven to Paradise in the morning, spent the day on the Nisqually Glacier, and been home by dinner. However, the 14,410-foot summit was most often the destination of my magazine stories. I have lost track of the times I have reached the top.

Most gung-ho climbers have their eyes on the summits and nothing else. Fred Beckey was one of the most cooperative and I photographed several of his first ascents. His dancerlike grace impressed me, as did the care he devoted to safety ropes and his concern for younger climbers. When I was working with Fred my tricouni-covered boots proved useless on rocks. With my boots scraping, Fred literally pulled me up a pinnacle named Tulip Tower, my one and only first ascent, listed as such in Beckey's *Cascade Alpine Guide, Volume 2*.

Some of the young climbers I photographed in the 1940s went on to glory. Beckey couldn't have been more than twenty-five when I did a story on his first ascent of Lighthouse Tower, and Pete Schoening, later world-famous for the belay that saved his party of seven on K-2, was still in college. Jim and Lou Whittaker were teenagers the first time they posed for me.

I have, on occasion, climbed the mountain in two days as most climbers do. However, on a two-day climb there is little time for pictures. For an in-depth magazine story I need to spend four or five days to reach the top, searching out interesting glacier formations along the way.

From Paradise, on the south side of Mount Rainier, the climb starts from the parking lot at 5,420 feet where a National Park ranger checks everyone's equipment. The first day's destination, a five- to six-hour hike, is Camp Muir at 10,000 feet. The first mile is on the busy paved trails to the edge of the Muir Glacier, covered with year-round snow and showing only a few small crevasses.

Climbing glaciers or spending a day on snow, we smear "Clown White" on our faces to prevent sunburn. Clown White (a zinc oxide derivative) is a paste that completely blocks the sun rays and doesn't sweat off, but it does come off on clothing and sleeping bags. It takes soap and water to remove the paste, which may be in short supply on a climb. There are sunblocks on the market now that do almost as well.

For me, climbing up the Muir Glacier is the worst part of the trip. Out in the middle of the glacier there are no landmarks and no shade and packs are always heavy, while Camp Muir is in sight the whole time, one weary step after another; hour after hour is like a treadmill that goes nowhere and Camp Muir seems no closer.

Camp Muir is in a narrow saddle between the Muir and Cowlitz Glaciers. In the 1930s a stone cabin was built to house twenty or so climbers, and there was a smaller cabin for the guides. The large cabin was cold, damp, and dark, and I have only stayed in it one stormy night. The rest of the time I either camped outside under the stars or leveled the snow and set up a tent. Camp Muir is a wonderful place to watch a sunset on the lowlands and see Mount Adams, Mount St. Helens, and Oregon's Mount Hood turn a strawberry pink. One time when I wasn't aiming for the summit, I took a sunrise picture from my sleeping bag that ended up as an eighty-foot-wide transparency in New York's Grand Central Station.

On those days when I was headed for the summit, my climbing partners and I would get up at midnight, have a cold breakfast, dress in warm clothing, strap on crampons, tie into our climbing rope, and step onto the Cowlitz Glacier. By starlight and flashlight, we crossed the Cowlitz Glacier with our crampons crunching on the frozen snow. By the time we crossed over the Ingraham Glacier the eastern sky would be glowing, and we would be well up the Emmons Glacier when the sun appeared.

The mountain rising over a mile above the surrounding hills stands high in the sky like a huge white cloud. When the sun climbs over the horizon the snow-covered glaciers turn a strawberry-ice-cream color, which changes into gold as the sun gets higher and finally to white. The reverse happens at sunset.

To climbers high on the mountain the sunrise is amazing. While on the horizon the high peaks turn a

Left: *Cowlitz Glacier while filming* Ice Climbing on Mount Rainier. Top: *Bergschrund in the Chocolate Glacier blocks the way to the top of Glacier Peak.* Bottom: *Resting in the steaming crater rim near the summit of 14,410-foot Mount Rainier.*

rosy pink, but standing in the middle of it the eyes play a strange trick and the brilliant colors seen from afar never amount to much. It is the same quick adjustment the eyes make going from a room at home with a bright white fluorescent light to a room with an amber-colored light. The same phenomenon occurs during a sunrise as the eyes quickly adjust to the color change. The only clue that something different is happening is the shadows, which turn an intense blue. Many climbers are so disappointed in the sunrise they see that they do not stop for pictures. However, film, unlike the eyes, records the true color. With a bit of luck and a lot of faith, some amazing pictures can be made.

Hopefully, by 8:00 A.M. we have reached the crater rim on Columbia Crest, highest point of 14,410-foot Mount Rainier. The rim is warmed by volcanic heat, so there are warm rocks to rest on, enjoy the view, and eat before starting down.

In good weather, one would like to spend a few hours on top, but the stay has to be short. In early summer crevasses are covered by the previous winter's snow that bridges and hides the void below, by midsummer many of the bridges have collapsed, and by late summer there are so few bridges left that a glacier-wide crevasse may completely

Below: *Ice cave in the Ingraham Glacier on Mount Rainier. The rope is tied to me.* **Right:** *Early morning on Glacier Peak's Chocolate Glacier.*

block the way. Some bridges are obvious while others can only be detected by a slight sagging in the snow. All are dangerous, and the reason climbers are roped together is that the weight of one person may be enough to break through the bridge. This is also why climbers must get off the glacier before the sun warms up and softens the snow.

MOUNTAIN SAFETY

Ice bridges do break and climbers fall into crevasses and are trained in self-rescue techniques to get out. Except for deliberately breaking through a bridge for pictures, members of my team have never had a problem. However, we did have a close call. Leading a rope of three, we crossed a crevasse I knew was hidden by snow.

I was followed by another rope of two people. The first climber had just crossed the bridge when, with a big *whomp,* the bridge collapsed for 100 feet each way, leaving a 20-foot gap and a very deep hole between the first and last person on the rope. While my rope waited, the two still tied together detoured around the end with the rope between them dangling over the open crevasse.

Photographing a climb takes three or four times longer than simply reaching the summit. We had to find a spot that challenged the climber (or looked in the picture as if it did) but had a solid ledge of rocks or ice to stand on and perhaps set up a tripod.

Some of my pictures have been taken looking up from the depths of a crevasse. It is an eerie feeling and a bit frightening to be lowered with all that space below my feet, but combined with what can be a spectacular blue in the ice, the giant icicles, the geometric shapes, and lights and shadows, make the experience hard to forget. There is no way I can take the picture I want swinging from the end of a rope, so before going down, I make certain

Teenager Carol Marston on the Cowlitz Glacier.

there is a ledge to stand on. As the ledge could break, I always remained roped.

When Pat became pregnant she had no problem hiking fifteen miles in a day, but she was prohibited from climbing because her doctor said the rope around her waist could strangle the baby if she fell, so I lost my favorite model. Fortunately, in the early 1950s, I was very involved in The Mountaineers Climbing Course, helping plan and photograph training films. In turn, the Climbing Committee kept eyes out for possible models. Gary Rose, Dave Nicholson, and the Marston sisters, Joan and Carol, were four of the greatest teenagers I have ever worked with. The five of us took a week-long expedition to Camp Muir. We had a picnic exploring glaciers and photographing the fantastic ice formations. We spent a night in Mount Rainier's summit crater, and were joined on that part of the trip by Bob who was doing a movie entitled *Ice Climbing on Mount Rainier.* Inside the crater rim we leveled off the volcanic rubble, pitched tents, and melted snow in a pot placed over a steam jet. At night the tents were warmed from beneath by the heat of the not-so-dead volcano. These four teenagers stayed with me for a number of summer stories, but eventually grew up and had to work for a living.

The next group of teenagers, Christine Nelson, Darline Goit, Dick Strand, and Bruce Hunter, also recommended by the Climbing Committee, were equally good. In a repeat of the Mount Rainier expedition, we camped two nights on the Ingraham Glacier at 10,000 feet, then moved up to 12,000 feet on the Emmons, and finally spent a night on top. One of the boys left his parka partly out of the tent and in the morning the portion touching the ground was bleached from the sulfur fumes.

On another trip I spent two nights on top of Rainier doing a story on a geologist. We camped in our usual place, again warmed by the dormant volcano. During the day we explored the steam caves in the snow-filled crater, melted there by the internal heat of the volcano, and hiked a mile to Liberty Cap, one of Rainier's three summits, 400 feet lower than Columbia Crest on the crater rim.

I had always wanted to photograph the lights of the Puget Sound cities at night from the top of Rainier, but each time the sun went down the wind picked up and it got much too cold to leave the cozy tent that was heated by radiant heat to sit around for a time exposure.

ELDORADO PEAK

I was always looking for new story angles, and in the summer of 1959 my inspiration was the All Ladies Expedition to the North Cascades (women's lib had not yet made "ladies" a put-down). All-women expeditions are common now, but thirty years ago they were almost newsworthy and certainly story-worthy. We were able to leave our two kids with grandparents, so for once Pat could come along. We had a total of six women. I had counted on Pat for protection, but most of the time all six ganged up on me. We drove to the end of the Cascade River road, hiked to Boston Basin, traversed to a camp on the Inspiration Glacier, and from there climbed Eldorado Peak. (Ginny Mohling and Ann Curtis made a first ascent of a needle and named it Bandanna Spire.)

The life of the party was Betty Manning, who played her recorder and kept the evenings lively. Poor

Above right: *Betty Manning during the "Ladies Expedition" to Eldorado Peak.* Right: *On a week-long climb of Mount Rainier, my teenage models start dinner at our camp at about 11,000 feet on the Ingraham Glacier.*

Betty. She had two children at home and it really had been a long time since she had done any serious climbing. The top of Eldorado was no easy feat for anyone, the last 300 feet a traverse along a knife-thin ridge of snow high in the sky with a drop to the Inspiration

Mountain guide Willi Unsoeld belaying a client up the Grand Teton, Wyoming.

Glacier on one side and a mile-long drop into Marble Canyon on the other. If one person on a rope were to slip, the next person on the rope would have had to jump off the other side of the ridge just to save themselves. The airy ridge shook us all, but Betty was almost in tears. In the middle she cried out, "Mother, I need you." On the summit she said, "If my kids or Harvey ever want to see me again, they will have to come up here, I am not going back along that ridge."

THE GRAND TETON

I have never felt confident on steep rock, but in 1956 I found myself doing a story on the Teton guides for *Time* magazine. The chief guide that year was Glenn Exum, who lined me up to photograph a man and his teenage daughter on the Grand Teton guided by the young Willi Unsoeld. I was impressed with Willi from his first friendly smile. He was absolutely great with his clients, taking them over airy spots like they were on the sidewalks of New York. But not me. Roped to my friend, John Carter, I dropped back to take a picture of Willi on the narrow ledge called Wall Street. At "Fat Man's Misery," the ledge thins out to nothing and a long step must be taken over space. When my turn came I couldn't do it, not until John went first and set up a belay. That was the worst place on the way up. Most of the route was a continual series of short, airy pitches interspersed with steep scrambles.

I was amazed at the view from the top, or lack of it. The Grand Teton stands virtually alone above ranchland and foothills. In a quick minute Willi named all the mountains in sight. In the Cascades, even the most experienced mountaineer needs a lot of time and has a lot of trouble identifying all the mountains upon mountains sprawling to the horizons.

The descent was easier for me until we came to a 120-foot rappel. I had often rappelled with Fred Beckey, but he did it very cautiously, never putting blind faith in his anchors. Willi expected clients to just back over the cliff and sail away. I tried it but, like Pat when I met her at Monitor Rock, my knees were shaking so hard I couldn't back off. Much to Willi's disgust, I slid off the cliff on my stomach, as I had seen Fred do so many times.

A few years later Willi moved to Seattle for graduate work at the University of Washington, and we had good trips with him and his wife, Jolene, and their four children. Willi subsequently became famous for his climbs in the Himalaya, climaxed by a first ascent with Tom Hornbein of the West Ridge of Mount Everest.

In 1972 the Unsoelds agreed to let me do a story on their family. We chose Eldorado Peak. Vicky was with me, and Willi and Jolene had three of their four teenagers. The trip was a riot. Willi was in his usual happy spirits, one minute philosophizing on world problems and the next minute telling funny stories, usually on himself. I was particularly impressed by his oldest daughter, Devi. She had Willi's appetite for adventure and his great feeling for humanity. She also had a sharp mind and surely would have accomplished great things in her life had she not died on Nanda Devi, the mountain for which she was named. A few years later Willi was killed in an avalanche on Mount Rainier.

THE PICKETS

In 1965 Bob and I were assigned by *National Geographic* to photograph an article by Supreme Court Justice William O. Douglas on proposed wilderness areas in Washington. Bob accompanied the justice on a horse trip into the Cougar Lakes region (which nineteen years later became the William O. Douglas Wilderness). I led a group of six on a ten-day hike into the Northern Pickets (which three years later were included in the North Cascades National Park). It was a pretty discouraged group that hefted heavy packs and started up the Ruth Creek trail in a drizzle that never stopped as we crossed Hannegan Pass and descended Chilliwack Creek, nor did the rain stop the next day as we ascended Brush Creek to a second camp on Whatcom Pass.

Air view of the rugged North Cascades. Klawatti Glacier and Eldorado Peak, left, and Glacier Peak in the distance.

The third morning had not a cloud in the sky, and we gasped at our first glimpse of some very impressive glacial scenery. We broke camp and climbed a shoulder of Whatcom Peak to an unnamed glacier, made a difficult traverse around the peak to Perfect Pass, and then crossed the Challenger Glacier to a spectacular campsite overlooking the sawtooth summits of the Northern Pickets.

Fury, Phantom, and Crooked Thumb were beyond our ability, but Challenger, the highest of the Pickets, was relatively easy. The summit stood only 3,000 feet above camp, but with detours for photographs we were a whole day on the climb.

We spent another day exploring and then headed home, avoiding the difficulties of the Whatcom Peak traverse by an easy-looking shortcut on Easy Ridge. The route truly was easy, 99 percent of it. The 1 percent was a vertical impassable cleft. We could throw a rock across but to climb across would have required a lot of pitons and hours. To get past we had to descend 1,000 feet and then climb 1,000 feet back up.

THIRD TIME IS NOT A CHARM

Mount Stuart has been a bugaboo for me. Bob and I first tackled it in 1939 while going to college in Ellensburg. Having only one day, we left town before dawn and were on the trail by 8:00 A.M. However, the nine long miles over Beverly-Turnpike Pass to Ingalls Creek took us three hours, so it was getting on toward noon when we started the 5,000-foot climb to the top. At four o'clock we reached the false summit, seemingly a stone's throw from the true summit, but neither of us owned a flashlight and we wisely gave up. Our last two miles of trail in pitch dark were not so much walked as groped.

My next Mount Stuart failure was in the spring of 1941, on a Mountaineers scheduled climb, a two-day trip. We had plenty of time but impossible weather.

My third attempt was over a three-day weekend the spring of 1968. Pat and Vicky and I parked the camper at the trailhead and packed over Beverly-Turnpike Pass to a camp at Ingalls Creek. The day was hot, the snow

Marge Mueller on the Challenger Glacier of the Northern Pickets, taken for a National Geographic *assignment and used twice by that magazine.*

almost boiling, streams were torrents, and Ingalls Creek was impassable. Next morning the water was down and we crossed without much problem. Pat had a bad knee and elected to stay in camp. On the mountain I began to feel sick to my stomach and just short of the false summit had to give up. On returning to the valley we found Ingalls Creek again bankful with meltwater and rising. We managed to cross a log with an inch or two of water rushing over it. One step from safety, Vicky dropped her ice axe and it was immediately swept away. We were greeted by Pat, who cheerily said she had a nice pot of fruit Jell-O cooling in the creek. It sounded great for a couple of thirsty people but, when she went to fetch it, pan and Jell-O had joined the ice axe. The next morning, the water having lowered and quieted some, we found Vicky's axe, but the pot of Jell-O is still somewhere in Ingalls Creek.

We loaded up and headed for home. A mile down the road the front of the truck was engulfed in a cloud of steam. I opened the hood and was amazed at the mischief done by some vandal. Over half the rubber water hoses had been cut and the radiator had gone dry—fifty miles from a service station. When the engine cooled I discovered the vandal was a porcupine that had crawled up onto the engine. Teeth marks on the rubber tubing, scratches on the paint, and a bunch of quills told the tale. I was able to cut off the damaged parts and reattach the shortened tubing to the engine and, after three hours' labor, I had the motor running again.

That was my last assault on Stuart, but two years later, working on a revision of our *102 Hikes*, I again parked our camper overnight at the Beverly Creek trailhead. The memory of the porcupine was still fresh, but we assumed the same thing couldn't happen twice, especially as we would spend the night in the camper. The next day we explored the County Line Trail, returned to the camper, and headed for home. A half mile down the road, again the cloud of steam arose, I opened the hood, there were the same teeth marks and porcupine quills. He had struck again. The moral of this story is beware of the Beverly Creek porcupine with a very expensive taste for oil-smeared rubber.

And no! Betty Manning is not still sitting on the top of Eldorado Peak waiting for her Mother, Harvey, or her children to come. After resting and a snack of crackers and cheese, she walked across the knife edge like it was a sidewalk.

• CHAPTER 9 •

A Climbing/Photo Seminar

or
A Fun Week at Camp Muir

Lou Whittaker demonstrating how a Jumar ascender works.

In 1970 Lou Whittaker, chief guide at Mount Rainier, contacted me to do a five-day photo seminar at Camp Muir. I think I had ten students who were interested in learning both climbing skills from the guides and mountain photography from me. The school was based at Camp Muir where, with three guides, we roamed the nearby glaciers looking for dramatic lighting on crevasses and ice walls. At a good location I would first talk about photography and then, using the guides as models, would help the students get dramatic pictures. Then the guides would take over and put the students through their paces. Sometimes we spent an hour or more at one location, which gave me a chance to point out how the shadows and highlights change as the earth turns.

Ethics and responsibility were an important part of

While I explained how the sidelighting gives texture to the ice, Lou and one of his guides climbed this ice wall. With the variety of shapes in a glacier, even at noon interesting lighting can be found.

my talk. Climbing photographs have a powerful influence on people. Most of the time the pictures are just admired and climbing techniques are not important but, to a few, a spectacular picture is a challenge they will try to emulate. Therefore, climbing techniques in photographs must be sound. An expert climber might safely pick his way across a glacier unroped, even stepping across a small crevasse, but the untrained climber watching or viewing a photograph might not recognize where the hazards are. If there is a potential hazard or even if it looks like there could be one, the climber must be properly safeguarded. With something as hazardous as mountain climbing, there is no margin for sloppy techniques. I am very disturbed when I see a dramatic picture published that shows irresponsible and dangerous techniques. How many fatalities have such a picture caused? Maybe none, but *maybe* has no place in the mountains.

My students were great to work with, and I made certain they got some excellent pictures. I would like to have repeated the seminar every year, but I

Above left: *The Camp Muir stone hut, built in 1921 at the 10,000-foot level of Mount Rainier, is high camp for many of my climbs and was also used for this photo seminar.* Above: *My seminar students, working from a snow-filled crevasse, watch a guide demonstrate crevasse self-rescue. Each student had to practice the rescue techniques.* Opposite: *Demonstration of both photograph lighting and crevasse self-rescue techniques.*

was already committed to spending the next year in Japan, so someone else took my place.

Mount Rainier has a long history of guides. It may have started when the Indian guide Sluiskin led General Hazard Stevens and P. B. Van Trump as far as Sluiskin Falls.

In the 1890s Len Longmire was the first to qualify as a professional guide. Sometime about 1920 Rainier National Park Company became owner of the guide service. When I started working at Paradise Inn in 1937, Gene Jack was the chief guide, and there must have been about four summit guides and six assistant guides who helped the summit guides lead ice-cave trips.

In the summer of 1941, when I operated the Paradise photo shop, Clark Sherman was chief guide and brought in a whole new set of summit guides. Two, who became my lifelong friends, were Dee Molenaar and Maynard M. Miller. During World War II the demand for guides dropped dramatically. After the war, guiding came back and Bob and I built many of our climbing stories around the guide service featuring Bill

Dunaway, Bob Craig, the Whittaker twins, Dick McGowan, and Gary Rose, and the guide service became a year-to-year concession for the next ten years. Only three or four guides were needed and they barely broke even at the season's end. It wasn't until 1968 that Lou Whittaker and Jerry Lynch formed Rainier Mountaineering, Inc. (RMI) and put guiding back into a profitable business. RMI now employs sixty people, and through publicity and great service the guides lead climbers to mountains around the world, from Kilimanjaro to Everest.

Lighting, shapes, climbing techniques, and the responsibilities of photographing dangerous activities are the subject of the week-long seminar held on the Cowlitz Glacier a short distance from Camp Muir. In the photo opposite, Lou demonstrates for the climbers what ice screws can (and cannot) do on an overhanging lip of a bergschrund. Even before everyone had a chance for pictures, the screws pulled out and Lou came down.

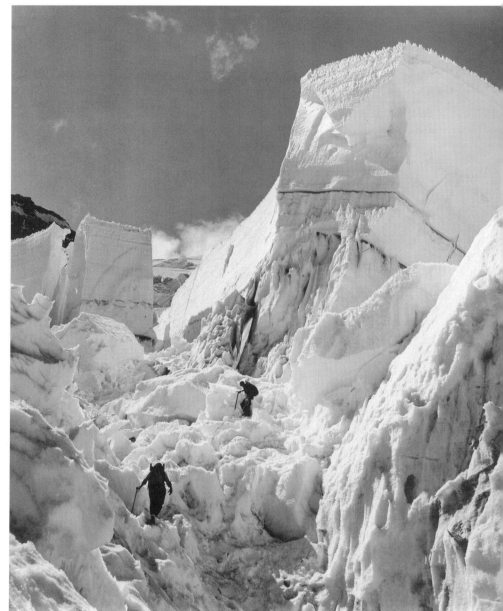

A jumble of broken blocks. The lines in the ice represent one year's accumulation of snow.

Mountain rescue team pulling Bill Degenhardt off Mount Snoqualmie after he broke his hip in an avalanche.

CHAPTER 10

Mountain Rescue

or
Call Ome

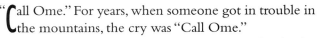

Ome Daiber.

"Call Ome." For years, when someone got in trouble in the mountains, the cry was "Call Ome."

Ome started it all back in the 1930s with a list by his telephone of climbing friends who were willing to go on rescue missions. Ome cared about people, and he became a one-man mountain rescue team, always ready to answer a call for help. When an emergency call came, he would phone some climbers and take off, leaving his wife, Matie, to organize a support group.

No one can talk about Northwest mountaineering without mentioning the Mountain Rescue Council and the "Big Three": Ome Daiber, Wolf Bauer, and Dr. Otto Trott.

Wolf Bauer has been a man of many careers and has excelled in all of them. He was a scientist and a brilliant ceramics engineer. As a skier he won the old cross-country Patrol Race from Snoqualmie Pass to Stampede Pass and placed (he finished on one ski!) in the Silver Skis Race, a 4,500-foot drop from Camp Muir to Paradise. As a climber in 1935 he made the first ascent of Ptarmigan Ridge on the north face of Mount Rainier, and that year with a group of eager young climbers he launched The Mountaineers Climbing Course, the first school of its kind in the world. After World War II he introduced foldboating to the Northwest, organized the Washington Foldboat Club, presented a course for novices, and pursued the sport as it evolved into kayaking. Ever fascinated by the possibility for interaction between man and nature, he even experimented with surfing on the Washington coast.

Wolf designed chemical plants around the world. From one of his many recreations he built a second area of expertise, with knowledge gained while paddling, to become the Northwest's leading consultant on shoreline management.

Most significant to mountain climbers, hikers, and hunters, Wolf was the leader in establishment of the Mountain Rescue Council (MRC), patterned after organizations in Europe. He began within The Mountaineers, whose "rescue patrols" had grown out of the Climbing Course, and subsequently broadened into a separate organization serving the entire outdoor community.

Dr. Otto Trott was a doctor in the German Army in the early 1930s. He was an ardent ski mountaineer and mountain climber, and some of his early exploits

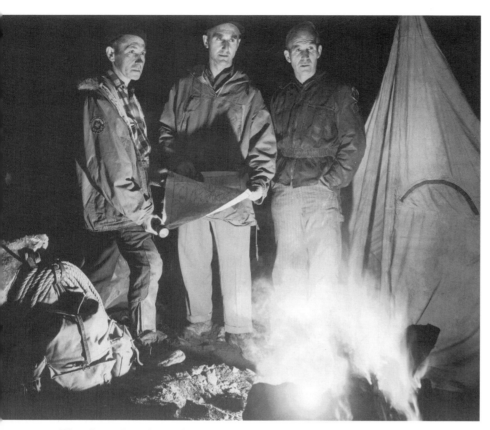

The three founders of Mountain Rescue. Left to right: Ome Daiber, Dr. Otto Trott, and Wolf Bauer.

exploring unnamed mountains. In 1935 Ome and two companions conquered Mount Rainier's Liberty Ridge, at that time the nation's outstanding mountaineering feat.

To the general public, Ome was the most famous climber of the times and became the first person called when someone got in trouble on a mountain. A respected Boy Scout leader, Ome helped pioneer the new concept of Explorer Scouting. When the Scouts' national headquarters heard that Ome and Wolf were teaching mountain climbing to the George Vancouver Rover Explorer Clan, they called a halt. The now "ex"-explorers formed the Ptarmigan Climbing Club. On the legendary Ptarmigan Traverse of 1938 they gave Ome's name to a noble peak but failed to record it, and Mount Daiber became Mount Formidable.

As the region's first full-time "professional" mountaineer, he manufactured and sold mountaineering equipment, invented Sno-Seal to waterproof leather hiking shoes, developed the Penguin sleeping bag with arms and legs that permitted a person to walk around on cold mornings without getting out of bed, and designed a stainless-steel cup known to old mountaineers as the Ome Daiber Cup (I still use one), to World War II GIs as an Army Cup, and in California as the Sierra Club Cup. Unfortunately, Ome was a few years ahead of the times. His equipment was ingenious, excellent, and expensive, but there weren't enough mountaineers or hikers back then who needed that quality of equipment to keep him in business. Plus, his one-man store was frequently closed because someone had "Called Ome." He fell back on his other occupation, a carpenter—but many a house languished incomplete when he was summoned to the wilderness on a mercy mission. Ome was featured in a *Saturday Evening Post* story that Bob and I took pictures for.

The Mountain Rescue Council could be said to

in the Alps must have shook up even the Weohrmacht. He didn't like what was happening in Germany, so he immigrated to the United States before the war, and set up a practice in Seattle. As an ex-German soldier, he was monitored by our intelligence authorities and once, to his disgust, was called in to explain a postcard of Mount Shuksan he had mailed to his family in Germany showing a new climbing route he had pioneered, a big X marking the bivouac site. Failing to penetrate the minds of nonclimbing, nonintelligent officers, he blew up and told them the line on the photo was a tank route to the top of Mount Shuksan and the X was a gun emplacement to rid the world of intelligence officers.

These are two of the "Big Three" who founded the MRC and guided its early years. Best known was Ome Daiber, already renowned in mountaineering circles of the 1930s for his part in Alaskan expeditions to

have its roots in Ome as the inspirational figure, Wolf as the student of European rescue organizations, and Otto as the first doctor in America to recognize the need for rescue personnel trained in specialized mountain first aid for times when an M.D. wasn't available.

The Mountaineers' Climbing Course maintained a call list of trained climbers ready to go when telephoned by the "Call Girls." The MRC—the Big Three—took this small system into a public organization that linked forest and park rangers, police departments, the Coast Guard, and the military. Bob and I were on the call list and Pat and Norma became "Call Girls," rounding up a rescue team by day or, more likely, after midnight; I also served a term on the board of trustees.

The Big Three were joined by a mountain-climbing banker, Dorrell Looff, who had the know-how to raise money for equipment; Max Eckenberg, who developed the Explorer Scouts' Search and Rescue program; and others who added special expertise. The pattern established in Seattle very soon was copied nationally, and the MRC became a unit of the International Congress of Rescue Groups, or IKAR. The English translation of Wastl Mariner's *Mountain Rescue Techniques*, made by Otto Trout and Kurt Beam, was adopted by IKAR as its official manual, in preference to the German original!

The next time I saw him was in 1947, shortly after I moved to Seattle. The *Seattle Times* sent me to photograph a search for an army plane that had crashed on Mount Pilchuck. I drove to the Verlot Ranger Station and found Ome in charge. He put me in the advance party, breaking trail through waist-deep snow. After a night's bivouac we skied to the wreckage and found the crew dead. When I turned my pictures in, the *Times* editor wanted to know why I was so late, where I had been, and why in the heck I was there. All he had wanted was a picture of the rescue crew leaving the ranger station. After that Mount Pilchuck experience, I became involved in mountain rescue and faithfully helped whenever called. I learned that sometimes there may be opportunities to take pictures, but the first priority is always to attend to the injured. Then, and only then, is it time to bring out a camera. A photographer must be part of the team ready to give a hand carrying the stretcher and never get in the way.

The rescues I was involved in showed the tragic side of the out-of-doors. I was along when we were called out to recover the body of a young boy who had climbed Mount St. Helens in smooth-soled shoes, glissaded down without being able to stop, and ended in a crevasse. Another time a boy with a gun was

OME

My first encounter with Ome Daiber was the winter of 1940 at Mount Rainier. On our group's very last run of the day on Devil's Dip one of the fellows broke a leg. Dismayed, we huddled around debating what to do. Streaking skiers went swooshing by, barely missing us. Then one came side-stepping back up the trail, introduced himself simply as Ome, and took over the operation. He used a wire mesh from his pack to tie up our friend's leg and pulled out several small sticks and some twine to turn the victim's skis into a passable toboggan, and off we went to Narada and our car. Once the boy was in the car, Ome disappeared.

A fatal accident on Mount St. Helens.

shooting at icicles inside an ice cave above Lake Twenty-Two. The shots collapsed the cave and we spent six hours in a pouring rain shoveling huge blocks of ice before we found the body.

AVALANCHE

My most memorable rescue was in 1952 when our good friend Bill Degenhardt was caught in an avalanche on Mount Snoqualmie and broke his hip. "Memorable" not only for his being a friend but also because we were able to bring him back alive. As soon as the call came in, twenty of us dashed off to Snoqualmie Pass, put on skis about 8:00 P.M. and reached Bill about midnight. We warmed him, and Otto Trott injected a bottle of plasma and then applied a splint. Bill was put on a ski stretcher and pulled and pushed up and down over steep slopes of a traverse, and we reached the cars just at dawn.

MOUNTAINS DON'T CARE

Bill's avalanche demonstrates that no mountaineer, however experienced, is immune to misfortune. However, the majority of accidents happen to beginning climbers and to hikers new to the wilderness who get into difficulty when they leave the trail. To educate people about hazards, the MRC set up speaker's bureaus. The program, though successful, was time-consuming and reached relatively few. To make better use of their time, the council decided to produce a safety movie. Of the minimum of $20,000 considered necessary, by the spring of 1955 only $3,000 had been raised. Bob and I volunteered to do what we could with that.

The outline story was to show how easy it is for the inexperienced to get in trouble, and then have experienced mountaineers show the same people the right way to do things. We started the film with a young couple wandering hand in hand across a glacier. The boy slipped into a crevasse and had to be rescued. Our intention was to continue the story using the same couple, with Matie and Ome Daiber as the experienced mountaineers to show the young couple how to hike safely. Before we could photograph the next scenario the boy got a job and the girl became Seattle's Seafair Queen. Lacking funds to reshoot the glacier scene, we made a slight change in the text and carried on with a new couple as the beginning hikers.

We photographed the four on a climbing trip in

Top: *A climbing accident on Mount Lincoln.* Bottom: *One of the opening scenes from our mountain rescue film,* Mountains Don't Care, *taken on the Nisqually Glacier at Mount Rainier.*

the North Cascades near Cascade Pass. The film had Ome explaining the right way to hike, and then as we left the trail to cross over Cache Col he explained how to find the way off-trail and more important how to find your way back. Ome picked a spectacular campsite overlooking Mount Formidable—where Ome had his first look at the mountain the 1938 Ptarmigan group had named Mount Daiber.

The next day in bright sunlight we crossed the Middle Cascade Glacier to climb Spider Mountain. The filming was so time-consuming we were benighted on the return. The night was clear, we had plenty of extra clothing and food, and we looked forward to a night under the stars on a bed of soft heather. Then a cloud towered out of nowhere and lightning struck Formidable. Closer and closer came the cloud and soon the heavens let loose a bombardment of lightning, thunder, hail, and just plain rain. Our nice soft heather beds became streams and we spent the rest of the night huddled under a tarp. In the morning we were between two layers of clouds. As soon as it was light enough to move we headed back to our tents, but long before we got there the rising valley clouds joined the lowering upper clouds and we groped our way through a dense fog—a textbook example of how fast weather can change. We couldn't have improved on the story if we had had a million-dollar budget.

A Seattle film producer put sound to our footage for an excellent film, *Mountains Don't Care*, which was

Top: *In a thick fog Ome checks his return route near Cache Col.* Bottom: *Bob filming Ome checking his route with map and compass near Cache Col.*

shown thousands of times in schools and churches, to Scout troops, and elsewhere. Over fifty copies of the film were printed and continued in use almost twenty years—with a marked drop of accidents.

I took a long chance with this short cut!

1 "When a gaping crevasse yawns in your face on the Columbia Icefields of British Columbia, you can spend all day circling its end... or you can *jump* it. Traveling's no fun 11,000 feet up in thin air. Jumping looked easier," writes Walter Gonnason, an American friend of Canadian Club. "My guide planted his ice axe solidly, belayed the nylon rope around it and wished me luck. 'Here goes,' I said, and...

2 "I missed! My ice axe slipped off the lip of the crevasse, and down I plunged. The rope broke my fall... but I nearly broke my ribs slamming against the chasm wall. Chunks of ice hurtled into the crevasse, and *I never heard them hit bottom*...

3 "No more short cuts for me, I decided, after inching one foot at a time up the sheer ice wall. One close call was enough to scare us both. We took the long way around to stay on the safe side. Skirting smaller crevasses, many of them deceptively bridged by fresh falls of snow, was slow work, but it got me home in one piece.

4 "This is the height of *my* ambition,' I said when my host suggested a go at Mt. Columbia. I was content to relax at his lodge—over a drink of Canadian Club!

5 "Peril lurks at every turn on Canada's icefields. But you're playing it safe when you order *the best in the house*. That means Canadian Club almost everywhere I travel."

Why this whisky's worldwide popularity? Canadian Club is *light* as scotch, *rich* as rye, *satisfying* as bourbon ... yet there is no other whisky in all the world that tastes quite like Canadian Club. You can stay with it all evening long... in cocktails before dinner and tall ones after. That's what made Canadian Club the largest-selling imported whisky in the United States.

IN 87 LANDS ... THE BEST IN THE HOUSE

"Canadian Club"

6 YEARS OLD
90.4 PROOF

IMPORTED IN BOTTLE FROM WALKERVILLE, CANADA, BY HIRAM WALKER & SONS INC., PEORIA, ILL. BLENDED CANADIAN WHISKY.

Walt Gonnason falling into a crevasse for a Canadian Club whiskey ad.

• CHAPTER 11 •

Assignments

or
How to Get Rich and
Have Ulcers

Filthy though it may be if you get too much, lucre in proper doses can be delicious. The best supply of the filthy stuff for a photographer is assignments. Bob and I got our first major taste from the *Seattle Times*, photographing The Mountaineers' 1946 Summer Outing circling Mount Rainier on the Wonderland Trail. We made an overkill, both having Speed Graphics and tripods and shooting the same scenes, in black and white and in color, but the payoff was huge, getting us started with a bang. The *Times* gave major space and subsequently we sold the same story to a travel magazine and the *Toronto Star,* along with individual pictures to calendars and books.

The success spoiled us a bit. Assignments can pay big, as did this one. A day or two of work may bring a

---

Canadian Club whisky ad, photographed on the Columbia Icefield in the Canadian Rockies with my 4x5 view camera. To be certain of one good picture, Walt Gonnason jumped the crevasse twelve times.

good month's income. However, the jobs are hard and fast-paced, one hassle after another. A photographer I know was sent on an overnight flight to Greece for a single day of shooting and then had to carry his films back to New York that same night.

There is a catch—and a big one. We had to first find clients. In our early years, the Freelance Photographers Guild brought us a number of good assignments. Agents take 50 percent of the net but are worth it—50 percent of something is better than 100 percent of nothing. One intriguing assignment I liked was for *Liberty Magazine*, illustrating a story on a safecracker after he had served his time on Alcatraz, retired to a farm in British Columbia, and taken up social work and writing. His autobiography was like a detective novel written by an expert.

Invariably on assignment, time was in short supply. In the Northwest, so is sunshine. Eastern art directors never understood how we could have three weeks of steady rain. Sometimes we were able to get extensions to finish an assignment, and sometimes we lost the job without ever exposing a film. Much to our agent's dismay we eventually quit the rat race. We did, however, continue to go after assignments on our own, providing the subject was interesting and there was ample time to wait out the weather.

CANADIAN CLUB ASSIGNMENT

Our first real break came when Bob, on one of our New York sales trips, contacted the advertising agency for Canadian Club whiskey. Every month during the 1950s and 60s a full-page Canadian Club ad ran in all the national magazines. The ad was always a picture story of an American in a foreign land, in some adventurous and dangerous situation. The story endings were

Twin brother Bob ready for Walt Gonnason's snowbridge to break.

always happy, the American and his foreign friend sitting down to sip their favorite whiskey. The photography was fun, but, I must admit, the big attraction was the money. These were among the highest-paying assignments in the business. One or two would pay our gas and rent for a whole year and all the peanut butter we could eat.

The first assignment was supposed to be on a cougar hunter using a bow and arrow. We traveled all over Vancouver Island and had four professional hunters ready to call us when they had one treed, but we ran out of time before we ever saw a cougar. The agency nevertheless paid our expenses and gave us a second assignment, to photograph a climber jumping a crevasse. All Canadian Club adventure ads had to take place outside the United States. We chose the Canadian Rockies. Our American model was a powerful climber, Walt Gonnason. Walt, Pat, myself, and a couple of helpers drove to the Columbia Icefield. Our "foreign" friend for the story was a Jasper National Park warden, Peter Withers, a friendly fellow who did more than pose—he carried sixty pounds of our camera and camping outfit eight miles up the Athabaska Tongue to the crest of the Columbia Icefield and set up camp on the ice near Mount Columbia. Peter had to return the same day and we watched him hike the eight miles back down the glacier, for a round-trip total of sixteen miles. Later we learned the reason he had to get back was for his seventieth birthday party.

We located an eight-foot-wide crevasse with a ledge partway down where I could stand. Walt jumped the crevasse twelve times just to be sure I got one perfect exposure. I did, and the ad was a complete success. The art director even wrote a "thank-you" note for producing the best ad he had ever had and complimented Pat on her hand-knit sweater the model was wearing.

Pat and I stayed on a few days to do a story on Peter Withers for *Ford Times*. He was a small, wiry man who, at seventy, could have passed for fifty. Summers he was a National Park warden and winters a physical education teacher at Jasper High School. Peter was a strong advocate of exercise, and urged young people to do strenuous activities such as tennis, skiing, and climbing, the kind of exercise that made sturdy bodies with strong hearts and lungs. Golf was not for young people, according to Peter, but was great for older people and he, too, intended to take it up when he reached his eighties or nineties.

Our crevasse-jumping shot for Canadian Club got us a half-dozen more assignments, including a climber crossing a fifty-foot-wide chasm on a tyrolean traverse. On another we photographed a climber on a glacier, crossing a snow bridge. The bridge was to break and the climber fall into the crevasse and rescue himself, unhurt. We used the Nisqually Glacier on Mount Rainier. The very first crevasse we came to had a perfect snow bridge for pictures, with room at the bottom for both Bob and me to stand. We were down in the crevasse, each intently holding a camera with finger on the shutter. When we were ready, our model, Walt Gonnason, very carefully stepped onto the bridge, expecting it to break any moment. It didn't. He jumped up and down on it and still it didn't break. He jumped again. Still didn't break. Nothing was happening. Bob and I had been tense so long we were getting shaky. Walt stopped jumping and we lowered our cameras to discuss how we could weaken the bridge a little. While we were talking, it broke and Walt fell in as planned, and rescued himself as planned. However, Bob and I had been caught with our cameras down, and we both missed the picture. It took us most of the day to find another bridge, not as photogenic, but more cooperative, and everything went fine. When the picture was finished, as if we had taken the action in the Canadian Rockies, we drove up to a resort on Lake Louise to toast our favorite whisky with one of our Canadian climbing friends.

We were very happy with the Canadian Club account and the agent was very happy with us but, as happens in the business, Canadian Club changed advertising agencies, the new art director had his own pet photographers, and we lost out.

OTHER ASSIGNMENTS

At different times Bob and I each photographed the big log drives in Idaho, Bob for the *Saturday Evening Post*, and I several years later for *True* magazine. On the Clearwater River log drive, the men lived in floating bunkhouses called wanigans and were transported about the river in eight-man boats. The first three years we watched, the boats were powered by oars, outboard motors considered unreliable in the rapids. This was certainly the hardest and most dangerous work we ever

Priest River log drive, a Saturday Evening Post *assignment in 1950.*

photographed. The men often spent hours waist-deep in ice-cold water. To fortify them, for breakfast the cook served stacks of hotcakes, pies, cakes, eggs, cereal, and a half-pound of bacon or ham per person. For lunch they had soup, vegetables, bread, salad, pies, cakes, and one pound of chicken or fish per man. Dinner was a repeat of lunch except there was one pound of beefsteak per man. There was always coffee, but when the wanigan was close to a road, the men also drank gallons of fresh milk. On the theory that warm wet was better than cold wet, on frosty mornings the men poured hot water in their already wet shoes before putting them on. These were genuine lumberjacks in the Paul Bunyan tradition. When the drive was finished, however, instead of tearing the town apart, they went home to their wives and kids.

Times have changed. A power dam put an end to the log drives, the misery whip has been replaced by a lightweight power saw, trucks have replaced the trains, and the most prestigious job of all, the tree-topper, has been replaced by a portable spar pole. In the process, logging roads have eliminated hundreds of miles of hiking trails.

Somewhere we picked up an assignment for Jantzen Sportswear to take mens' fashion pictures in mountain-climbing situations. We made arrangements with Dick McGowan, a guide at Mount Rainier, to provide models and help with logistical problems. Dick and I spent a day scouting the Nisqually Glacier for photogenic spots. The next day Bob and I went with Dick and a couple of guides who were to act as models, each with a clothes rack strapped to his back containing sports coats, shirts, and pants. We were accompanied by Dick's wife, who helped with the fitting, and an art director from the ad agency. Two ranger friends, on their day off, came along to laugh at the spectacle. We had a great time and

Right: *Setting up the 100-pound, 8x20-inch Colorama camera for an Eastman Kodak assignment, Mount Shuksan.* **Below:** *New York's Grand Central Station, displaying one of our eighty-foot-wide color transparencies*

Jantzen used a number of the pictures in national ads and on posters.

In 1960 I spent two weeks in New York visiting clients. While there I made a side trip to Rochester, home office of Eastman Kodak. The art director fell in love with a winter scene taken in the French Alps of a village church and bought it on the spot. Eastman made good use of the picture in its advertising, though, much to my disgust, they cut off the top of a beautiful mountain in the background. From that contact came an assignment in 1962 to produce a wintertime Colorama picture. The Colorama was an eight-foot-high by eighty-foot-long backlit transparency that hung in New York's Grand Central Station. At that time the Colorama was taken with a view camera using 8X20-inch film. Eastman loaned us the camera, supplied the oversize film, and developed and enlarged the picture in a swimming pool that had been converted to a darkroom.

In a howling windstorm I made this picture on Mount Rainier's Panorama Point for a cloth- manufacturing firm.

I flew to Los Angeles to pick up the camera and get instructions on its use. At the airport the camera weighed in at 104 pounds (this included film holders and tripod). The assignment was a winter picture of Mount Shuksan with a skier using a Kodak Instamatic camera. The first location was, fortunately, a short distance from the road. Still, setting up the heavy camera in ten feet of snow was a major operation. The biggest problem was getting the huge camera in focus. There was no depth of focus in the monster lens; it just had a bunch of tilts and swings to fool with until every corner came into focus.

Over the years we did eighteen Coloramas. The 104-pound camera could be separated into three parts, the heaviest about forty pounds, so I needed help, and chose for models young mountain climbers with strong backs. Twice we carried the camera a mile on skis to Artist Point in the Mount Baker Ski Area. Once we even put it on a horse and took it to Camp Muir for pictures on the Cowlitz Glacier. Kodak eventually developed a 5X7 camera for the Colorama but we never got to use it. The photo editor we worked with retired, and the new man purchased a large mobile home for the staff photographers as they traveled about the country. Now they even use 35mm cameras.

Many a Northwesterner has told us how he arrived on Manhattan Island homesick in an alien land and been surprised and thrilled and cheered to walk into Grand Central Station and see in living color, big as life, a picture of his favorite mountains.

From the great success in the 1950s and 60s, Bob and I have gone backwards. Our newspaper stories led to magazine stories, our magazine stories gave us a national name that led to books, and the books opened the door to ad agencies. However, when Bob turned to tourist travel and I became involved in trail guides, neither of us had time for magazine stories or picture books. Without magazine stories, our name was soon forgotten, without a name, ad agencies forgot us, and we no longer had that open door.

• CHAPTER 12 •

Books, Books

and
More Books

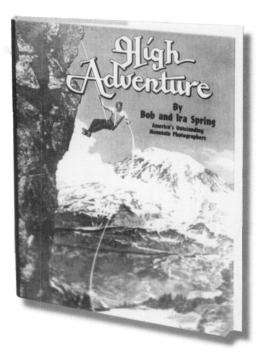

Our first book, published in 1952.

It probably was a brash idea back in 1950, after only three years in business, to think of a book, but our success with mountain-climbing stories in newspapers and national magazines gave us a reputation that opened doors. We assembled a sample book of forty to fifty black-and-white prints with simple typewritten captions and bound them in a volume that looked quite professional. Our first choice, Seattle's one and only publisher at the time interested in photo books, was Superior Publishing. The president and owner, Al Salisbury, was a student of Indian and pioneer history, and he and his wife, Jane, had written a successful book, *Two Captains West*. Al reacted enthusiastically, suggesting a lot of good ideas for the text and pictures, including revolving the book around Norma's and Pat's experiences married to mountain photographers.

To get climbing pictures of ourselves for the book,

"The Little Valley Pounder," taken at Klapatche Park by the combined efforts of two photographers, two wives, and two grandparents. Bob and I made fifteen exposures between us. We don't know which of us took the prize picture. Considering how many times it sold, the time and film were well repaid.

Bob, Norma, Pat, and I spent a couple of days at Camp Muir. Then, with Bob and Norma's eighteen-month-old son, Terry (the only kid the two families had at that time), and two grandparents, we did a family-camping sequence at Klapatche Park. The star player was Terry, carrying a pack following his mother's footsteps. The kid was uncharacteristically irritable, not yet having learned to accept mosquitoes, and it took all six of us to keep him in the right spot. We took over a dozen films, and I don't know which one of us actually snapped the shutter on the winning picture. When Bob and Norma took Terry home they found the mosquitoes weren't all to blame for his bad mood—he was coming down with measles.

The picture quickly became the most popular of our joint careers. It ran in the *Seattle Times* as a cover picture entitled "The Little Valley Pounder" and, even today, over thirty years later, people who ask what has become of the little valley pounder are startled to learn that the measles-mosquito-tormented child now has a big, bushy beard, a family of his own, and does wizard electronic things for a TV station.

To illustrate High Adventure, *the four of us camped at 11,000 feet beside the Nisqually Icefall of Mount Rainier. The camera was set on a tripod and a friend tripped the shutter.*

Despite the outrageous price of $8.50, our first book, *High Adventure,* published in 1952, was, by standards of photo books of that era, a rousing success. The printing of 3,000 copies didn't earn us much in the way of royalties; however, we were amazed at the prestige it brought us with magazine photo editors and account executives of advertising agencies, who were supposed to have seen everything and been impressed by nothing. But the volume opened the doors of New York to us. Al followed up by publishing the four little *Camera Adventuring* travel books and, a few years later, *This Is Washington* and *This Is Alaska,* written by Byron Fish and Norma.

In 1959 I teamed up with Harvey Manning, a mountain-climbing friend and author, for *High Worlds of the Mountain Climber,* a picture book telling the climbing history of the Northwest. Harvey has an unusual sense of humor, and even after reading *High Worlds* a dozen times I still get a chuckle each time. Harvey and I did four more books for Superior, all with lots of color. But with each book the quality of the reproductions became poorer and so did sales. We then tried a guide to *Wildlife Areas in Washington* and to *Wildlife Areas in Oregon.* Pat and I had a lot of fun in the state and national wildlife refuges, and the books had a lot of good information. Their only fault was that no one bought them.

I was then helping the Climbing Committee of The Mountaineers with photographing various techniques used in the Climbing Course lectures and as reference material for the club's textbook then in preparation. After a five-year effort The Mountaineers published *Mountaineering: The Freedom of the Hills.* To everybody's surprise, sales were so brisk that there was a sizable profit—a sum representing the money that would have gone to royalties had not the work been done by unpaid volunteers. A Literary Fund Committee (LFC) was established to employ sales income to publish other books serving the purpose of the club, notably, "to preserve the natural beauty of Northwest America."

100 HIKES IN WESTERN WASHINGTON

The LFC recognized early on that the rapid growth of backcountry travel cried out for hiking guides. Saving trails by putting boots on them, thus making new friends for trails, new defenders against the onslaught of machines, was a primary factor. But so was meeting the needs of newcomers. As Tom Miller, creative genius of the LFC, put it, "Come the first good day of spring I can't get any work done. People flood my office from all over the company, asking directions on how to climb Mount Si." This was probably happening in every office in Seattle.

Bob and I probably took the brunt, for all week long we got calls from strangers asking where to go hiking. I'd been thinking of guidebooks but, in spite of the phone calls, didn't think a strictly hiking guide would sell. I was promoting a camping guide with a few trails snuck in. I'd pitched the idea to Al Salisbury, but it wasn't his kind of book. Then I got a phone call from Harvey, chair of the LFC, informing me that the committee wanted my camera for a book. I said, "Great!" and told him what I had in mind. He said, "Great! We'll do that next. But first. . . ." I was darn skeptical, but Tom Miller came to our meeting with an English guidebook to 100 hikes in the Alps that excited everyone. The English volume was a "cookbook," giving in detail specific recipes for each hike—a sketch map for orientation, text giving directions, and a photo showing why. Although still doubtful, I agreed.

Our work had taken Bob and me on many trails, but the average hiker didn't realize the variety and number of trail opportunities available to them. Ardent hikers were apt to return over and over again to a few favorite places rather than be disappointed by a strenuous hike that gave lesser rewards. Before our guidebook, finding new trails was mostly by word of mouth, which tended to congregate people on a few trails to super-good views or lakes. When one of our mountain stories was printed in the Sunday *Times*, the next weekend that trail would be mobbed.

Tom led the committee in drawing up a list of 100 longtime favorite hikes. Marge Mueller, a graphic artist and climber, was recruited for the maps, outdoor writer Louise Marshall for the text, and I was wanted for the pictures. As it happened, I had already worn out several pairs of boots on the wanted trails—sixty-odd of the 100 trails, in fact. Bob was spending the summer in Alaska on an assignment so the other forty hikes were up to me. Pat and I, usually accompanied by John and Vicky, did the remaining hikes during the summer of 1965. Unfortunately, Louise, although an ardent hiker and good writer, had only done a dozen of the wanted trails and Harvey stepped in for her.

In August 1966, *100 Hikes in Western Washington* came off the press. I thought we would be lucky to sell a thousand. How wrong could I be! Tom had ordered a printing of 5,000, expecting that to last two years. But REI put stacks by the cash registers and every member checking out a load of hiking gear picked up a copy, and the two-year supply sold out in three weeks. Another 5,000 lasted through September, and another 5,000 had to be printed for Christmas.

Obviously, 15,000 copies sold in half a year would have a huge impact on too few trails. There could be no delay. Already by the summer of 1967 remarks were heard about "100 Hikes Not to Go On." The

Top: *Cascade Pass and Eldorado Peak. The publisher printed 5,000 copies of this, the first* 100 Hikes *book in our series (and in the nation), expecting this to be a two-year's supply. The book went on sale August 1966 and was sold out in three weeks.* Bottom: *Vicky's picture of Harvey Manning after he had walked 3,000 miles researching his* Footsore *series.*

Pat photographing cliff penstemon on the Sleeping Beauty trail for Mountain Flowers, *printed in 1970.*

Club whiskey and Grand Central Station Coloramas sort of accounts, whose art editors come and go. Although less lucrative, guidebooks fit my lifestyle much better than walking the streets of New York looking for new accounts.

Backcountry use kept growing so much that even with three guidebooks there was still a need to disperse hikers. The final step was dividing the mountains into four 100 hikes books and the 50 on Mount Rainier. This covers about 90 percent of the trails of interest to hikers.

The grand total of 450 trails (over 500 if counting the trails we hiked and rejected) took eight years to hike. Occasionally John and Vicky would help, and Vicky eventually took on *100 Hikes in the Alpine Lakes* as the principal photographer and researcher. Harvey, while translating my notes into English, interjected his own opinions on trails he knew and did some of the week-long walks in the North Cascades that he, married to a wealthy school librarian (ha ha), could afford, but I as a slave to my boots couldn't.

backcountry population had to be dispersed. Moreover, the preservation agenda required attention to the many other trails in danger of being lost to roads.

The second phase of the guidebook program began at the request of the Mount Rainier National History Association, *50 Hikes in Mount Rainier National Park*. Then, while the original *100 Hikes* kept on selling like hotcakes (totaling more than 50,000 copies before we could retire it), Harvey and I drew up lists for *101 Hikes in the North Cascades* and *102 Hikes in the Alpine Lakes, South Cascades, and Olympics*. I had used up all our existing file of trails on the first 100 hikes, so for the next two 100 hikes we had to start from scratch, which took three summers. The guidebooks became so time-consuming that I couldn't keep up with the Canadian

HOW WE HIKED 500 TRAILS

Pat and I developed an efficient method of researching trails. We would drive our small, rugged pickup camper to a trailhead and spend the night. As soon as it was light enough to see we were on our way, usually by 4:30 or 5:00 A.M. (daylight time). It is cool at that time of day, and carrying only day packs we made good time. There were other benefits, too. Bugs aren't awake yet, wildlife is more visible, and I could take advantage of the early morning light for pictures. On a hike we recommended as a one-day trip we often reached our destination by 8:00 A.M. and were back to the camper by 10.00 A.M. Recommended overnight hikes took a little longer, but we were generally back by noon. We often found hikers at our destination still

Mount Rainier from Sourdough Mountain, featured on the cover of 50 Hikes in Mount Rainier National Park, *printed in 1969.*

in their sleeping bags. We looked forward to the three- or four-day hikes, where we shouldered heavier packs and spent a night out.

I didn't take notes on the way but made it a firm rule to sit down at the camper on our return and write down impressions while still fresh in my mind. When this was done, I would close up the camper and move to the next trailhead.

In three summers, Pat and I generally hiked a different trail almost every day, rain or shine. I wore out three pairs of boots. My feet sweat so much it doesn't matter whether it rains or not. After a day of hiking my shoes are wet, so I keep two pairs of shoes with me and alternate them, wearing one pair while the other dries.

It was exhausting work but we enjoyed every mile—well, almost. We didn't have time for an overnight trip on the Wolf Creek trail near Winthrop and

Three Fingers Lookout, featured in the 1981 Lookouts: Firewatchers of the Cascades and Olympics, on which I collaborated with well-known writer, Byron Fish. Pat and I had a great summer climbing to places like this and searching for abandoned trails to former building sites.

did a round trip of twenty-four miles in one day. On the way in we encountered hundreds of cows. On a narrow stretch of trail we inadvertently got between a cow and her calf. No matter how fast or slow we hiked, the calf would stay just in front of us bawling for its mother, who was puffing and bawling at our heels. When we tried to pass the calf it would go faster and so would the mother—bawling in front of us, huffing and puffing at our heels. On the way back we were stuck a good five miles behind a parade of cows, and the last one in line had a terrible case of diarrhea.

When choosing a trail for a guidebook, we look for a variety of experiences to please everyone, short trails, long, strenuous trails, trails to lakes, to spectacular viewpoints, through virgin forests and alpine meadows, and trails where solitude can almost be guaranteed. The most popular routes are those leading to mountain lakes or spectacular views. Besides describing these trails, we made a point of including those so unused the tread is lost in fields of heather and alpine flowers. We found miles of delightful paths where one can be lonesome. Even after being in a guidebook for twenty years, some of my favorite trails are still walked so little that more animal tracks than footprints are seen.

In the Northwest, Harvey Manning's text was an early exponent of minimum-impact travel. Together, we have a very good working relationship with Forest Service personnel here in Washington. We closely follow their recommendations on what trails to describe, what environmental problems to discuss, and where to camp for the least damage to the landscape. At their request we even have left trails out. Information from maps and rangers helps us determine whether a trail is worth researching; however, actually seeing it for ourselves is the only way to be certain.

Our hiking books have drawn a lot of mail, not all complimentary. We've been blamed for overcrowding the backcountry. But Wyoming had a trail guide ten years before ours, and trails there didn't see an increase in use until the same time as Washington. People don't go to a bookstore, open pages of a guide, and run off to buy boots. Something else sends them to the hills. What? Who? John Muir preached, "Climb the mountains and get their good tidings." That was written almost a century before *100 Hikes*, and nobody blames Muir for the population explosion. He is credited with inspiring the wilderness movement, and the national park movement. If by chance we had something to do with the increase in hikers, then we should be given some credit for the trails that have been saved from the bulldozers and for how our books helped convince Congress that there were enough hikers to warrant dedicating new wilderness areas.

Another complaint is the added impact of our books on trails that are already heavily used. We have often been told that we should leave out the popular trails, but how could one have a complete guidebook to the region and omit Cascade Pass or Snow Lake? We feel that wouldn't be fair, and after discussing the problem with the Forest Service and officials of environmental organizations, we decided to include such trails but warn hikers of the problems and what they must do to avoid creating environmental damage.

The *100 Hikes* series isn't the whole of our guidebooking. We've done a row of others, including one about the sagebrush steppe of the east slope of the Cascades and another on—believe it or not—the Alps. With Harvey, we did the four volumes of *Footsore: Walks and Hikes around Puget Sound*. Harvey did the research for those, walking 3,000 miles, noting where I could get good pictures. When that series was retired, he and his daughter Penny collaborated on two books, "the Sons of Footsore," covering the cream of the lowland beaches and foothills, and again my camera was there.

Adding another string to our bow, Pat started carrying a 35mm camera to photograph wildflowers, and this led to a flower book on the Rocky Mountains and several in Washington.

What have we got from all this besides a lifetime "vacation"? Not much money. Though The Mountaineers have printed half a million copies of our books, we've earned barely minimum wages. Unlike our competition who use third-party information to write their guidebooks, our trails have all been hiked by us. Doing a hundred hikes for one volume takes a lot of time, a lot of gas, a lot of peanut butter. Then when the information gets old, a revised edition is required—more time, more gas, and more peanut butter. One or more of our guides always is in revision. Boots still are getting worn out. But if not out hiking, where else would we be? And since we do our hiking as a business, the peanut butter is tax-deductible.

• CHAPTER 13 •

Winter Wonderland

or
How to Keep Cool without Trying

Mount Baker ski area, 1950.

Our first mountain ski tour could easily have buried us. Growing up in Shelton, Bob and I had no contact with the mountaineering world. All we knew was what we read in popular magazines that dealt with sensational events, not down-to-earth instructions. We had read about avalanches wiping out villages in the Alps but didn't realize our Olympic Mountains that we had roamed in the summertime had dangerous avalanches in the winter.

The last days of 1937, when we were freshmen at Ellensburg, we attempted a major ski traverse in the Olympics. The day after Christmas, loaded with seventy- to eighty-pound packs topped by pairs of skis, Bob and I, each carrying a camera, climbed the trail to Upper Lena Lake at 4,600 feet. The winter had been

mild; there was less than a foot of snow at the lake. Flakes began floating down as we built a fire and set up our homemade tent. The next morning we crawled out into a foot of new snow, which kept coming all day, getting deeper and deeper as we broke trail up the side of Mount Lena and headed toward Mount Stone. The going was slow and by dusk we had covered only three miles. We had a terrible time starting a fire on top of what was now five feet of snow to heat our dinner, and the tent had no floor to keep our blankets dry, but we were too innocent to be worried.

When we hoisted our packs the third morning, three more feet of new snow had accumulated and was still coming down. Even a foot of fresh snow can be an avalanche hazard. We know that now, but didn't then. We struggled on with a visibility of only a hundred or so feet, and around noon started a long, steep traverse leading up to Saint Peter's Gate on the side of Mount Stone. Halfway up we heard a tremendous roar in the fog behind us. In a few minutes came an equally loud roar in front of us that we couldn't see. We suddenly

Spring skiing in the Cascade Pass area, 1965. Since then, this small glacier in Boston Basin has almost disappeared.

• 121 •

realized our danger. We didn't dare go back the way we had come and to go forward was suicidal. We took off our skis and walked straight down the hill, slipping and sliding over what would be difficult cliffs in the summer, reached the safety of timber, and made camp. The next day we found our way out to a logging road and hiked ten miles back to the car. We were very lucky to have survived our first lesson in avalanches.

All the extras one needs for ski touring make for heavy packs; add to that a heavy camera, film, film holders, and changing bag, and winter photography with a 4x5 view camera is not easy. To protect the ground glass during a fall, the camera has to be buried deep in the pack, which means taking the pack off and digging deep to get to the camera. In very cold weather, while opening the camera and calculating for the film exposure, one can get a painful frostbite. In zero weather, the shutter slows down and the lens must be removed and warmed next to the body—taking care the lens doesn't frost up coming from a cold to a warm, moist place. In subzero weather the film becomes brittle and can break when wound around the sharp corner in the film holder. (Film holders aren't made that way anymore.) There is one other hazard in zero weather—the metal viewfinder may freeze to your face and stick just long enough to yank off a bit of skin. I haven't been out in subzero weather with my 35mm camera. I don't know how all its electronic gizmos would react, but I assume at least the batteries would be useless unless carried in a warm place next to your stomach.

For a *Seattle Times* story in 1950 we spent a winter week in an icebox, a three-sided shelter at Van Trump Park on Mount Rainier. To provide for a pretty luxurious trip, that fall we had carried in a week's supply of food and cut a huge pile of firewood. Just after Christmas, Bob, Norma, Pat, myself, and three friends skied the four miles from Longmire to Van Trump, where the shelter should have been. No shelter! Just a big snow-covered meadow! The shelter had to be here. There was a very slight bump in the snow and we dug in; five feet down we struck the roof of what became our home for the next five days. When we built a warming fire, we were smoked out. If we didn't, we were frozen. The first four days were overcast and stormy, but the last day cleared. We supposed skiing down to Longmire would be easy, so spent all day taking pictures and left the shelter as the sun was setting. In the dusk we missed a turn, ended up in the Kautz Creek drainage, and didn't get to Longmire until one o'clock in the morning. Instead of being reprimanded for doing the wrong thing, we were greeted by the park superintendent like long-lost sons and daughters.

You would think Bob and I would have learned something, but in 1957, again right after Christmas, we left Paradise with a couple of friends and climbed into the clouds at Panorama Point. Partway there, as we paused to catch our breath, we heard the "cluck, cluck" of a ptarmigan. Bob is good at imitating sounds, so he "cluck, clucked" back. The ptarmigan walked between us and right over Bob's skis. It was pure white except for black feet and a red patch over its eyes. There wasn't time to dig out cameras, safely stored deep in our heavy packs, and the bird probably wouldn't have shown up anyway on our black-and-white film.

Our destination was the small

Bob's and my December 1937 camp below St. Peter's Gate in our homemade, floorless tent.

Headed home after our week-long stay at Camp Muir. Little did we realize it would take two days to reach our car at Paradise, only four and a half miles away.

guide hut at Camp Muir, where we were to spend a week shooting a story on the testing of sleeping bags. The door to the guide hut was blocked by a snowdrift, which we dug out. That night, although clear, was windy, and as we slept the snow drifted up against the *outward-opening door*—we were trapped! Heaving against the door opened it a couple of inches, just enough to reach out with a kitchen spoon and dig. The whole rest of our time we didn't dare close the door, and covered the opening with a tarp. No matter. A major storm moved in. It was a doozy, with winds up to 100 miles per hour that blew up a huge drift covering the entire front of the building. We thanked the wind for that and dug a snow tunnel out the doorway and down over the bank to the Cowlitz Glacier. A second tunnel gave access to a chilly privy.

The storm raged for days, drenching Western Washington in heavy rain, the freezing level rising to 8,000 feet. The last full day at Muir was clear and we made

good use of it, taking pictures. The next morning, to save weight, we ate the last of our food and used up the rest of the stove gas. At noon we left Muir for the two-hour descent to Paradise, easy skiing until we reached the 8,000-foot level, where the heavy rain had turned the snow to solid ice. Fast skiing gave way to slow creeping. Instead of a quick romp to the car, we spent hours belaying down gentle slopes. The winter night came early, forcing us to bivouac at Panorama Point with no food or water (but plenty of sleeping bags) and finish the descent the next morning.

The last ski tour Bob and I took together was about 1959, to try our hand at movies. Besides our usual 4X5 cameras, we carried thirty pounds of movie gear—a

Rolex camera, a heavy tripod, and film. The plan was a three-day trip from Paradise to Camp Muir, across the Cowlitz, Ingraham, and Emmons Glaciers to Steamboat Prow, and finally down to the White River road. For once we were blessed with good weather; while it was foggy at Paradise, we climbed into sunshine above a sea of clouds. We had a great time skiing among the crevasses, difficult any time but especially when roped together. The movie and still pictures were good, and because we happened to show a scene of cooking Zoom, a popular hot cereal, the film entitled *Skiing above the Clouds* was sold to the Zoom manufacturer and shown thousands of times.

Another memorable winter trip was at Ed LaChapelle's research station on the Snow Dome at the edge of Mount Olympus' Blue Glacier. Bill Fairchild, whose plane was equipped with wheels for the airstrip in Port Angeles and skis for mountain snows, flew me in. As we approached the glacier we seemed to be aiming right at the sloping side of the mountain, certain to crash. Just as we were about to do so, Bill pulled up the nose at the same angle as the glacier and we touched down smoothly a few feet from the cabin. I spent a week following scientists around the Blue Glacier, sometimes to within a few feet of the summit. At the week's end Bill returned for me. Landing on the glacier had been scary. The takeoff was a heart-stopper. Headed downhill the plane was still on its skis when we went over the rounded edge of the glacier and dropped like a rock. As our speed picked up we were suddenly 3,000 feet above the floor of the Hoh River Valley and flying.

Winter mountains do not always pose prettily for the camera. Year after year we pilgrimaged every weekend to Mount Baker, and maybe once or twice a winter we'd get a perfect day that was worth taking cameras out of the pack. During a long week in the Alpine Club of Canada's cabin at Lake O'Hara, I never

Opposite: Little Tahoma and the Emmons Glacier, while filming our movie, Skiing Above the Clouds. Top right: Bill Fairchild's breath-stopping take-off over the edge of Snow Dome on Mount Olympus. Right: Roped skiing in Boston Basin from our winter camp near Cascade Pass.

Bob's wondrous star-track photograph of Mount Shuksan. He set his 4x5 Speed Graphic on a tripod for a one-hour exposure.

saw more than a hundred feet ahead of me. Therefore, I especially appreciate my two ski tours to Cascade Pass in perfect weather. May is the best time to tour there. Snow is still plentiful in the high country, the days are longer, and by then the road is usually driveable a few miles from the trailhead. The hiker trail crosses the track of frequent avalanches, but we found a safe route in the timber that took us all the way to the top of Sahale Arm. One of those trips was made especially memorable by ptarmigans. We must have camped on their favorite roosting place because every night a half-dozen gathered around our tent and scolded us for hours, taking care to disappear when it got light enough for pictures.

A year or two before the establishment of Glacier Peak Wilderness banned machines from the face of the (wilderness) earth, eight of us hired Bill Fairchild to fly us to the Honeycomb Glacier. Four days we skied there, including to the top of Glacier Peak. The fifth day we slid on down to Kennedy Hot Springs. In summer they may be hot. In winter the six-foot-deep pool blasted out of solid rock is surrounded by snow, the steaming water at first pleasantly warm contrasted with the freezing air, but after a few minutes feeling less warm—in fact, a little chilly. We agonized over getting out in the freezing air to dry and dress, but finally it became a case of get out or stay in and succumb to hypothermia.

In 1962 three of us took the twice-weekly train from Vancouver around Howe Sound, past the town of Squamish, and twenty miles farther to Garibaldi Station, the trailhead (now accessible by road) to Garibaldi Lake in Garibaldi Provincial Park.

Austin Pass warming hut on one the rare days with both fresh snow and sunshine.

In late afternoon we and three Canadian skiers from the University of British Columbia got off the train in a sleet storm. The Canadians headed for the tiny waiting room and its potbellied stove, dry wood, and kindling for a "spot of tea" before starting out. We elected to see how many of the five miles we could do before dark. The snow was the consistency of newly mixed cement. Alternating the lead frequently to break trail, we made only one and a half miles, in two hours, before it was dark. We set up our tent and crawled in. The rain stopped during the night and the temperature dropped a bit.

The next morning we were up bright and early and underway by 7:30 A.M. The soggy snow of the day before had been strenuous. Today was worse: The surface was covered with a breakable crust. At each step the skis slid under the crust, which had to be broken before another step could be taken. The Canadians caught up with us about ten o'clock, having spent the night in the waiting room. Our broken trail let them do in an hour what had taken us five hours. Relieved to have help we gratefully let the younger ones take their turn breaking trail, but in a half-hour they stopped for a brew-up and afterward remained behind us just out of sight. About 1:00 P.M. fresh snow fell and, as the crust was covered, breaking trail became easy. The Canadians then passed us at high speed. Exhausted, we didn't reach the cabin until after dark.

The cabin was a three-story chalet owned by the British Columbia Provincial Park Service. Having conserved their energy by not breaking trail, the Canadians had built a fire in the kitchen and had a pail of snow melting. Too exhausted to eat, I found a vacant bunk on the second floor, crawled in my bag, and instantly went to sleep.

Well past midnight a Canadian came clumping down the stairs from the third floor and, in passing, mumbled something about fire. The words didn't register in my half-sleep until he came clumping back up

carrying a pail of water. Then I realized he had said that the roof was on fire. Then It Really Registered. *"THE ROOF IS ON FIRE!"* I heard crackling noises as I jumped out of bed, put on clothes and boots, woke my companions, and ran up to the third floor in time to see the Canadian heave the pail of water at the burning rafters. The fire was too high to reach and the water fell back down on the Canadians' sleeping bags. The flames were around the stove pipe. Fortunately the five feet of snow on top kept the flames from spreading very fast. We dashed outside, climbed up on the roof, and with an axe cut away enough shingles to reach in and smother the fire with snow. I returned to bed, lulled to sleep by the sounds of the Canadians drying out their sleeping bags.

Two days of the Garibaldi week were good enough for us to ski five miles across Garibaldi Lake to camp on a promontory with a view of Mount Garibaldi. Remembering the difficulties of our trip in, and knowing that if we missed the ten o'clock train there wouldn't be another for two days, we left the chalet a day early. We were glad we did, as the Canadians tried to do it in one day and missed the train (our hearts bled).

We expected to sleep in the waiting room out of the rain, but firewood had been stacked there and the only open space was two small benches. We had dinner and contemplated setting our tent up in the wet snow. An empty boxcar on a siding looked more appealing. We set up the tent inside the boxcar, snuggled into our bags, and had just drifted off when— WHAM!—we were hooked onto a freight train. We were in the process of evacuating the boxcar as a brakeman walked by. He held up his lantern, saw our tent, and said, "Wow, hobos with a tent!" Saying nothing more, he walked away, came back in a few minutes and told us, "The train is headed for Prince George, but we'll leave the boxcar for the next trip and you can go back to bed."

When we boarded the passenger train the next day, the conductor, in a smart uniform, asked if we had a good night's sleep. Sure enough, it was last night's brakeman.

Opposite: *Artist Point in the Mount Baker Ski Area*
Above right: *January picture of Comet Falls.* Right:
Clark's nutcracker

GETTING SOFT

The sixty- to ninety-pound pack one needs for winter camping eventually got to be too much for me. Since then, Pat and I have made three winter tours to Yellowstone National Park to photograph wildlife, "bivouacking" in Old Faithful's Snow Inn.

February through March of 1982 we rented a deluxe condominium on the edge of a snow-covered golf course in Jackson Hole, with a great view of the Grand Teton right from our bedroom window. Moose often browsed on the golf-course shrubbery. One morning an ermine ran by the window. In good weather we explored Jackson Hole and the nearby Gros Ventre Range on cross-country skis and photographed the snow-covered scenery as well as moose, elk, and coyotes. The prettiest days were the coldest. I had lots of trouble using my 4x5 view camera at minus thirty degrees. Between pictures, I practiced what I preached and put the lens in my shirt pocket to keep it from freezing. However, I forgot and put my face against the metal viewfinder, which froze to my nose—ouch. In poor weather we stepped outside our door and skied across the golf course. In horrible weather I stayed indoors and wrote the first draft of this autobiography.

Opposite: *In 1950 the plowed road ended at Narada Falls. Without the road Paradise was a scene fit for a Christmas card.* Above right: *Despite bright sunshine, at 18 degrees below I found it difficult to set up my tripod for this photograph of the Snake River and Teton Mountains, Wyoming.* Right: *Moose browsing shrubbery at the front door of the house we rented in Jackson Hole, Wyoming.*

Shoveling out the Army rescue plane stranded by deep snow on the Taku Glacier during the 1953 Juneau Icefield trip.

• CHAPTER 14 •

Juneau Icefield

*or
How to Do a Ten-Day Trip
in Thirty-Seven Days*

Dr. Maynard Miller, Director of the Juneau Icefield Research Project, Alaska.

My first trip to Alaska was in 1953, when Maynard Miller invited me on the second winter expedition to his research station on the Juneau Icefield. Maynard had arranged for us to fly to the glacier in an experimental air force rescue flying boat equipped with skis under the wings and one on the keel to land on snow. We were to spend a few days on the glacier, then ski thirty miles back to Juneau. He estimated the whole trip would take about ten days. In fact, he had to get back that soon because his wife was expecting their first child in two weeks.

In 1941, the year I managed the Paradise photo shop at Mount Rainier, Maynard, the same age as me, was one of eight mountain guides, so I frequently photographed him leading tourists to the ice caves. While World War II sent me to the South Pacific, Maynard stayed in the mountains. Maynard's interest was glaciers, and he was well on his way to a doctorate degree when I joined him on this expedition.

Maynard, Irving Herrigstad (a radio expert with the Mountain Rescue Council), and I flew into Juneau on a commercial airline and waited for the air force

plane—and we waited. The fourth day our air force craft arrived and we took off in the rain, the three of us, the six-man crew, and a couple tons of equipment and supplies. The plan was to fly to the Alaska–Canada border, the highest point on the icefield, at an elevation of about 6,000 feet, where most of the supplies were to be unloaded. Then the plane would fly us eighteen miles down the glacier to the main research station at the 3,000-foot level.

The plane landed at 6,000 feet, as planned, and supplies were unloaded in a neat pile four feet high. Maynard expected us to return here in two days and spend five days doing his experiment. I wondered what sort of experiment required a stack of lumber, two big generators, two large tents, three drums of gasoline, cases of food, and a number of sturdy boxes. We were getting back in the plane when Maynard had an afterthought that came from years of experience with mountain weather. He went back to the pile, took an eight-foot-long 2×4 from the lumber pile, and propped it up like a flag pole.

The plane taxied down the gentle slope of the glacier—

Dropping fifty-gallon drums of gasoline on the Juneau Icefield and finally taking off after being stranded ten days on the Juneau Icefield.

and taxied and taxied. The ski design was for dry Arctic snow, and in October the snow so near the coast was wet, and there was so much friction between the wet snow and the belly of the plane, that even with full power the pilot was not able to get enough speed to become airborne. After a half-hour the motors became too hot and had to be shut down to cool off. In hopes the snow would be firmer and the air denser at a lower elevation, it was decided to taxi down the glacier. Taxiing a half hour, cooling a half hour, repeat and repeat. Nine miles down the glacier the plane ran out of gas.

The hour was too late to get help. The crew stayed with the plane, using its emergency survival equipment, while we three skied the remaining nine miles to the research station. Darkness fell before we had gone three miles, so most of the way was navigated by compass. About midnight the building loomed in front of us, a wooden building with every comfort of home. We had a bite to eat and collapsed in bed. I woke up about 3:00 A.M. to find Maynard cooking a giant dinner.

While Irv stayed in the cabin to man the radio, early next morning, Maynard and I skied back to the plane to help with the refueling. Shortly after we arrived an air force plane came over and parachuted eight fifty-gallon drums of gasoline and free-dropped five-gallon cans of de-icing fluid, but no food because the plane was expected to take off in an hour or two. The drop technique needed some practice. Six of the eight gas drums came loose from their parachute harnesses and fell free. The pilot's aim with the de-icer was so good that one free-dropped can just missed us and buried itself next to the fuselage between the wing and tail! Loading the gas into the tanks was a mean job. First the drum had to be hauled to the plane; then the gas was hand-pumped into the wing tanks. First, though, the six drums that had fallen free had to be dug out. The one I worked on was buried five

feet deep in the snow and upside down. I shoveled out a hole big enough to turn the drum over. It being too heavy to pull out of the hole, we pumped the gas into an empty drum, hauled that to the plane, and pumped it into the wing tank.

Night was falling when at last the plane was ready. The temperature had been dropping all day and the snow was in good shape for takeoff. Despite Maynard's shaking his head in disagreement, the weather report was good for the next two days and the captain, worried about the surrounding mountains, elected to wait until daylight to take off. The crew again bedded down in the plane and the two of us skied back to the station.

The weather turned foul. The station was enveloped in fog, wind, and blowing snow. The next morning Maynard and I again made our way to the plane, this time carrying food for the crew, in good spirits though hungry and cramped in their small quarters. The storm raged on. The fourth day we again skied the nine miles with more food to the plane. Four feet of snow had fallen and the plane was buried almost to its wings, so we dug it free and shoveled out a ramp. The plane taxied up out of the hole to the new surface of the glacier and, in so doing, exhausted its safety margin of fuel. The crew, getting cabin fever, decided the next day to taxi down to the research station.

Maynard had a project on the glacier in front of the buildings measuring the temperature of the ice inside

Research cabin above the Taku Glacier on the Juneau Icefield.

a crevasse. The day was so foggy we couldn't see anything, but off and on we heard the roar of the plane's engine taxiing. Then there would be a long pause while the engines cooled. The sound came closer and the plane loomed out of the fog. As we watched, it seemed to drop, then bounce up, before finally coming to a stop a hundred feet away.

The pilot went back along the track to see what had made the plane bounce and found a gaping hole into which the plane had collapsed a hidden snow bridge over a deep crevasse. Maynard was delighted by the new hole and within the few minutes it took to rig climbing ropes was inside taking readings before outdoor air could affect the ice temperature.

It looked for a while like there was going to be a new research station buried right in the glacier. The air force actually wrote off the airplane as unsalvageable. Maynard might have been happy to have a laboratory in a moving glacier, but there was no way we could ever have led the six nonskiing, nonmountaineering crewmen (all from South Carolina) back to civilization. By radio Maynard urged the air force to give it one more try.

Ten days after the plane had set us down on the glacier, the weather turned clear and bitterly cold. An air force plane again came in and dropped more gas and de-icing fluid. This time the drums were properly attached to the parachutes. By midafternoon the plane was stripped of extra gear and ready to go. The temperature dropped to ten below, the snow was dry, and the plane took off with ease as I took pictures.

TO WORK AT LAST

On day fifteen of our ten-day trip, Maynard was ready to start his own work. The three of us headed eighteen miles back up the glacier to the high cache. The weather was clear and cold, but it might as well have been storming for the powdered snow drifted in a vicious ground blizzard. Facing the wind, we made only ten miles the first day and spent a miserable night in a two-man tent. Drifting snow built up outside the tent, squeezing it even smaller. I felt suffocated and was happy when morning came. We pushed on to the cache.

What cache? There was nothing to see. The cache had disappeared under ten feet of new snow and was lost in a four-mile-wide plateau. Looking for a needle

in a haystack, we spread out and searched for three hours. No needle, nothing but miles of snow. We were running out of daylight but agreed to each make one last quarter-mile circle before giving up. Sticking above the wind drifted snow, Maynard stumbled on one inch of the eight-foot 2x4 he had planted as an afterthought seventeen days before.

We pitched a big army tent and made a comfortable living quarters. Next, we set up the generators, built a large tripod, and wired up an electric drill Maynard had invented as an experiment to determine the density of ice layers in the glacier. It was like an oversized soldering iron with a hot point that melted a hole 100 feet down in the ice. All we had to do was keep the generator going and record how fast the drill melted the ice. But nothing ever comes that easy. Maynard needed to measure the water content of the early snowfall, so we had to break our backs digging several 15-foot-deep holes.

Ten days at the cache site, then five more at the research station, and on day 32 we headed back to Juneau on skis. Maynard calculated we might be able to cover the thirty-some miles in one day, but, just to be safe, we took a two-day supply of food. If we had trouble, there were two caches along the way we could use. Or thought we could. The temperature was minus eighteen, the snow was deep, and our packs were heavy—mine was at least ninety pounds and Maynard's heavier. We made well over half the distance that first day and camped in view of the spectacular 8,600-foot Devils Paw (Mountain). Getting a big camera out of a ninety-pound pack is time-consuming, so I had postponed taking a picture until we stopped, but by then it was dark. Dawn was beautiful. I slid out of my warm bag and set up my camera. Having taken my lens to bed with me to save the shutter from freezing, I exulted in my winning series of pictures of our little tent in the middle of the huge glacier, with Devils Paw in the distance. Much to my dismay, while developing the pictures at home, I found the film had broken from the cold and I had nothing but blanks. What a crying shame. To actually have sunshine in that dramatic setting and then goof up. I had remembered to keep the lens warm but had forgotten what minus eighteen degrees would do to film. I should have kept it warm, too.

With less than half the distance to cover, on day 33, we were sure we would make Juneau by nightfall, so

Research camp at top of the Juneau Icefield next to the Alaska–Canada border.

we did not detour to the first cache, but bucking a fierce wind made the going difficult and we didn't get far that day. The third day we were running short of food, and were glad to find the second cache on a windswept ridge overlooking Juneau Airport. However, this one did us no good either, as a sixty-mile-an-hour wind and minus temperature made it impossible to un-fasten the ropes that secured the cache without getting frostbitten hands. Within sound of Juneau Airport we pitched the tent, gaining little comfort from being able to hear, above the roar of the storm, planes taking off. Expecting breakfast in Juneau the next morning, we ate all the food we had left and used up all the gas for our stove.

The next morning, however, day 35, the ridge crest was solid ice. Maynard spent all day chopping steps while I belayed him, and then Irv, with a thirty-foot length of rope. The sun was bright in the sky, but the heat did not reach us through a ground blizzard driven by gale-force wind. It took us all of day 36 to descend 500 feet, and night caught us still a long way from Ju-neau. I dug in my pack and came up with a jar of jam and a bag containing two raisins. I mixed the jam with powder snow and made two quarts of very good ice

Above: *Headed back to Juneau on day 32 of our ten-day trip.*
Left: *Maynard bent under a pack of 100-plus pounds on the Taku Glacier.*

cream. That was our dinner. I debated how to divide the two raisins three ways and finally gave up and ate them myself. On day 37 of our ten-day trip we finally had breakfast in Juneau, and a mighty big one it was.

On a call home, Maynard found he was the proud father of a five-day-old boy. In the hospital, his wife, Joan, was being looked after by strangers who assumed she was an unwed mother, for they didn't believe her story of a husband stranded on an Alaskan glacier.

THIRTY YEARS LATER

Dr. Maynard Malcolm Miller has added some amazing facilities in thirty years. The research project now covers some 5,000 square miles. On my first visit in 1953 there was one small cabin and a few trail caches. Now there are seventy cabins in seventeen locations. Each year between twenty-five and fifty students and a dozen or more instructors turn the icefield into a vast laboratory to pursue studies of glaciology, climatic changes, geology, and botany. This is the only such project in the world, and it is due to Dr. Miller's ability to obtain funding from private foundations, government agencies, and individuals.

In the summer of 1983, just thirty years after that winter expedition, Pat and I hiked into the icefield. The weather was too poor to go farther than the windswept ridge where years before the three of us had spent a hungry night because we hadn't dared to open the food cache. The wind was still raging, but this time there was no danger of going hungry; the food cache had become a small city with eight buildings (tied down with steel cables), stoves, generators, and loads of food.

CHAPTER 15

Ocean Beaches and Justice Douglas

or

Beware of Slippery Rocks

Family dispute near Hole-in-the-Wall.

The Olympic Loop Highway wasn't completed until the mid-thirties. In 1929, when we were growing up, the drive from Shelton to the ocean at La Push was arduous. On our first trip the pavement ended at the edge of Shelton. A gravel road wound in and out of every little nook and cranny along the west shore of Hood Canal. I suspect the main streets of Port Angeles were paved, but the road was gravel around Lake Crescent, the miles of blackened forest of the huge Sol Duc Burn, to Forks, then to the Quileute Indian Reservation, through the village of La Push, across the mouth of the Quillayute River on a wooden bridge, to a cabin camp at Rialto Beach.

I don't remember much about the dirt roads except that they were washboard, which Dad blamed on Model Ts, something to do with the way their pistons fired. Of course Model Ts are long gone and dirt roads still develop washboards. On that first visit to the ocean, we hiked north along the beach to Hole-in-the-Wall,

Butch Eastman steering the dugout canoe into "The Indians' Secret Fishing Hole" for a **Ford** *Times story.*

a natural tunnel through a rocky point that was passable only at low tide, and then south past La Push to explore the three small arches against Quateata Head.

I didn't get back to the ocean until I started free-lancing. In 1951, when John was six months old, I had an assignment from *Ford Times* for a story on "The Indians' Secret Fishing Hole," featuring two Quileute boys who traveled by cedar dugout canoe (powered by outboard motor) eight miles south from La Push to the mouth of Goodman Creek.

We drove to Forks in brilliant sunshine but, descending the hill into La Push, entered a dense fog bank. The next day the fog persisted, and the next, and the next, for a week and more. The story couldn't be photographed because the boys never would have been able to find the narrow entrance to their fishing hole at Goodman Creek. The fog was so heavy we might as well have been camping in the rain. After several days we ran out of diapers. Washing was no problem, but hanging them in the fog made them wetter. Finally, we drove to a Laundromat in Forks. Wouldn't you know, a mile from the ocean we drove out of the fog into bright sun.

The time waiting for the fog to lift was not all

Top: *Quileutes fishing the mouth of the Quillayute River.*
Bottom: *Playing the Quileute bone game at La Push*

recalling the original town located atop the sheer cliffs of James Island, a natural fortress that the Quileutes' enemies never did succeed in capturing, and the time he walked with his father fifty miles down the beach to witness signing of the treaty with the whites.

From Charley Sailto we learned the "bone game," still played by the Quileute people, a simple guessing game using two small look-alike bones, one of which is marked. While a member of one team or tribe craftily shifts the bones from hand to hand, his companions chant, beat sticks, and pound drums. The opposing team attempts to choose the hand that holds the marked bone. In olden days household effects were wagered, and weapons, and wives, but poker chips are now used.

I photographed William Penn, another old-timer, constructing canoes from giant cedar trees by burning out the centers and hacking away with crude tools. The canoes today look the same as they have for centuries, though outboard motors have replaced paddles.

Eventually the fog blew away and the two teenage boys, Butch Eastman and Jim Black, and I piled into a dugout canoe and were soon moving out the Quillayute River into the ocean swell, one minute riding the crest of a wave with a panoramic view and the next down in a hollow looking up at walls of water that seemed certain to engulf our little craft. Never were we more than a mile from shore as we rode past and between hundreds of islets and surf-battered jagged sea stacks. I had many misgivings, but Butch seemed to know every rock and passageway.

An hour and a half from La Push, Butch pointed out the place we were headed. To my eye our destination looked no different from the miles of rocky shoreline we had passed. He headed straight toward cliffs rising a hundred feet above the water. A few yards from shore I still could see nothing but rock walls and surf, but a sharp right turn revealed the entry cleft. A quarter-mile through a narrow, twisting passage the cliffs dropped away and the waterway widened into a pretty little bay, into which flowed a creek accessible only by water, "The Secret Fishing Hole."

I explored the river bank while the boys fished. The river issued from a dark, damp forest, and a few hundred yards upstream I came upon an old campsite that must have been deserted for many years. In the sand beside the river were deer and elk tracks. When

wasted. Pat and I got acquainted with Chief Charlie Howeattle of the Quileute. He showed us around La Push and helped us do a story on his village. He described terms of the treaty that guaranteed the tribal right to net fish in the Quillayute River. During fish runs, the entire family turns out to pull in the nets. He introduced us to Stanley Gray, at eighty-six the oldest man in La Push, who told about the early days,

I returned the boys had a fire going and were cooking a fresh-caught fish. Late in the afternoon we packed up for the journey home. Several miles from La Push the fog came in so thick we couldn't see the shore. However, Butch recognized every rocky sea stack and, aided by the foghorn on James Island, had no trouble getting us back to the quiet harbor at La Push.

"A WALKIE TALKIE"

Except for a ten-mile stretch at Kalaloch where the highway parallels the ocean, and two Indian villages, fifty miles of the Olympic ocean beach is wilderness. To correct this obvious oversight, local chambers of commerce and tourist organizations were pushing for a road along the Washington coast to compete with Oregon's famous coastal highway. The Washington State Highway Department was willing, though it pointed out that unlike Oregon our ocean-side slopes were unstable and the road would have to be built back from the beach, giving few views of the ocean from a moving car or even a parked car. They also observed that our vegetation is heavier than Oregon's and brush ten feet high would interfere with views. Facts did not deter the tourist industry's demands.

To preserve the last remaining wilderness beach in the contiguous forty-eight states, in 1953 conservationist Polly Dyer organized a three-day, twenty-mile march from Lake Ozette to La Push, led by Supreme Court Justice William O. Douglas. The press was invited as well as any interested individuals, either for or against the road. Fifty marchers from conservation groups were augmented by at least twenty of us from the media. Commentators and cameramen from Seattle television and radio stations attended, as well as reporters and photographers from Port Angeles, Bremerton, and Aberdeen newspapers. The *Seattle Post-Intelligencer* had both a photographer and a writer,

and I represented the *Seattle Times*. Pro-road tourist-industrialists were invited to come along on the hike but preferred to stick to the roads, where they held up signs, "Bird Watcher Go Home," (meaning the Justice).

It was quite a gang that left Lake Ozette and hiked the four miles to Cape Alava, site of our first night's camp. The big wheels of conservation were there. The Justice and his wife, Mercedes, Olaus and Mardie (Margaret) Murie, Polly Dyer, and Dan Beard (Jr.) are a few I recall.

This was my first meeting with Justice Douglas and I was impressed. He was a quiet, friendly man who preferred to listen rather than talk. He must have been a disappointment to the news people. In the morning everyone started hiking together, and photographers who were on their toes got pictures of the Justice leading the pack. But once on his way, few people could keep up. I was the only representative of the press who was a hiker and I had my own problems. I'd get ahead and find a photogenic spot, hurry to get the camera

Justice William O. Douglas putting on dry socks and giving a photographer a chance to catch up.

out, take my picture—and by the time I put the camera away the Justice was a small dot way down the beach. If you asked him to stop for a picture, he was very willing to oblige, but you had to catch up with him to ask.

The march was well covered. The *Seattle Times* used my story, and from my notes Byron Fish wrote a column entitled "A Walkie Talkie." The demand for a coastal road died down and the wilderness beach became famous, drawing hikers from all over the country as the longest of its kind in the lower forty-eight states.

I saw Justice Douglas a number of times afterward. He wrote the foreword to our book *High Worlds of the Mountain Climber*, and we collaborated on a North Cascades story for *National Geographic*. Some ten years after the beach hike Pat and I, by chance, met him on

the trail to Cascade Pass. He now had a heart-pacer, which slowed him down but made it easy for us to stay with him.

The Justice was a very outspoken and controversial man and worked prodigiously both on the bench and during his "leisure" time when the rest of the court was relaxing. He wrote more than fifty books on law, conservation, and his childhood experiences. He lectured, wrote stories for national magazines, and was on the board of directors for several foundations. On the Supreme Court he wrote more briefs than any other justice.

When the question came to the Supreme Court of who, public or private power companies, should build a dam in Hells Canyon, Justice Douglas sent it back to the lower courts to determine the best use of the canyon. We now have a free-flowing river. He raised an uproar with a story for *Playboy* magazine, calling the

Above: *U.S. Supreme Court Justice William O. Douglas leading the pack out of camp the second morning. His pace soon strung out the line. Not many hikers and no other photographer could keep up with him. Above right: A tidal pool near Hole-in-the-Wall. I didn't have a Polaroid filter, which would have gotten rid of the sky reflections, so I found someone to hold my dark cloth to block the reflection. Right: Toleak Point, where I broke my ankle and got a ride home in a Coast Guard helicopter.*

Army Corps of Engineers "America's Number One Public Enemy," an article that helped pave the way to the requirement for environmental impact statements on major construction projects.

I did a story for the *Seattle Times* on Justice Douglas,

Top: *Near Ruby Beach.* Bottom: *Turnstones playing "chicken" with huge waves.*

and mail that letter. It is a stay of execution scheduled for next week." Holding someone's life in my hands, I was a nervous wreck until I reached the post office at Trout Lake and handed the letter to the postmaster.

Much to my editors' embarrassment, the owners of the paper did not like the Justice and killed the story. No problem—I sold it to a national magazine.

SLIPPERY ROCKS

The sea stacks along the wilderness beach are a favorite subject of both Bob and me. Ten years in a row Pat and I rented a cabin at La Push for a New Year's weekend. In general, we have better luck with sunshine in winter than in summer. However, the nights are so long we confine our beach walks to day hikes. The La Push beach isn't nearly so interesting as it was when I first saw it in 1929. About 1950 the Corps of Engineers blasted away the three photogenic arches at Quateata Head to quarry rock for a jetty at the mouth of the Quillayute River.

Our favorite, and most photogenic, beach is Toleak Point near the mouth of Goodman Creek, "The Indians' Secret Fishing Hole." On our 1979 hike there the weather was beautiful but cold and I had my hands in my pockets to keep them warm. I slipped on a seaweed-covered rock and as I went down my foot twisted under me. The initial pain was fierce but

his wife, and two grandchildren living in a mountain cabin some twenty miles from the Trout Lake post office and the nearest telephone. When the pictures were finished he handed me an envelope to mail. The last thing he said as I was going out the door was, "Be sure

within a few minutes was gone. I knew I had done something bad to my ankle, but before pushing the panic button I tried walking. I took a couple of steps and my foot flopped sideways and I fell. Again the pain was so great I almost threw up, but in a few minutes it

Waterfall on Taylor Head.

was gone again. The leg swelled up, making its own cast, and never again gave me any pain. But I knew now I could never get back to civilization on my own power. Son John carried me above the high-tide line and ran for help. Daughter Vicky and Pat stayed with me. We were sheltered from the wind and the sun was warm, and by chance some friends happened by, so I was comfortable and well entertained.

John made good time to the car and four hours after the accident a Coast Guard helicopter from Port Angeles came to my rescue. I was taken to the Forks Hospital and given emergency treatment. John loaded me into the back of his van and took me to Group Health Hospital in Redmond, where the ankle (broken in three places, plus a dislocation) was patched together with a metal plate and four or five screws.

I spent a frustrating two months in a cast, but my ankle is completely healed and, except for a scar, I wouldn't know which ankle had been broken.

While in a cast and confined to crutches or a wheelchair, I decided to build a lean-to greenhouse on the end of our garage and equip it with a hot tub. I did everything I could to reach from a chair or from crutches, but I had to enlist Pat to do the high work. The only real frustration was watching her pound nails. She just never did get out of the apprentice stage in carpentry. However, we ended up with a nice green-house and a hot tub that has soaked away many a sore muscle after hiking and skiing.

• CHAPTER 16 •

Wildlife Encounters

or
When to Photograph and When to Run

Bald eagle on San Juan Island keeping an eye out for rabbits.

To coin a phrase, wildlife *is* wilderness. Some of my best friends . . .

At the age of 104, my father shared his favorite memory about a night spent on the side of Mount Stone in the Olympics in 1939 when a large bull elk with huge antlers was silhouetted by moonlight on a cliff above our camp. Our parents taught both Bob and me to enjoy wildlife, just as they taught us about wildflowers, so the love of wildlife was instilled early in my life.

One of the fringe benefits of researching all our hiking books has been the occasional encounter with wildlife. Besides hiking in the cool of the morning, my

Sometimes I do live right. For this brief encounter at White Rock Lake I only had one color film left in my camera and it turned out so perfectly that I have been accused of carrying around a stuffed deer. Beyond are the Dana Glacier and the cliffs of Dome Peak.

policy of parking the camper at the trailhead for the night and hitting the trail at daylight has had the double benefit of often finding wildlife grazing by the trail. During the heat of the day, when most people hike, the animals are in the forest hiding from bugs and resting. My encounters with wildlife during the early hours are so short and the light so poor, I seldom get pictures, but they add up to wonderful experiences and memories.

I wanted to pass along my fascination with wildlife, so I compiled a book full of photographs and my experiences with animals, which was published in 1975. In my mind the book was excellent, but it was not a good seller. Not daunted, in 1976 I coauthored a book on "where to find wildlife" in our state. This was followed two years later by a similar book on Oregon. Unfortunately, they, too, did poorly.

PLAYING HIDE AND SEEK WITH DEER

Where deer are not hunted, as in Yellowstone National Park, they are very indifferent to people. Outside of such refuges deer run at the sight of man. It would be easy to be antihunting, but hunters have been leaders in protecting animal habitat and lobbying for the wilderness.

One morning Vicky and I were hiking to Holland Lakes in the Bob Marshall Wilderness, and at one point the trail angled up a cliff on a long five-foot-wide ledge. We were just starting up when two bucks started down. They saw us, turned around, and ran out of sight. The ledge was the only way down the cliff, so Vicky and I sat down to see what would happen. Sure enough, in a few minutes one poked his head around the first corner, saw us, and disappeared. Not wanting to harass the deer, we hiked on up the ledge. Near the top, its head behind a bush and rear end fully exposed, was one of the deer, safely "hidden" as we passed, but almost close enough to reach out and pet.

Hiking in the Wyoming Range, I sat down to rest in the shade of a tree. When I was about ready to get up, a five-point buck crossed the meadow in front of me. I kept perfectly still. The deer knew something was wrong because he kept staring in my direction. I didn't dare reach for my camera—any movement would have made him run—so I just sat there enjoying that beautiful animal until it was out of sight.

In 1977 Pat and I camped two nights at White Rock Lakes, highlight of the Ptarmigan Traverse. I spent all morning taking pictures on my 4x5 view camera. I had only one sheet of color film left and started back to our tent to reload, but got sidetracked by a ptarmigan wandering around camp, just begging to be photographed. I got my 35mm camera and followed the bird until it jumped up on a small rock with a mountain behind it. I knelt in an awkward position and focused. I was concentrating on getting everything lined up perfectly, when in my viewfinder a deer walked between the bird and the mountain. I looked up so fast that in my awkward position I fell, making a sudden movement that startled the deer, which ran away. I dropped the 35mm and grabbed the 4x5 and followed it across the knoll. Two beautiful bucks were waiting for me. One ran, but the other stood in front of Dome Peak just long enough for me to focus and shoot my last color film. Then it was gone. Sometimes I do live right.

My favorite wildlife picture was the deer at White Rock Lakes. Unfortunately, it is so perfect I have been accused of using a stuffed animal—preposterous of course, considering it takes three days of fast hiking to get there and would probably have taken days longer carrying a prop that size.

ENCOUNTERS WITH ELK

Our encounters with elk have been different. I needed elk pictures to illustrate a booklet on Olympic National Park. In Yellowstone National Park elk are never hunted and are not afraid of people, but the Olympic elk migrate outside the park during hunting season and are easily spooked by man, with or without a gun. To get close enough for pictures, we bought an elk call that worked almost too well. We backpacked up on High Divide and made camp in a meadow in an area with lots of elk tracks. There were elk all right. We heard them crashing through brush and bellowing all night. Early in the morning when it was just getting light, Pat awoke and practiced blowing the elk call to get the hang of it. She did. Wow! A big bull elk (it gets larger every time we think about it) came charging out of a nearby forest, bellowing. When he saw our tent, he stopped his charge and stood there pawing the ground. Then with a swish of massive antlers he tore out a small alpine tree growing nearby. We were speechless and ready to make a dash for the closest large tree when, satisfied he had silenced his scrawny competition, the bull turned around and walked away. While we took pictures that day of a herd of cow elk, that big beautiful bull stayed out of sight.

During the rutting season, elk are nothing to fool with. I remember when I was still living in Shelton, a neighbor fought a losing battle with a bull elk on the road around Lake Cushman. The elk was in the middle of a bridge and refused to move, so our neighbor eased his car closer and closer, but the bull just lowered his antlers and charged, cracking the radiator.

We took three winter trips to Yellowstone, where animals congregate near the thermal areas. One time I was maneuvering around to get in position to photograph an elk feeding along the Firehole River. I wasn't paying attention to the other animals until I heard an odd grating sound. I looked around and there was a bull elk less than five feet away, gnashing his teeth, his way of telling me I was in his territory and to move off before he clobbered me. He probably would have

Left: *Elk In Yellowstone National Park.* Above: *a ground squirrel at Crater Lake.* Below: *An elk harem on High Divide. The male who had responded to Pat's elk call stayed out of sight.*

Top: *Early one morning, hiking up Granite Creek in the Gros Ventre of Wyoming, we surprised a bull moose grazing in a small meadow. Too dignified to run, he kept casually moving away as I got out my camera. I just had time for one exposure before he stepped into the woods. There was a moment's pause and then, out of sight, he lost his dignity and we heard the sound of galloping hooves.* Bottom: *A salmon fighting its way up the Sol Duc River to its spawning beds.*

if I had stared at him, something he would have taken as a challenge.

Vicky and I were sitting on the shore of Shriners Lake eating lunch when we spotted a cow elk walking across a meadow toward the opposite end of the lake. We held perfectly still and the cow came closer. She obviously saw something but didn't know what, because as she walked she kept looking right at us. She was looking so hard in our direction, she walked right off a four-foot bank and plunged into the lake. After thrashing around in the water a bit, she climbed out and disappeared.

Maybe the most fun of all has been with young animals. Vicky and I were hiking in the South Wyoming Range when we surprised an elk herd, mostly cows who ran. However, a dozen or more calves, still in their polka-dot baby fur and grazing by themselves, evidently hadn't gotten the message. We walked up to them singing lullabies. The poor things didn't know what to make of us, couldn't make up their minds whether to join us or run. We just sang to them, took a couple of pictures, and left. As soon as we turned our backs, they ran for mama.

BUFFALO . . . WHEN TO RUN

One winter at Yellowstone's Firehole River thermal area, I was on skis photographing a buffalo. I have a great respect for these big animals so I was using a telephoto from a good safe distance. The buffalo started walking slowly away but then turned and started walking toward me, still slowly. *Okay,* I thought, *I will get out of its way,* so I moved off at an angle. The buffalo changed his direction too, coming slowly but straight at me. Worried, I turned and pointed my skis toward the closest tree. Looking over my shoulder I saw the buffalo charging at me full bore. I wish I could have taken the time to photograph him as he plunged through the stomach-deep powdered snow, a huge spray flying out as if from a speeding snowplow. I ran as fast as my skis would go to the nearest tree, took off the skis, and scrambled up. The buffalo stopped. He didn't look up at me but stayed there for a cold hour before moving off, letting me escape. I related my experience to the ranger at Old Faithful. He laughed and said the week before he had been chased up a tree, maybe by the same animal, only he didn't have time to take off his skis. He must

Buffalo at Warm Springs, Yellowstone National Park. Fortunately, this one was aware he had invaded "my space" and was bashful about it, so I didn't have to climb a tree as I would have had it been "his space." What tree? There was none near.

have had great wax. The picture I took before the charge has been used many times by *American West* magazine and was made into a huge poster.

Animals have their own personal territory and other animals enter that territory at their own risk. The problem is guessing where the territorial lines are. They vary with the individual animal and even with different times. Obviously I had entered that buffalo's territory. Another time the opposite was true. I was sitting on a rock photographing two buffalo near a steaming hot springs when I became aware of a thump-thumpety-thump behind me. I looked and a buffalo was walking by less than ten feet to my left, acting as if afraid I would attack him for entering my territory. I switched lenses and got a great picture.

ONE BEAR STORY AFTER ANOTHER . . .

On the trail to Mount Rainier's Shriners Peak we looked down on Shriners Lake and were thrilled to watch a bear swimming across the lake. We were too far away to take pictures, but we sat down and watched it thrash around in the water like a playful dog, get out, shake itself like a dog, and ramble away.

Back in 1940, camped alone under the stars at Mount Rainier, I put my pack between my bed and a large boulder to protect my food from the bears. During the night I woke with a huge weight on my sleeping bag. Startled, I reared up. A bear was sitting on a corner of my bag chewing my pack. I must have been sleeping soundly because my pack had been torn open and some of the food eaten, but what really hurt was the bear had bitten into my film.

Another time, hiking alone in the fall, I rounded a corner and met a bear feasting on blueberries not twenty feet off the trail. It reared up and growled. My hair stood on end but there was nothing I could do but ignore him and keep walking.

Left: Moving a "campground bear" from Mount Rainier to a logging camp in the Puyallup River valley. The ranger is marking the bear with paint so that next time it will immediately be recognized as a problem. Right: A visit from the landlord on Mount Olympus. This is the goat that collapsed our tent in the middle of the night. Bottom, left to right: Coyote in Yellowstone; Western bluebird; ptarmigan in summer plumage; pika that Pat photographed along the Granite Creek trail in the Gros Ventre Wilderness of Wyoming.

My final bear story was the time Pat and I were hiking up a gravel bar along the Nooksack River. In wet sand we found a large bear print. We glanced up the river and saw a bear walking toward us. There were no nearby trees, so we yelled to scare it away, but our voices were drowned out by the sound of the river. When it was about to bump into us it finally got the message and ran.

To prove that when people talk about bears even I cannot be trusted, for there is always one more bear story to tell, here's another one—but I promise this will be the last. This should have been an elk story. I once accompanied Louis Kirk, a National Park ranger, and his wife Ruth on a five-day trip to Olympus Guard Station, nine miles up the Hoh River trail, where we hoped to photograph elk through the cabin windows. I had made a morning trip to the outhouse and a few minutes later Louis followed me. He came back accusing me of mutilating the toilet paper. I denied doing any such thing, so we returned to the scene of the crime. It was my fault. I had left the outhouse door open and in the short time between my visit and Louis', a bear had looked in and taken a bite from the roll. Presumably it wasn't to his taste, but the teeth marks were clearly visible. I photographed some female elk through the window but never saw the bear or bulls. A week later Ruth went back by herself for another try. On her last morning, with a bucket of wash water in hand, she opened the front door and threw the water—on a big buck that was as surprised to see her as she was to see him. Of course it was gone before she could get her camera.

Snow geese at Tule Lake Wildlife Refuge

MOUNTAIN GOATS, KING OF THE MOUNTAINS

As chamois are to the Alps, mountain goats are to our western mountains. They are not rare, just seldom seen.

Vicky, Pat, and I hiked the eighteen miles to Glacier Meadows on Mount Olympus and camped on the moraine above the Blue Glacier. As we approached the moraine, we saw a goat near the spot where we were going to camp, so I put on a telephoto lens and snuck up on him. He saw us, but instead of running he came in our direction, so close all I could see in the viewfinder was an eye. I had to take off the telephoto to get a picture.

He grazed around our tent all night, keeping us awake with the noise of his eating and stomping. Evidently he was just curious, for there was much better grass a few feet away. Sometime in the darkest part of the night he bit through the willow branch the tent was tied to and down came the tent. Startled at that, he ran away. I tied the tent to a sturdier branch and a half-hour later the goat was back. At first light I looked out and a foot from the mosquito-netting door were eyes looking in, sharp horns inches from my face.

Mountain goats are common in the Cascade Mountains, but the Olympic Mountains are isolated and the goats never found their way across Puget Sound. In the 1920s, long before the area became a national park, hunters captured some goats in British Columbia and released them in the Olympic Mountains. Goats, like other animals, inherit traits. Some are

very curious and walk up to a human while others are timid and run. Away from a sanctuary, such as a national park, the curious are shot and only the timid survive to pass along their traits. While goats are fairly common in the Cascades, they have been hunted, and therefore they run away. Evidently it was just the curious goats that were trapped in Canada and released in the Olympics. The Olympic goats became a photographer's dream, for instead of running as they do elsewhere, close-up pictures were easy to get.

The population grew slowly at first, but then in the late 1970s the number seemed to explode and reached the point where they were impacting meadows and destroying some endemic plants. The impacts reached the point where the Park Service was ordered to reduce or eliminate the goats. Part of the reduction was capturing and transporting them to the Cascades, where we now occasionally find a goat that doesn't run.

FAVORITE BIRDS

Bird are extremely difficult to photograph. The great pictures in nature magazines are taken from blinds by photographers with far more patience than I have. However, I have had some luck using the car for a blind. Wildlife is a lot more tolerant of a person inside an automobile than outside, so instead of setting up a tripod I brace the camera against the open car window. To hide any noise I might make I leave the radio going.

For a number of years we have attended the Audubon's annual Memorial Day camp-out near Yakima, Washington. We are constantly amazed at how knowledgeable some of the members are. They recognize birds from just a twitter or glimpse. What we like best is their ability to give us lesser experts opportunity to photograph owls, wrens, and even bluebird nests.

I have many favorite birds. In the mountains there are the ptarmigan, Canada jay, and Clark's nutcracker.

At home it is the friendly chickadee. Along the water I am fascinated by the great blue heron stalking a dinner and the majestic bald eagle perched upright on a tree overlooking the water.

Some 50 to 60 pairs of bald eagles nest in the state of Washington and another 400 to 500 migrate here in midwinter to feed on dead salmon. Having been shot at in the lower forty-eight states, these birds are pretty wary of humans, so we were surprised at how tame and how numerous they were around the towns of Southeast Alaska. We saw them soaring over, perched on piling, and even on city light poles. Our biggest thrill was when an eagle soared a few feet above the hood of our car on a dock in Ketchikan, its six-foot wingspread literally blocking our light. Of course, no camera was handy. Near Petersburg we camped along the water and 20 to 30 eagles were feeding on a very dead seal washed ashore a short distance away.

I met a man on San Juan Island who invited me to take pictures of a nesting pair of eagles in his backyard. I had to set my camera on a tripod and work in the open. The birds recognized him as a human friend, but not me. Everything was fine as long as their landlord was with me, but when he left the birds became very upset. He finally had to return so I could finish my photographs.

Who would believe my run-in with a grouse? Vicky and I were hiking on the Heart Lake trail in Yellowstone National Park when we came upon a mother grouse and a flock of chicks. I swung off my pack, stooped over to get my camera out of the pack, and my rear end was ambushed. I got on the other side of the pack and that darn bird kept circling around to attack my back again and again. Vicky could have helped, but that miserable excuse for a daughter was laughing her fool head off. By the time I managed to get my camera out, the bird had gone off to look after her chicks.

Opposite: *On San Juan Island a bald eagle lands near its nest located close to a farmhouse. As long as the farmer stood with me, the eagle tolerated my camera, but became very upset when he left.* Right: *Pat and her models, Everglades National Park.* Bottom right: *Telephoto of a mighty yawn from a brown pelican, Redwood National Park.*

DANGER

On an overnight trip to Toleak Point, we were awakened by something in the tent. I turned my flashlight on in time to see a piece of salami disappearing through a brand-new hole in my tent. I went outside and a skunk was calmly eating my salami. What could I do? Yelling didn't impress the critter. Poked with a stick, it turned its tail as if to take aim at me. The skunk finished the salami and ambled off, leaving me to clean up a mess of shredded plastic wrappers and fix a hole in the tent.

• CHAPTER 17 •

Ptarmigan Traverse

or
Two Wonderful Weeks
in the Fog

Mount Formidable ("Daiber") from near Kool-Aid Lake.

My 1957 story on a week-long teenage expedition to the top of Mount Rainier was given a good spread in the Sunday color section of the *Seattle Times*. Sale of the same story to the *Saturday Evening Post* was almost final when they wanted to know what local publicity the trip had received; they turned it down when I told them of the newspaper treatment. However, they said they would be interested in another story providing they had first use. Over the winter I dreamt up the idea of four youths and an older leader attempting the Ptarmigan Traverse from Cascade Pass to Image Lake. The party I recruited had two teenagers, Peggy Stark and Russell Bockman; a young couple, Marge and Ray McConnell (Marge is now Mueller); experienced

Climbing fog-wrapped Sentinel Peak from our camp on the LeConte Glacier. We climbed a wrong peak first — probably a first ascent.

mountaineer Coleman Leuthy, a thirty-one-year-old schoolteacher; and myself.

There were then no United States Geological Survey (USGS) contour maps of the region, only Forest Service planimetrics maps done purely by eyeball surveys in the 1920s, largely sketches and guesses. They were not very accurate but did help us identify the peaks. I also had a few aerial photographs taken five years earlier. However, we had the advantage of knowing the route could be done. Four members of the Ptarmigan Climbing Club had made the trip in 1938, and Tom Miller's group in 1953 had brought back some great pictures. Had I asked, Tom would have given me a lot of firsthand information, but I have always loved exploring and wanted to find my own way. Aside from the fact that the Ptarmigans and Tom started their traverse at Sulphur Creek and ended at Cascade Pass, we knew virtually nothing about details of the route. In addition, we were pioneering a new route around Dome Peak to Image Lake.

Left: *Climbing a bergschrund at the edge of the Chick-amin Glacier.* Right: *A week of rain being steamed out of our socks and gear at Blue Lake.*

Pat drove the six of us to the road end and we hiked the two miles to Cascade Pass. We were just leaving the pass when Pat came running up the trail with my package of maps and aerial photographs, overlooked under the car seat. Lucky. The maps weren't much help, but as the trip progressed we found the photographs invaluable.

From Cascade Pass we traversed the steep slopes of Mixup Peak, ascended to 6,900-foot Cache Col, and dropped down to tiny Kool-Aid Lake, named during a Mountaineers Climbers Outing by members who one hot day calculated it was just big enough to make enough Kool-Aid to quench the party's thirst. The first two nights the weather was beautiful. I had a whole day of sunshine to take pictures while climbing Magic Mountain and Hurry Up Peak. In deteriorating weather we moved on, shuffling over the two-boot-wide Red Ledge, then set out on the crest of the long ridge we expected would take us directly and easily to the top of Spider Mountain; and it would have, had not the easy crest been sliced by a deep, impassable cleft. A

Climbers atop Magic Mountain.

difficult detour on steep heather slopes led to the Middle Cascade Glacier, which we ascended to the Spider-Formidable Col. From that grand vista of glaciers and peaks to the south we dropped to two small lakes not shown on our map. We called them His and Hers by whom bathed in which lake. Hers, the upper lake, was more private but was fed by a hidden snowbank that kept the water at a squealing temperature of about forty degrees. We fellows knew about the snowbank but forgot to tell. His was a cozy sixty degrees. Later we learned the tarns had been called by Tom Miller's group Yang Yang Lakes, the name now on the map.

The creation of the Glacier Peak Wilderness and its rules still in the future, and our backs expressing concern about the monstrous packs required by a two-week outing, we had left four boxes of food with a pilot in Sedro Woolley for an air drop. Clouds covered the peaks as we ascended the Le Conte Glacier on the side of Sentinel to the site of next day's drop. We scooped a flat platform in the névé and put up tents

A POST PICTURE STORY

Learning the Ways of Mountains

The Ptarmigan Traverse as featured in a 1953 Saturday Evening Post.

just as the rain started. In the morning the weather improved only slightly, and when the plane arrived the ceiling was barely 100 feet. The pilot did a noble job, but the low ceiling and a downdraft on the approach run gave him a problem. He dropped two of our four boxes on target but the third landed a half-mile down the glacier and burst open. The ceiling dropped to zero and the pilot had to give up on the fourth box. We roped up and retrieved the scattered remnants of the third box, but nothing could be found worth salvaging. We had found one good reason why hikers must be self-sufficient. Fortunately nowadays, with lightweight equipment and dried food, air drops are no longer needed. The fact that air drops are forbidden in wilderness areas forces hikers to be self-sufficient, and that's the way it should be.

After inventorying the food we realized we might get a little hungry before the trip was over, though never in danger of starving. In the afternoon, for something to do, we wandered in the fog to the top of Sentinel Peak, less than 1,000 feet above camp. We were surprised on top to find no sign of a previous ascent, and a brief clearing told us why. We had climbed the wrong peak. Having a whole afternoon free, we proceeded to climb the right summit, adding our names to those of the 1938 Ptarmigans and Tom Miller's 1953 group. Since obviously no one had bothered to climb the first peak, and it was pretty respectable, we claimed a first ascent and called it Mount Peg after the youngest member of our group, Peggy Stark.

The Le Conte Glacier was the wormiest icefield I'd ever walked on. In bright sunlight iceworms wiggle down beneath the surface and are so seldom seen that most climbers believe they are a barroom myth. After two days of clouds and rain they had come to the surface, and in places the glacier surface was black with millions of what look like miniature angleworms.

We descended to the South Cascade Glacier and then climbed up to its head and dropped to our next camp at White Rock Lakes, three tarns scooped out of granite by ice. The view here of Dome Peak and its giant glaciers across the West Fork Agnes Creek is one of the most awesome of the Cascade Mountains. The 1938 Ptarmigans never mentioned the lakes, maybe because the glacier still covered them. The name given by Tom Miller's group derived from the White Rock Sparkling Water, which comes in bottles with a half-dressed nymph on the label, kneeling on a rock and gazing into a stream of sparkling water. At the outlet of White Rock Lakes is exactly the glacier-smoothed rock where Bob Grant, one of Tom's party, felt the nymph ought to be.

The weather cleared for great pictures of Dome Peak reflected in the lake. I offered to photograph the girls dressed like the nymph but had to settle for girls in parkas, not as eye-catching but more appropriate for the ice-ringed and iceberg-flecked waters.

From White Rock Lakes we pioneered the new route to Image Lake. Our plan was to cross a rib of Dome Peak from the Dana Glacier to the Chickamin Glacier, traverse the Chickamin Glacier to Blue Lake, and then follow the Hanging Gardens on the very crest of the Cascades to the trail at Canyon Lake, and thence to Image Lake. Along the way we hoped, time and weather permitting, to do some climbs. Sunshine gave us a fine day on top of Spire Point, but on the Chickamin Glacier clouds snuggled down and visibility was less than 100 feet. The five-year-old aerial photos allowed us to navigate blind through the crevasse patterns but wouldn't be much help climbing Dome Peak.

While we had reluctantly passed up other peaks along the way because of rain, we certainly didn't want to miss out on climbing Dome Peak, the climax of the traverse, so we set up tents in the middle of the glacier to wait out the weather. For two days the rain never stopped, or even thought about it. Sleeping bags were soaked. We were bored stiff. When asked to define "misery," Camp Chickamin jumps to mind. We gave up and hiked on to Blue Lake, built a bonfire, and spent a day drying out.

The following day the weather improved and we climbed Dome Peak. The summit was fogged in—no view—but at least we were there.

On the next-to-last day of our trip, in rain and fog once more, we groped along Hanging Gardens' broad fields of lupine, each leaf of which held a large drop of water, the better to soak our pants and fill our shoes. At noon, having been hiking for hours in fog with no idea how far we had come, how far we had to go, or even if we were on the right ridge, tired and wet and discouraged, we silently ate what had to pass for a lunch without the usual good-natured bantering. Shouldering packs and trudging on, in a hundred feet we stumbled on an old miners' trail, not on our map, that led us right to Image Lake and a dry trail shelter.

Still sixteen trail miles from the road, we suppered on a pot of very watery soup. At least we could build

Above right: Dome Peak and the Chickamin Glacier during a brief clearing near Sentinel Peak. Right: Our two nymphs at lower White Rock Lakes, with Dome Peak in the distance

a fire to dry our clothing and warm our poor feet, which had been wet so long they were terribly tender. The final morning we limped our way to the road, where Pat and the Starks were waiting with a big dinner and, for dessert, all the peanut butter I could eat. To make a happy ending, *Saturday Evening Post* used the story.

RETURN TRIP

For some two years after our trip, nobody else (that we heard of) completed the Ptarmigan Traverse. In the mid-1960s one or two parties a year were doing it, and by the 1970s the number had grown to ten to twenty parties a year. We began to hear grim stories about what heavy traffic was doing to meadows along the route. Pat couldn't go along on my first Ptarmigan Traverse because of the kids. In 1979, she persuaded me to take her, and anyway I wanted to see for myself what was happening. Though my ice axe and bones were twenty-two years older, the scenery was as spectacular as before and this time, in perfect weather, we could see it. The meadows weren't in as bad condition as I had been led to believe. I would like to say they were as pristine as in 1957 but, of course, they weren't. The wilderness experience of exploring the route, retracing steps from dead ends and trying something else, wondering where we'd camp, all that was gone. This time it wouldn't have mattered if I had forgotten my maps— hundreds of feet had stamped an unmistakable trail across meadows, rockslides, and even glaciers. Campsites were well worn yet clean. Evidently the sort of people who do the Traverse appreciate the fact that no one is going to pick up after them, and the sort of people who don't practice "no-trace camping" never get that deep into wilderness.

We met three young men from Madison, Wisconsin, who had spent all winter planning their trip and poring over maps. I was impressed by how readily they recognized peaks they had never seen. At Kool-Aid Lake we met a guided party of young people. Exactly how young they were was made clear to us when a girl looked at Pat's wood-shafted ice axe and said, "That is just like my grandmother's."

(Lower) White Rock Lake, Dome Peak with the Chickamin Glacier, left, and the Dana Glacier, right.

CHAPTER 18

Foreign Affairs— The Alps

or

Off to New Adventures

Vicky doing first-grade math with chalk and slate.

Bob and Norma expanded their horizons by spending two summers exploring Alaska while Pat and I stayed close to home, tending to business. Then came our turn. As children we each had read *Heidi* and independently dreamed of living in the Alps. To have the experience we wanted, and get the photographs that would make the trip profitable, we needed a whole year.

In the fall of 1959, Vicky ready for first grade and John for third, we packed four steamer trunks with darkroom supplies, clothing, books, camping gear, and everything a family of four needed for a year's stay abroad. We went by train to New York, by the *Queen Mary* to Cherbourg, and by train to Paris. There we picked up an Opel station wagon and drove to Chamonix in the French Alps, beneath Mont Blanc, highest mountain in Western Europe.

It was mid-September when we arrived. The clouds were low and rain was falling. As we drove into the deep valley of Chamonix, through a break in the

Village church near our rented chalet at Les Praz de Chamonix, the Aiguille du Dru in the background.

clouds we spotted a cable car a mile above, seemingly attached to nothing. Said Pat, "You will never get me on one of those things."

We made camp at the edge of town and visited a real estate agent. He first showed us deluxe apartments proper for rich Americans. We wanted to rent a centuries-old farmhouse on a mountainside like that of Heidi's grandfather. The agent explained that those were summer farms and nobody lived there through the cruel winter. He made us understand that aside from the constant threat of avalanches that sent the farmers to the valleys, if we tried to stick it out we would be spending all our time cutting firewood instead of taking pictures.

The agent convinced us that living in one of the picturesque farms on a mountainside was not practical, but we did not want to live in a resort town like Chamonix. We settled on Chalet La Coucas, a couple of miles out of the city in the tiny village of Les Praz de Chamonix. Chalet La Coucas was a good substitute for Heidi's house. It was located in the middle of a large pasture and had picture windows that gave breathtaking views of Mont Blanc glaciers and the Chamonix Aiguille (needles). We had to bend our necks backward to look up to the spires of the Aiguille du Dru and the Aiguille Verte.

OUR HOME FOR A YEAR

The chalet had all the modern necessities: a small coal stove and a huge fireplace for warmth; a kitchen with a propane stove; and a small bathroom with washbasin, toilet, tiny bathtub, and an odd thing called a bidet, which made an excellent place to wash film. Wide eaves gave the windows some weather protection, though during storms the wind sounded like a freight train and we often wondered if the roof was going to fly away, or maybe the whole house. Every morning until the snows came, a little lady with gray hair grazed two cows outside our window. She always gave us a pleasant "*bon matin.*" The cows wore melodious bells around their necks and, as John pointed out, kept our lawn mowed. In the winter the cows disappeared, but in the spring the wildflowers turned the pasture into a riot of color. Again, we were awakened by cowbells. Our little lady had returned.

John and Vicky were enrolled in the one-room schoolhouse at Les Praz de Chamonix. The teacher, Mademoiselle Gruaz, could not speak English, and John and Vicky couldn't speak French. My high-school French, as well as that of my wife, was little help. Conversation with Mademoiselle was interpreted by a neighbor lady. In November Mademoiselle informed us the children understood French but wouldn't speak it. By January she reported they were both speaking French fluently and that Vicky spoke without an accent, meaning, of course, that she was speaking with the local Chamonix accent.

We purchased John and Vicky secondhand bicycles. This was Vicky's first bicycle, and although she could barely reach the pedals she practiced riding on the small street in front of our chalet. One day she was wobbling down the road just as a motorcycle turned into the road. The driver saw her coming and moved

Top: *Chalet La Coucas, our home for nine months beneath the Aiguille du Dru, at Les Praz de Chamonix.*
Bottom: *Real French bread direct from the bakery.*

Skiing above Chamonix.

to one side, and Vicky also moved to that side. The motorcyclist changed sides and so did Vicky. The frustrated man finally stopped his motorcycle and awaited the inevitable, a gentle head-on collision.

Close to our house were several small cable cars to prepare us for the big ones. Pat overcame her fears, but both our hearts stopped the first time the car bumped its way over a 100-foot-high pylon; since then we have ridden on cars dangling from wires a mile above the

ground, sometimes in clouds, seemingly attached only to a 50-foot piece of wire. Cable cars come in all shapes and sizes; some hold two people, others eighty. Many reach elevations over 10,000 feet. We were well acclimatized when we rode the high ones, but many tourists from sea level suffer symptoms of mountain sickness.

It was fall-color time in Chamonix, and from the moment we arrived I was busy taking pictures. Weekdays I went by myself searching out picturesque villages. Weekends Pat and the kids came along. In an October snowstorm we drove over Grand St. Bernard

Left, top to bottom: *John's and Vicky's favorite store; Mademoiselle Gruaz and the one-room schoolhouse in Les Praz de Chamonix; Pat shopping in Chamonix.* Above: *Zermatt and the Matterhorn*

Pass for a story I had promised a travel magazine. In December, when the snow came to Chamonix, we rode to the ski slopes in gondolas and I hired a ski instructor to pose for spectacular action pictures.

In November we had a terrible fright. John complained of a stomachache at school so Mademoiselle Gruaz put him to bed in her apartment above the schoolroom and sent Vicky home to get us. As the pain went lower and intensified, Mademoiselle called a doctor. He diagnosed appendicitis. John was put in the Chamonix hospital. The doctor conferred with the surgeon, who was dubious about the diagnosis and called for a blood test. The blood samples were

John, Vicky, and a neighbor boy on the Lake Blanc trail. Mer de Glace, Chamonix Needles, and the Mount Blanc massif.

sent to a laboratory in a city far enough away that by the time the tests results were back the appendicitis had turned to peritonitis and John was in serious condition. How serious we never knew, the doctor having a very limited knowledge of English. He could only tell us that "John was bad, very bad, but not terrible."

Many French speak German but very few will admit to English (a grudge against what Wellington did to Napoleon?). When we first arrived, the shopkeepers gave us dumb looks when we asked for something in English. That made us work harder on our French. After a few weeks they realized we were staying and trying to speak French, so they became friendly. Many conversations were carried on with a word of French and a word of English, and one of the older clerks even kept a French–English dictionary handy.

Winter wasn't what we had expected. In the Cascade Mountains at 3,000 feet, the elevation of Chamonix, snow gets 10 to 15 feet deep. Chamonix,

farther south, most commonly gets rain or wet snow. We never had more than a foot or two on the ground. The winter sun reaches the valley bottom only four hours each day. Our sunrise, over the Aiguille du Dru, was about noon; sunset, behind the Massif des Aiguilles Rouge, about four o'clock. However, cable cars took us up to ski slopes where the sun was brilliant all day and the snow was often deep powder while that in the valley was wet slop.

School was less than a mile away so John and Vicky walked even when there was snow. We bought an old sled and the few times we were snowbound used it to carry groceries. One time when I was away taking snow pictures, we ran out of propane for the kitchen

Farm buildings near Murren and 13,668-foot Jungfrau (mountain).

stove. Pat tied the heavy tank to the sled, pulled it two miles into Chamonix to be filled, and then pulled it back to our house.

Ed and Rhena Willgress, Pat's parents, joined a tour to Europe that spring, and they came two weeks ahead of the group to spend time with us in Chamonix. Pat's father spent many hours walking the roads and leaning on fences, watching the farmers plant spring crops. He always carried small packages of cigarettes and vegetable seeds in his pockets. He was quite frustrated at not being able to speak French, but his packages of seeds were a means of communicating. Years later, on a return to Chamonix, we learned he was fondly remembered by the farmers he visited.

With Chamonix lying just twelve miles from Switzerland, we frequently drove across the border. Usually we showed our passports and car-ownership papers and were waved on. On one trip the customs people wanted to know more. They poked half-heartedly at our (wet) camping gear, asking a question we couldn't understand. In a quarter-hour they gave up and let us pass. John and Vicky had understood every word but were too bashful to speak up. When we were on our way, John said all they wanted to know was whether we lived in Chamonix.

During summer vacation we took pictures throughout the Alps from France to Yugoslavia. In 1960, with Yugoslavia still behind the Iron Curtain, we had to get a tourist visa at a consulate in Italy. When we arrived at the border, an iron gate was opened to let one car across and then closed before another was let past. Camping was allowed only at a few designated sites, and each time a police report had to be filled out. The roads were narrow, which didn't matter because there was little traffic. Gas stations were thirty to fifty miles apart. We passed the Yugoslavian army on maneuvers, riding in horse-drawn wagons. The people were friendly and we enjoyed every minute of our three days there.

At the time we were in the Alps, women hiked in skirts and dresses. Pat had a favorite green skirt she

Vicky and a Yugoslavian family.

often wore. We are told cows are color-blind, but twice they nibbled on her skirt and once reached for a green plastic tarp on our roof rack. The last time we were there, most women wore shorts or knickers. In Italy we passed a mixed group of women, the older wearing long black dresses, a couple of the middle-age women in shorts, and some of the younger girls in very skimpy bikinis.

On the way to France we had stopped in New York to talk to clients, especially Selma Brackman at the Freelance Photographers Guild (FPG). I explained in depth to her our proposed trip. I knew she had a lot of great pictures available of the usual tourist spots in Paris, Rome, and the Matterhorn, so I promised mountains and quaint villages. Selma urged me to take the *classic* pictures of Paris, Rome, and the Matterhorn. I was certain she was wrong but followed her advice somewhat. Of the twelve months in Europe, we spent ten months photographing the quaint villages and skiing in the Alps and only a total of two months (a week here and a day there) taking the pictures FPG wanted. Though our year's adventure pro-

duced a profitable story in the *Saturday Evening Post* and one in *Friends* (Chevrolet's magazine), those two "tourist" months for FPG accounted for three-fourth's of our year's income. The very first picture the agent sold for us was a very conventional shot of Notre Dame in Paris. Since then, while I have never gone out of my way to travel through Paris, when I find myself there, I take the same pictures of Notre Dame as every other photographer in the world.

John and Vicky never complained, but there is no doubt that given a choice at their age they would have voted to stay home with their friends, toys, and familiar surroundings. It wasn't until they were grown that they began to appreciate the value of experiencing other cultures. Pat and I are often asked if we could notice how living in a foreign nation for a year and becoming bilingual had broadened our kids' education. Who can tell? We know they loved the hiking but weren't too impressed by the most famous peak. Europe's Matterhorn didn't look to them nearly as good as the one at Disneyland they had seen at home on TV.

• CHAPTER 19 •

Foreign Affairs— Japan

or
It's a Man's World

Dance of the Virgins, a local village celebration at the Sengen Shrine which I photographed while working on Sigemi's book.

Living in a small French alpine village for a year was such a rewarding experience and proved so financially successful that in the fall of 1963 we again packed our trunks and this time shipped them to Japan.

We rented a small house on Lake Yamanaka at the 3,000-foot level on the side of Fujiyama. The house was very small by American standards and so poorly insulated that papers blew off the table during windstorms, but the view was spectacular. There was nothing between our house and the mountain except a lovely reflection in the lake.

It was a typical Japanese house with tatami-covered floors and a *kotatsu* in the floor to warm our feet. We slept on the floor, ate sitting on the floor, and took a bath in a family-sized tub of boiling-hot water.

Planting rice near our house on Lake Yamanaka, with Mount Fuji rising above.

The Japanese language and alphabet ruled out putting John and Vicky in a public school, so before leaving home we enrolled them in the Culvert Correspondence School. Although teaching was time-consuming, it left us free to visit Kyoto and Nara during cherry-blossom season and spend the night during the spring equinox in an ancient monastery on a mountaintop located at the exact point from which the sun could be seen to rise directly behind Fujiyama.

We needed help in Japan, being at a complete loss with the language, written or spoken. In Europe we could understand labels in the stores and decipher maps and road signs, but the Japanese alphabet stopped us cold. We hired Yoshi Nishihara, a young woman who spoke English, daughter of a Christian minister who had finished his schooling in Seattle. Japan is a man's world. For a Japanese, Yoshi was fairly liberated but, even so, everything I did or said (even if I was wrong) was right and instantly obeyed, except when it came to having a glass of beer. To Yoshi, drinking and smoking

Above, top to bottom: *Sigemi, her mother, and her sister shopping; our interpreter, Yoshi Nishihara; tea at Sigemi's family home (Sigemi had disappeared and is not in this picture).* Above right: *Daytime living room and nighttime bedroom in our house.*

were cardinal sins, and she couldn't bear seeing me go astray. Fortunately for our relationship I have never smoked, but to her dismay I do like a little beer on a hot day.

In addition to the usual stock pictures, I contracted with American publishers to do the photography for two books, both authored by Ruth Kirk. Ruth was the wife of the Olympic National Park ranger I accompanied to photograph elk at the Hoh Guard Station. Ruth is a painstaking researcher and I admire the depth of understanding she has of her subjects. She did such a beautiful job of writing that one of her books received an award from the Book of the Month Club's Junior Division.

One of the books was a supplemental reader for junior-high students and the other a children's story of Sigemi, an eight-year-old Japanese girl who was a blend of traditional and modern Japan. Sigemi lived in a small village on the side of Fujiyama. Her father worked in a modern watch factory and her grandparents owned a mill that processed silk cocoons into thread. The family also had its own rice paddy. I en-joyed working with Sigemi and her family as well as photographing the various aspects of Japanese life and industry for the junior-high book.

A VILLAGE FESTIVAL

The small village where Sigemi lived had an annual Sengen Shrine festival. The villagers, including Sigemi's father, carried the spirit of the village goddess from the shrine overlooking the village in a special little house to the village Shinto shrine, where it was seated in the throne room for a few hours before being car-ried back. Because I was photographing the book on Sigemi, I was allowed to photograph the entire festival, from the carrying of the goddess on the shoulders of four men into her house, to the dance of the virgins, and fi-nally to the transferring of the spirit from her house to the throne room. For this a huge curtain was drawn so no one could witness the transfer, but I was invited be-hind the curtain and only the priest and I, and a small boy who crawled under the curtain, actually saw the spirit. I don't know about the small boy, but I promised not to tell what I saw, so I won't.

Farmhouse near Lake Yamanaka.

The second day of festivities took place on Fujiyama, where men in costumes waged a mock battle. I looked twice at the "men," and there hidden under huge, fierce-looking masks were John and Vicky,

Top: John, Vicky, and a Shinto priest at Sengen Shrine festival. Bottom: A 106-degree Japanese hot spring bath.

recognizable only by their American jeans. They had been enlisted by the fun-loving men who conducted the festival. We could guess but never knew if they were the good gods or the bad.

In the middle of winter our house froze every night. We would stand the cold as long as we could, then drive down to sea level to one of the many hot spring resorts and spend hours in a 104-degree bath. A Japanese bath is quite different from an American bath. Before getting in, you must first wash with soap and rinse with water. Only when perfectly clean can you step into the bath, and you cannot dirty the water with any clothes. The resort baths were mixed but were so steamy it didn't matter.

During our stay in Japan we took two hikes in the Japanese Alps and climbed Fujiyama four times. We first climbed Fuji in October on a cold and miserable day when all the warming stations and tea houses were closed. We climbed it again in June but had to go up two more times before we got a day clear enough to take pictures. Fujiyama, at 13,395 feet, is probably the most-climbed mountain of its height in the world and certainly the most-climbed major mountain in Japan. On a single day 20,000 people have made it to the top, and an estimated 200,000 climb it every year. A road to the 7,000-foot level still leaves more than a vertical mile to climb, no easy feat for people who live at sea level and are not accustomed to high elevations.

Fujiyama is so woven into Japanese culture it's no wonder that climbing the mountain is a common ambition. We saw people of all ages making the ascent, some on religious pilgrimages, others "because it is there." Four major trails are wide enough for 3 people to walk abreast, which we often saw clubs do in groups of 100 to 200, like army regiments, the leaders carrying club flags. I saw one large group emerge from a fog bank, the leader and the rear guard communicating with walkie-talkies. To avoid the heat of day and watch the sunrise from the top, many start up at nightfall, their flashlights an

unbroken line snaking up the trail. Inns and restaurants are numerous along the way, and on one of our climbs we spent the night at the 10,000-foot level, looking down on the lights of Tokyo.

Our most emotional experience in Japan was the New Year's Eve we visited a nearby Buddhist temple and a Shinto shrine. At midnight, to the sound of a temple gong, we walked from our house along the shore of Lake Yamanaka to the temple. It was a very cold, clear night with a full moon and everything sparkled with frost. Fujiyama glowed in the moonlight, reflected perfectly in the lake. At midnight the Buddhist priest, reciting each of man's 107 sins one by one, struck a large bell-shaped gong after each sin, a ritual that took several hours. After photographing the Buddhist priest, we visited the Shinto shrine where people were receiving the blessing of the priest for the coming year. He waved his wand over us, too, and it must have worked, as we had a wonderful year.

Top, left and right: Fog or sunshine, Fuji is climbed by hundreds and even thousands every summer day, keeping track of each other by radio. Bottom: Monk ringing the village temple bell 107 times (for man's 107 sins) at midnight on New Year's Eve.

CHAPTER 20

The World at Our Feet

*or
Adventure for Fun
and Maybe Profit*

"The Little Mermaid" in Copenhagen. I photographed her during a 4:00 A.M. sunrise, at high noon, and during a 10:00 P.M. sunset. My time was well spent— the pictures sold well.

Jet travel has changed our world. In 1638, my ancestors, passengers on the *Susan and Ellen,* crossed the Atlantic in ninety-nine days. In 1887, Pat's grandparents crossed in ten days by steamship. In 1959, on our first trip to Europe, the *Queen Mary* took us across in five days. Our return trip a year later on a Boeing 707 was only a few hours. Thanks to the International Dateline, Pat and I arrived home ten minutes *before* we left New Zealand. Now a person has less adventure visiting the Taj Mahal.

Jet travel has enlarged our file to include Poland, Hungary, Bangkok, Borneo, Peru, Ecuador, Machu Picchu, castles in Spain, and snake-charmers in Morocco. On returns to our favorite, the Alps, we are likely to run into a neighbor from down the street. What will travel be like when our grandchildren get to be

our age? Will they fly to the moon? Probably old stuff. Maybe Jupiter.

Scandinavia in 1967 was our final trip abroad with the family. John and Vicky were now in junior-high school and could not be taken out a whole year, so we settled for a shorter trip.

The success of our Japanese trip established a profitable formula, and this time I had contracts for three books and several magazine stories. One book was a supplemental reading book for junior-high students, similar to Ruth Kirk's award-winning book on Japan, and the other two were children's books, one about a boy, Lars Olaf, in Norway, and another on Leise Abrahamsen, a Danish girl. This time I teamed up with Harvey Edwards, the American writer I had worked with on a ski story while we lived in Chamonix.

I left for Scandinavia in March and joined Harvey in Copenhagen, where he had rented a house that we used as headquarters. Harvey and I immediately took off for Lapland to spend a week photographing Lapps in their winter quarters. Snowmobiles being a new

Tour boat in Geiranger Fjord, with. Seven Sisters Falls on the left.

Lapp family at Kautokeino, Norway, back when reindeer were more reliable transportation than snowmobiles

off, again racing. I had no idea what direction we were going. It was snowing and we could see only a quarter-mile. There was no visible trail and no landmarks, just rolling hills with occasional birch trees. Furthermore, the Lapp was sitting with his back to the reindeer and made no attempt to steer. Mostly he was steering a bottle from his coat to his mouth.

When racing neck and neck, the reindeer didn't veer much from the occasional birch trees, just squeezed by, sometimes giving the sleigh a punishing blow. They stopped only from exhaustion. When one stopped, they all stopped. When one took off, they all took off, and woe to the passenger not aboard. At one stop we were stomping about to get warm when the reindeer took off. We all made flying leaps for our sleighs, my reins tangled with the interpreter's sleigh, and in the midst of the race we had to untangle the mess. Out of the corner of my eye I could see Harvey had caught hold of his sleigh by just one hand and was being drug along in the snow.

The weather was deteriorating, snow was falling, and the temperature was zero. Visibility also was almost zero, and even if we found the herd I wouldn't be able to get any pictures, so about ten miles out we gave up and returned to Kautokeino. The tracks we had made going out were completely covered by blowing snow, and I was glad I wasn't the leader because I was lost.

development and very expensive, most Lapps were still using reindeer for transportation. (As one told me, if you get caught in a blizzard and run out of food you can't eat your snowmobile.) The Lapps are proud of their heritage and, at least during the winter when we were there, wore their colorful costumes for work, play, and school. Most lived in houses, but one family I photographed still lived in a reindeer-skin tent that looked like an Indian teepee.

At Kautokeino we made arrangements to visit a herd of 10,000 reindeer about twenty miles from town. We hired a Lapp to take us by sleigh. Each sleigh held only one person and was pulled by one reindeer. There were four of us, including a local resident who came along to interpret, and four sleighs. The reindeer started off sedately enough but soon began racing each other over the rolling Arctic steppe. They raced out of control for a half-hour until they stopped from sheer exhaustion, tongues hanging out, sides heaving. We got out, stretched, and got back in, and the reindeer took

Back in Copenhagen we recruited ten-year-old Leise for our child's book. She was a talented girl living in the ancient village of Dargor, a few miles from the city. Her home was several centuries old. The roof was thatched. The streets were cobblestone. I photographed Leise off and on during the six months I was there. She didn't speak English and I didn't understand Danish, but we had no problem communicating. I spent many hours photographing another wonderful girl in Copenhagen, the Little Mermaid. She posed for me at

Olaf, his older brother's name, a composite of both his grandfathers' first names.

I liked Geiranger Fjord so much that when Pat and the kids joined me when school was out in June we spent a whole month there. This is probably the most photographed fjord in Norway. Ocean-going cruise ships sail into the narrow gorge all summer, dwarfed by the towering cliffs. The surrounding hills are only 3,000 feet high and the peaks 5,000 feet, but the ridges were snowcapped, giving the feeling of being at the foot of impressive mountains. Our favorite hike was to a farm high on a bench halfway up a cliff overlooking the fjord. A trail had been blasted down the cliff to the farm and from the farm down to a boat landing on the fjord. We were told that before the trail was constructed rope ladders were used by the farmers. When marauders or the tax collector came near, the ladders would be pulled up.

I returned home with an excellent collection of pictures and the three fine books, but the income barely paid our way. I discovered there wasn't nearly as much American interest in Scandinavia as in Europe and the Far East. The only pictures that sold very well are those of the Little Mermaid and Geiranger Fjord.

OFF TO SEE THE WORLD

When John and Vicky left home, I was no longer under pressure to make every trip at home and abroad profitable. Not worrying about the bottom line opened a world of opportunities for travel and adventure. Pat and I were free to go to the Amazon, the Sahara Desert, Hong Kong, Indonesia, and the Taj Mahal, or return to the Alps. I had no trouble selling the pictures, but with the travel costs sometimes all I made was my expenses.

By boat, train, balloon, and elephant, Jules Verne wrote about going around the world in eighty days. Pat and I took twenty days. However, jet speed made our trip a lot easier. As most of our stops were at famous landmarks, the trip was very profitable.

For a week in Bangkok we had signed up for an

sunset, in the middle of the day, at sunrise, even in the rain, and never complained. She was extremely profitable, too—I sold over $5,000 worth of her pictures.

We drove to Geiranger Fjord in Norway and there found an eight-year-old boy, Stale, for our Norwegian book. The hills above the fjord were still covered with snow when we first photographed him and his school friends skiing. We returned in summer for hiking and boating pictures. The book editor thought the Norwegian name Stale wouldn't go over too well with readers in the English language, so with his parent's permission, for the book we changed Stale to Lars

inexpensive room in a deluxe hotel. When we got there we were given an expensive room costing four times as much, and I objected. They explained that the cheaper rooms were in the old wing lacking the air-conditioning that every American wanted. We asked to see the old building and were enchanted by a charming, semi-antique room with high ceilings, electric ceiling fans, and huge windows opening onto a grove of trees full of noisy tropical birds. Exactly what we had read about in novels. During our second night a violent storm knocked out the power for twelve hours. Guests sweltered in air-conditioned rooms with windows that wouldn't open and were baffled by elevators that didn't move. We just opened our windows, and our two-story wing lacked elevators anyway. We had a good laugh at that and enjoyed the swimming pool and the dining room on the river bank—and an all-too-short week exploring temples and waterways.

In Greece we spent two nights in a small Athens hotel photographing the Acropolis, but, with campgrounds so abundant, we rented a car to explore the site of the original Olympic games. Not knowing that grocery stores were open only in the morning, we had left our shopping until later, and the first night had to eat at a small restaurant adjacent to our campground. The friendly proprietor was so happy to have American guests that he sat with us describing his years as a guerilla fighter in World War II and his restaurant experience in New York and raved about what a wonderful place Greece was to live. When we were ready to leave, he brought out a guest book and said he liked to have guests he enjoyed sign. When we wrote our names, I glanced back a couple of pages and there were Herb and Jean Belanger, longtime mountaineer friends from Seattle. It truly is a small world, considering the hundreds of campgrounds in the country, and this was the only restaurant we visited in Greece.

The stone money of Yap was one of the world's enchantments that intrigued me in school days. The stones are hardly pocket change, round with a hole in the center, varying in size from one foot to six feet, and weighing up to several thousand pounds. While U.S. money is common in Yap, the famous stone money is still used for major purchases, such as real estate or boats. Size is a factor, but value is mainly determined by the stone's history. No names are on the stones, but each is owned by an individual or a village.

Where in the world is Yap? If you can't locate it on a map, buy a ticket on Continental Air Micronesia and they will find it for you. There was no problem finding the stone money—some 6,000 stones line village streets and trails.

Fascinating as their stone money is, even more so are the people. Some who live on the thousands of

Opposite: Grindelwald, Switzerland, the beginning of many great hikes **Above right:** *Stone money on Yap Island, one of the stories that had intrigued me in my school books over sixty years before.* **Right:** *Yap's Independence Day Festival, an endangered lifestyle.*

islands and atolls that dot the Pacific have guarded their traditional lifestyle and live by choice the carefree life, much the same as when Magellan found them in the 1500s. The natives of Yap are in transition, a mixture of traditional and modern. In Yap's one city, Colonia, most women wear colorful skirts and blouses and the men shirts and pants. Outside the city, boys go to school wearing only a loin cloth called a *thu* and women are often seen topless. The people of Yap are in no hurry to join the Western world: Their lifestyle has served them well for thousands of years—more than we can say about ours.

EAST IS EAST AND WEST IS WEST, BUT THE TWO DO MEET

Pat and I would not trade our Northwest wilderness mountains for all the mountains in Europe, but we came along at a time when we could have the best of

both worlds. In 1976, to combine work and play, we undertook a hiking guide to the Alps in partnership with Harvey Edwards, the friend who lived in Chamonix and wrote the Scandinavian books. We estimated the research would take three to four months of hiking every day. To make this project fun rather than an ordeal, we stretched the hiking over three years. Harvey helped us buy a secondhand Citroën and camping gear in France and bought a garage in Chamonix to store everything. One trip we were accompanied by John and on another by Vicky and a girlfriend from the Peace Corps. Our book included the French Pyrenees and the Alps of France, Switzerland, Liechtenstein, Germany, Austria, Italy, and Yugoslavia, a lot of the Alps we hadn't seen before.

Regardless of the local language, we have never had much trouble finding familiar food—except peanut butter, which I dearly love for a noontime sandwich. Peanut butter is good on any bread, especially the tasteless Italian bread. On French bread it is like adding ice cream to apple pie. For me, home is where the peanut butter is, so when going abroad I take a couple of jars in my luggage. I first freeze the peanut butter solid in the deep freeze, and then if a jar does break, the peanut butter won't ruin our clothes in our baggage.

We noted changes, good and bad, since our first trip in 1959. Much of the green space around Chamonix had been lost to large apartment buildings. Even the pastures around our old chalet, La Coucas, now were built up. Zermatt, which had very little green space to start with, was worse. We noted with dismay that the Swiss were building roads to remote alpine farms and to water developments, ruining many miles of mountain trails.

We also found more cable cars. We had always enjoyed riding up in mornings, looking down on people harvesting hay or herding cows and sheep, spending the day exploring alpine trails, and walking back down to

Left: Pat and her assistant. (Actually the cow had her eyes on Pat's green daypack.) Opposite: Geiranger Fjord. John and Vicky were tied to a rope, with Pat belaying. On Tom and Vicky's Scandinavian bicycle trip, Tom posed with his bicycle on the same overhang. No belay, and it was an expensive bike, too.

Left: *Grand Canal, Venice, Italy.*
Below: *The small village of Moret-sur-Loing near Fontaine-bleau, France.*

Left: *Skogafoss Falls, on one of the rare sunny days in Iceland.* Top: *Entrance to the ancient city of Fez, Morocco.* Bottom: *Segovia Castle, Spain.*

Top: *Ibex on Piz Languard near the top of the chairlift, just where the hotel proprietor said they would be.* Bottom: *Edelweiss, alpine cousin of our pearly everlasting. (This is not the plant I stepped on.)*

the valley floor. However, enough is enough. As in the United States, Europe has environmental groups striving to preserve a way of life. A very strong tourist industry wants more cable cars, as well as more groomed ski slopes with wide, graveled ski runs for beginners replacing alpine flower fields and pastures.

On the positive side, wildlife is increasing. In the last twenty years European countries have set aside Naturalist Reserves. We saw and photographed deer, marmots, chamois, and the endangered ibex. Chamois were

the most common, One morning Pat and I were just getting started on a trail when we spotted two chamois running full steam down the mountain. They crossed the trail a hundred feet in front of us and then, without stopping, circled and recrossed the trail a hundred feet behind us, and still running full steam disappeared up the mountainside. Another time I watched five chamois running back and forth and up and down a steep snow slope, evidently just because they were exhilarated by the beautiful morning.

Our biggest thrill was our encounter with ibex. The mountain ibex was hunted to virtual extinction in the 1800s and only a handful remained in the Grand Paradiso, a private hunting preserve of the Italian kings. A pair were smuggled into Switzerland and from that meager start there are now 4,000 to 5,000 in Naturalist Reserves scattered through the Alps. We heard that one especially good place to see them was on 10,699-foot-high Piz Languard, directly above the Swiss resort city of Pontresina. We took the chairlift from Pontresina up 1,000 feet and then climbed on foot another 3,000 feet to a small hotel-restaurant only 300 feet below the top of the mountain, with gorgeous views of glaciers flowing from Piz Palu and Piz Bernina. As we climbed, a huge thunderhead formed over the Bernina Range and started moving our way. A short way from the top we saw some chamois and even got close enough to photograph two female ibex, but it was the males with their long curved horns we sought.

We arrived at the hotel to find the proprietor closing his shutters and shooing all the guests off the mountain before the thunderstorm hit. He took a moment to tell me that at that time of year we would find the male ibex 3,000 feet below, near the top of the chairlift. His parting words were, "Just look up at the cliffs at the last bend of the trail." Pat and I ran down the trail and sure enough, atop a cliff a short distance from the lift where we had started was a male ibex only a couple hundred feet above us. We were halfway up when the thunderstorm hit with flashes of lightning, crashes of thunder, hail, and pelting rain. We crawled under our ponchos to wait it out. When the storm started, the ibex came down the slope we were climbing. It looked as if he was going to join us under our ponchos, but a few feet away he turned toward the cliffs and laid down under an overhang. Pat pointed out that the ibex was smarter for it had a nice dry spot. I

Cape Adge, la Plage naturists (who are not, as we thought, naturalists).

disagreed and said he should read The Mountaineers' book, *Freedom of The Hills*, which says to stay out of caves and overhangs during lightning storms.

We sat watching the ibex and he lay watching us. The air was so full of flying spray, I couldn't open my camera. The storm blew over and the sun came out; the ibex stood up, joined three other males, and I took pictures.

While hiking in a French Naturalist Reserve, I was walking across a grassy field when Pat yelled, "*Stop!*" She pointed at my feet. Under my hiking boot was the first live edelweiss either of us had ever seen. The poor plant was badly crushed, so I shoved it back in shape and took some pictures. A bit farther was a whole field of edelweiss. Symbol of the Alps, the flower is seldom seen. Happily, it is not really rare. It just grows in a very special environment, and once we figured out where to look we often found it.

Our first summer working on the guidebook we had a long siege of bad weather in the Alps and decided to see if the sun might be hiding from us in the Pyrenees. The road skirted the Mediterranean for sixty to seventy miles, with beaches broad and sandy and large campgrounds almost continuous. Late in the afternoon we pulled into one with a camping symbol, signed NATURIST LA PLAGE, which we assumed meant it was a naturalist reserve with a beach and camping. We

soon learned the difference between "Naturalist" and "Naturist." While the missionaries are persuading the South Pacific natives to put on clothes, the Europeans are taking theirs off. We found there are maybe a thousand naturist beaches in Europe. Aside from the freedom to wear whatever you wanted, or nothing, it was a delightful mile-long sandy beach, the water warm, with small sailboats to rent, and sailboards to fall off of. We were lucky to be there after the summer crowds left. The campground had a capacity of 15,000 people; three hotel condominiums had apartments for another 35,000. There was a complete village with two supermarkets, restaurants, banks, a post office, beauty parlors, and a Baskin-Robbins. We soon became accustomed to the lack of clothing. The people looked very natural in all-over tans. Upon closer inspection, what appeared to be bright red bikinis on some was actually the skin of new arrivals that was usually covered by tiny bathing suits, and was now sunburned.

We had planned to sell the car and garage when the Alps book was finished, but having gotten used to so easy and economical a way to see Europe, we kept them another six years, returning for about a month each year. One summer we toured England, another summer Holland and the coast of Brittany. Other summers we have gone back to our favorite places in the Alps.

Once in the Sella Dolomites of Italy we "hiked" to the Rifugio Pisciadu on one of their engineered "trails"—a combination of steel steps, short ladders, bridges, and cables—all hanging out in the middle of the sky. Although the exposure is the same, one could hardly compare this kind of climbing to the first ascents I have watched Fred Beckey make. At the bottom we tied a very short climbing rope with a carabiner around our waists, hooked ourselves to a safety cable attached to the cliff, and worked our way up on natural footholds, and/or steel bars anchored in the rock, knowing that if we did slip the cable would hold us. However, every few feet the carabiner came to an eye bolt anchored to the cliff and we had to unsnap and reattach to the cable above the anchor. During each such moment we were vividly aware of all the air beneath us. If so inclined you could easily spit 500 feet. Other than that, we felt very safe and the climb was lots of fun. Pat had obviously come a long way from her shaky knees when I photographed her for the first time on 15-foot-high Monitor Rock before we were married.

• CHAPTER 21 •

Return to My War Memories

or
From Hell to Paradise

Mary, my "Island of Love" model on Kuiawa Island.

"Paradise Islands!" I couldn't believe it. The beautiful travel brochure was calling Papua New Guinea "Paradise Islands." The very same islands where I had spent three years dodging bombs, swatting mosquitoes, and sloshing around muddy airfields during World War II. "Paradise Islands" my foot! "Nightmare Islands" was more like it.

My three years as a photographer in the 13th Army Air Corps started in New Caledonia in 1942 and then leapfrogged to the Solomon Islands, to the Admiralty Islands, New Guinea, Morotai, and, as the war ended, the Philippines.

Adventure and photography made my three war years palatable. Whatever island I was on I looked for places to hike on days off. My favorites were jungle trails that ended in fascinating native villages where I could take pictures and make friends and see the jungle

1944 victory celebration at Sangowo village, Morotai Island.

life I had read about. I seldom found another GI to go with and, in retrospect, it wasn't too wise to go traipsing off in the jungle by myself, especially when no one knew where I had gone. There were Japanese hiding out on many of the islands, still armed and, as I found out later, crocodiles in the rivers I waded. Some of the islands I explored had a reputation of being home to headhunters and cannibals, but there were only smiles when I met someone on the trail and, being young, I never worried.

The "Paradise Islands" brochure prompted me to dig out my old photos and my wartime diary that I had kept for those three years. Yes, it was just as bad as I remembered—day after day, week after week, of rain, mud that stuck like glue, swarms of mosquitoes, and always heat and humidity. Some "Paradise"! But there was more. I had recorded fascinating villages and encounters with wonderful natives who accepted me as a friend. When I overlooked the mud and misery, my diary and photographs began to look and read a lot like the brochure. The more I read, the more intrigued I became. *Maybe,* I told myself, *just*

1943 photograph, left, and 1990 photograph, right, of pipe-smoking women on Guadalcanal. Only the size of the basket has changed.

maybe a vacation might be a lot different from a war.

The diary and old photographs reminded me that fifty years ago I was just beginning my search for adventure that became such an important part of my life's work. If I went back, how much change would I find? Would I find the villages and the friends I had made? Most of all, how much change would I find in myself?

On November 1, 1942, I had left San Francisco on a troop transport and arrived in New Caledonia twenty-one days later. In 1988, a 747 flew me there in eighteen hours. My first priority was a pilgrimage to the places I had been stationed, and I wanted to go at my own pace. Plane reservations were made for me in advance and, thanks to guidebooks, I had no trouble finding hotels on my own. Things did go wrong, but nothing that a bit of patience couldn't resolve.

I had a terrible time finding my old campsites. In New Caledonia our camp had been on a hill overlooking Tontouta Air Base, a small airfield. Try as I might, I could not find the hill and concluded it had been leveled to make room for the mile-long runway of the new Tontouta International Airport. The airport reminded me of the hours I had spent there inside a warplane trying to focus the large 4X5 view camera in a tiny space, and how much simpler the job would have been with my new automatic-focus, automatic-exposure, "point-and-shoot" 35mm camera.

On Guadalcanal, where there had been hundreds of campsites like ours scattered around the jungle, no one could remember where the 13th Air Force had been located. On Manus Island I knew where to look, but the jungle had completely engulfed our campsite. Even the roads leading to it were lost in a tangle of 100-foot vines. I didn't have any better luck locating the natives and villages I had photographed. Everything near our old campsites had changed. I walked for miles and showed my wartime pictures to anyone who would look, but no one could recognize the villages or the people. However, it was a great way to make friends. When the older natives realized I had been there during the war, they greeted me like a long-lost relative.

While the old army camps were hard to find, war relics are scattered from one end of the Pacific to the other. Tanks, airplanes, and half-sunken ships are

Left: *A 1943 nine-women-powered canoe, and (below) a 1990 photograph of a similar seventy-five-horse—powered canoe.*

found throughout the South Pacific. I remembered from fifty years ago watching some of today's relics being made. During a bombing mission over Rabaul on the island of New Britain I rode along to photograph the drop pattern of a cluster of bombs. With someone holding my feet, I laid over the open bomb bay door. My view was straight down 10,000 feet. I was so fascinated by a smoking volcano next to the airfield, I almost forgot to take pictures. Now, some of the best displays of warplanes are the damaged Japanese craft still sitting in jungle-covered bunkers next to the smoking volcano at Rabaul Airport.

Changes were everywhere. The muddy airfields and roads I remembered had been paved. Around the main cities, the traditional houses with thatched roofs had been replaced either by houses of sheet metal salvaged from the war or by modern wooden buildings. Near the cities and paved roads, most of the women I photographed topless during the war were now wearing Western clothing.

A few things hadn't changed, mainly the natives. Unlike other third world countries that endured hundreds of years of colonial rule, Westerners had not exploited the natives of Papua New Guinea. They may now be wearing Western clothes near the cities, but they still bubbled with the friendliness I knew during the war.

Outrigger canoes looked the same. In 1943 on Manus Island I

The "Island of Love" Yam Festival, 1990. Normally there are an equal number of men and woman in this dance, but the men's attire was so brief and so erotic they did not let me take their picture.

Outrigger canoe that carried us from Kiriwina to little Trobriand Island of Kuiawa, Papua New Guinea, 1990.

even though they were well known during the war. The primitive natives in the New Guinea highlands had been discovered only ten years before, and soldiers were encountering tribes that had never seen a white person. These tribes were of little interest to the GIs who were longing to see the people (girls) of Trobriand. For emergency purposes, a landing strip was leveled on Kiriwina, largest of the Trobriand Islands. American pilots who, for one reason or another, had made "emergency" landings brought back fascinating stories of the those "Islands of Love." On my 1988 trip I had time to visit places where the old customs are still part of daily life; however, these places are best visited with a guide who can speak the language.

The Trobriand Islands are referred to as a missionary's nightmare, where young girls are urged to sample a variety of prospective husbands. The "Island of Love" fame has its drawbacks. Tour boats visit the main island of Kiriwina and the jaded natives demand $2 for each snap of the shutter.

Thanks to the small size of our group, we were able to sail by outrigger canoe from Kiriwina thirty miles across the Solomon Sea to the small island of Kuiawa,

photographed a very large canoe steered by one man and powered by ten fierce-looking, noisy women. In 1988 the ten fierce women had been replaced by one noisy seventy-five–horsepower outboard motor.

Some places in the South Pacific are still remote,

Men of New Guinea highlands, 1990.

population 200. We were only the second or third tourists to ever visit the island, and the natives loved to have their pictures taken, especially when I gave them instant Polaroid pictures of themselves. They were as curious about us as we were about them. We lived in their houses, ate their food, and joined them in their native dances. Skirts of grass or cloth were usually the only clothing worn by either men or women. Our visit was marred by a malaria epidemic. The native medicine helped, but some victims had high fevers accompanied by miserable headaches. To relieve their aching heads, the native chief made deep cuts on the victims' foreheads to let the headaches out. Evidently the cuts hurt enough so they would forget the pain inside.

To see the fascinating highland people I had heard about during the war, I made a four-day trek with a guide through the Wigmen tribes in the Southern Highlands Province of Papua New Guinea. The Wigmen tribes are famous for their "Sing Sings," where the people paint their bodies in colorful clays. The elevations were between 4,000 and 7,000 feet and the climate was invigorating. The natives who met our airplane and carried our packs wore bright, colorful clothing, and everyone had a friendly smile and handshake. But behind those smiles were men armed with machetes, bows, arrows, and spears, ready to wage war against neighboring tribes over a lost pig, or the kidnapping of a woman, or to punish an unfaithful wife. Several doctors I met said their most common emergency treatments were for spear and arrow wounds.

In 1944, on the Dutch side of New Guinea, now part of Indonesia called Irian Jaya, an American transport plane crashed in a 5,000-foot valley and the survivors discovered a whole new culture. Isolated by fifty miles of swamps and surrounded by rugged mountains, the survivors named the place Shangri La. There are still no roads to Shangri La, yet the main city, Wiema, with a population of 50,000, has paved streets, cars, trucks, hotels, and even bathtubs all carried in by air. The peaceful natives are farming as they have always done. Except for tiny gourds, men still roam the city streets naked, and out in the countryside women wear only tiny grass skirts.

MOROTAI AT LAST

September of 1993 I returned to the small island of Morotai in the northern Moluccas where I had spent six months in 1944. The friendly people I remembered so fondly from the war gave me a royal welcome. Morotai is not easy to reach, which may be why I was the first American veteran to return to the island and may explain my wild reception.

In 1944 I had spent three weeks on a slow boat from the Admiralty Islands to Morotia and arrived in the middle of an air raid. In 1993 I flew Garuda Indonesia Airline from Los Angeles to Biak and took the daily flight to Ternate, the closest jetport to Morotai. Arriving on a Monday I had planned to go on the

Fishing canoes, Morotai Island, as seen in 1943, left, *and 1994,* right.

Husking rice hasn't changed in fifty years at Dayo Village. Top right: *The 1943 photograph I took of Mrs. Bola.* Bottom right: *Mrs. Bola showing me the same picture fifty years later.*

weekly ferryboat to Morotai on Tuesday. However, my guidebook was out-of-date and the ferry had left Monday morning. Anticipating trouble, I hired an English-speaking guide named Fauzy. He found we could ferry from Ternate to Halmahera Island and board the bus for a five-hour ride across the island to Tobelo, where, for a small fee, I could hire a motorboat to Morotai.

We were underway late Tuesday morning and had no problem getting to Halmahera. However, the bus to Tobelo only ran when filled with six paying customers. Fauzy and I being the only passengers, I had to pay for the empty seats, a total fare of ninety dollars. The road was under reconstruction and we got stuck four times, and I mean stuck. Much pushing and lots of debates put the bus back on the road four times in the grueling 120 miles, and we didn't reach Tobelo until 9:00 P.M. The discomfort was soon forgotten because, as I had written in my diary October 8, 1944, *"Tomorrow I will be in Morotai."*

Wednesday morning we learned that ninety dollars was the "small fee" for a powerboat! Which reminded me of David Niven and his bag full of money in the movie *Around the World in Eighty Days.* Looking for something cheaper, we stumbled on a ferryboat leaving for Morotai in a few hours. Aboard the ferry I showed my World War II pictures to a woman on her way home, which chanced to be Dayo, the village I had often hiked to visit. Five years old when I had taken the pictures, she began to shed tears, recognizing many of the people in the photographs.

"Morotai at last!" were the words I wrote October 10, 1944. Arriving in 1993 resembled a rerun of my

Carrying garden produce, Morotai Island, 1943, left, and 1994, right.

war diary. Then I had been impressed by a smoking volcano across the water on Halmahera and the air raid in progress. The ferryboat landed at Daruba, the same harbor as fifty years ago. This time giant clouds obscured the volcano and instead of an air raid, Thor was hurling thunderbolts and lightning.

Fifty years after my first visit I set out with Fauzy to find my old camp. The only clue was my diary, which said it was about a four-mile hike to Dayo. However, in what had reverted to a coconut plantation I couldn't find any sign of the buildings or tent sites where thousands of GIs had lived.

Although I didn't find the camp, the scene brought back some awful memories. Night after night for four weeks Japanese bombers harassed us. Most of the time our fighter planes and anti-aircraft guns kept them away, but not always, and several times they damaged our airfields but seldom hurt anyone on the ground.

After a silent moment to think about that terrible night when bombs did hit our camp and destroy my tent, killing a boy next door, Fauzy and I took a bus to Dayo. I remember the walk as an easy four-mile stroll on a sandy beach with two streams to ford. The streams were still there and so were long stretches of sand.

Either the beach had changed (quite possible) or I had forgotten (also possible) the cliffs that would have stopped me at high tide, and the rocky sections, and a mangrove swamp that had to be skirted.

At Dayo Village I finally found a person I had photographed during the war. Mrs. Bola, although she did not remember me, remembered having her picture taken while husking rice. When I gave her a large print, the villagers were so pleased several put on their best clothes and let me take their pictures in the same pose.

One of the highlights recorded in my wartime dairy was dated Saturday, November 25, 1944, Sangowo, Morotia.

I have just witnessed an interesting pageant at Sangowo village that could have come out of the National Geographic*, or a Hollywood production.*

The festival started with a parade up the wide village path. First came the dancers followed by a band, and then colorful banners followed by a flock of kids. The band was using complicated looking homemade bamboo instruments which sounded something like bagpipes. Not bad. There must have been 30 players, young and old, in the band.

The dancers were the most interesting. Three men and three women were dressed in very colorful clothing, beautifully made but looked old enough to be heirlooms. One woman had a very elaborate headgear that included a bird of paradise.

Bamboo band at Sangowo village, Morotai Island, 1943, left, and 1994, right.

There were three arches along the path where the dancers did some extra turns. The last arch was at the village square where the men dancers were met by three men giving a wild imitation of a battle. They each had a long javelin made of teak in one hand and a shield made from teak inlaid with mother of pearl in the other hand. After a mock battle with the dancers, they suddenly stopped, smiled at one another, shook hands, and then they all started dancing together. They were rather wild. I got spattered by dirt from their feet several times. Oh yes, there was also a large drum, too big to be carried, and some metal gongs. Some men were pounding out a rhythm as hard as they could hit them. What a noise.

On my return trip in 1993 I wanted to see Sangowo again, so Fauzy and I took the bus the few miles beyond Dayo. The reception of my festival pictures was overwhelming; the villagers got quite emotional over some of the pictures and happy over others. They recognized most of the people and were very excited by the dancing man with a beard. He had died a few years before. Except for children in the background, now adults, I didn't find anyone in Sangowo I had photographed.

The villagers were so pleased with the pictures I gave away, they put on an impromptu parade just for me, complete with band and dancers. The band was playing the

Yali girls at Angguruk village.

same bamboo instruments as fifty years ago plus some homemade horns. Because so many people crowded around, I had a terrible time getting pictures. When it was time to leave, everyone wanted to shake hands. One of the men and several women wanted to hug me—*wanted* to? I couldn't stop them. I wonder what reception other Americans will receive? The band gave me a royal send-off, playing, of all things, "Pistol Packing Mama," the same tune my diary noted the village kids singing during the war.

CHANGES: ARE THEY GOOD OR BAD?

Reflecting on my trips I have many mixed feelings. There are roads to many of the villages I hiked to. Beyond the roads people still live and dress as they did fifty years ago. Their canoes are the same except some have outboard motors. Communication between villages has never been good and, because they do not speak the same language, there is often troubles between villages. Dense jungles and steep mountains so isolated villages from each other, that each valley and each island developed its own language. Papua New Guinea is said to have over 3,000 separate languages. However, the government is changing that. I found schools in all but the most remote villages teaching a common language that may create better relations.

The primitive cultures of the South Pacific are as endangered as the endangered animals and birds that we are trying to protect. Should we try to influence the native's decision of whether to join the twenty-first century? If so, which way? While older people are happy with the life they lead, the young, learning in school about the rest of the world, are eager to leave. The transition has been painful for natives who leave their jungle and mountain villages to look for nonexistent jobs in the cities.

I just happened to be in Papua New Guinea during a political campaign, which is similar to our system, to elect a president. I shook hands and talked to very astute native politicians who were campaigning even in remote villages reached by jeep tracks. Unlike other third-world countries where military coups produce a "president for life" and resources are exploited to enrich the leaders, Papua New Guinea's government seems astute enough to use their oil resource and rich

Top: *Missionary plane landing at the Yali village of Angguruk.* Bottom: *Arriving at Tari Airport in New Guinea highlands at the beginning of a five-day trek.*

nickel, copper, and gold deposits wisely. Although environmental organizations have legitimate concerns over the influence of Western corporations on government and the destruction of native cultures, the people I talked with convinced me that elected officials of Papua New Guinea are truly for the people, and the very islands where I spent my war years dodging bombs, swatting mosquitoes, and sloshing around in the mud may well be "Paradise Islands."

• CHAPTER 22 •

My Favorite Mountain Pictures

or
Why Do Some Pictures Sell and Others Don't?

A minor eruption a month before the May 1980 blast that changed the shape of one of the most famous calendar views in the west.

I am annoyed when people say they are "locked out of the most beautiful views in the country." They, of course, are referring to the 1969 Wilderness Act, which prohibits wheels of any sort in designated wilderness areas. Heaven forbid a person might have to walk. How un-American can the Act be! When someone claims they are "locked out," they have no idea what they are talking about. The most beautiful scenery in the country is reached by cars traveling on paved highways. The judges are the many art directors who buy our pictures. They prove time after time the best scenery can be reached by road.

An art director for an ad agency or calendar company sitting in an eastern office doesn't give a darn how hard you worked to get a picture. All the director looks for is a photograph that fits his layout. It doesn't matter one bit who took the picture, or that

Mount St. Helens before the 1980 eruption.

the photographer spent two weeks backpacking to get it, or if the photographer just set the tripod up right beside the car. In spite of all the beautiful places I have hiked to, over 90 percent of the mountain pictures I sell were taken within a few feet of my car.

If the best views are readily accessible by car, why do people rave about what an art director would class as a mediocre scene? The answer is that old adage that one appreciates something most when he has to work for it. So why do pictures taken from the roadside sell and my favorite wilderness pictures don't? Could it be that I, too, am influenced by how much energy I used to take some of my favorite pictures?

Assuming the plane ride taken to get pictures of the North Cascades and Mount Waddington, a boat ride across Spirit Lake to get a reflection of Mount St. Helens, and the paved trails walked to get photos of the flower fields of Mount Rainier qualify as "easy access," then the 90 percent is accurate. The exception is the couple of times I have sold the breathtaking view of Image Lake reflecting Glacier Peak some sixteen miles

Above: *Sunrise on the Goat Rocks and Mount Adams from Camp Muir, at 10,000 feet on Mount Rainier. This was taken from my sleeping bag.* Opposite: *Lake of the Hanging Glaciers and the Commander Range in the Purcell Mountains of British Columbia.*

from the nearest road. From a bottom-line standpoint, my thousands of hikes have been to illustrate guide-books, and long backpacks to illustrate adventure stories in magazines.

The real exception is the photo of sunrise from Camp Muir, which has sold very well. However, I don't know if it should be classed as easily accessible or difficult. It is a grueling trek to 10,000-foot Camp Muir, but I was already there during my week-long photo/climbing seminar. Unlike the summit climbers who left Camp Muir at midnight, my students got to sleep in. The weather was good, so instead of sleeping in the crowded hut I moved my bed out under the stars. Between watching shooting stars, hearing the summit climbers taking off at midnight, and a wonderful sunrise every morning, I didn't get much sleep. But that one morning, with clouds in the valley, I didn't even get out of bed to take the picture that has sold many times, including being enlarged to an eighty-foot-wide, backlit transparency for Eastman Kodak's Grand Central Station Colorama.

Opposite: *Those little dots are climbers on their way to the summit of Mount Rainier.* Above: *Berg Lake and Mount Robson, the highest mountain in the Canadian Rockies. I made two attempts to climb this mountain.* Right, top to bottom: *Hiking to high camp on Eldorado Peak; Mount Baker from the portals on the end of Ptarmigan Ridge; Earling Strom's lodge, Lake Magog, and Mount Assiniboine, a British Columbia Provincial Park.*

CHAPTER 23

Through the Years with Boots and Camera

or
Wearing out Six Trapper Nelsons and Thirty-eight Pairs of Boots

Ira at work on the Emmons Glacier in 1954.

Bob's and my photographic interests, never exactly the same, gradually diverged. He liked cities and events and nice hotels. My tastes ran to mountains, hiking, climbing, a tent in the rain, fighting brush, and slapping mosquitoes. Initially the differences were our strength, giving us a broader range of pictures. Eventually, though, the differences caught up with us. Bob felt too many of my mountain trips were weathered out and a waste of partnership resources. I felt he was spending far too much time in Alaska for the returns we were getting. After a year or two of bickering, in 1967, we revised our partnership to simple coopera-

Paradise Inn, almost buried under twenty feet of snow, 1951. When this became a Seattle Times cover photograph, the Park Service put up a "Keep Off" sign.

tion, each going our own ways, paying our own ways, and receiving our own incomes, while helping each other with sales and, of course, preserving the "Bob and Ira Spring" identification we had worked twenty years to establish.

The new relationship has been good not only for family relations but also for business. Free of partnership restraints, Bob focused on travel promotion, first on a contract with Alaska Airlines and then with Exploration Cruises, a company with five small ships, each capable of carrying eighty passengers and designed like a wartime landing craft to be beached, allowing passengers to walk a gangplank directly onto land. The combination of deluxe travel, local color, and natural history has suited Bob and Norma perfectly. They have planned many of the cruises and photographed them, and Norma has written the brochures.

While Bob has traveled to exotic places around the

When Bob fell ill, I finished his assignment to photograph a Choco village on the Moque River in Panama's Darien Jungle.

When Terry and I arrived, Bob was still pretty groggy but was stewing about the pictures he should be taking on an Exploration Cruise out of Panama City, so, using Bob's cameras and film, I joined the cruise to take his pictures. There was space on the boat for Terry, so he went along, too.

The first part of the cruise was through the San Blas Islands where we landed at four different villages and, thanks to the unique ship design, passengers could step ashore without getting their feet wet. The native people were very colorfully dressed and everyone enjoyed visiting the villages, taking pictures, and shopping for souvenirs.

On the west side of the canal, the ship cruised south along the coast of Panama and anchored off the mouth of the Mogue River within sight of the Darien Jungle. The jungle is the missing link of the Pan-American Highway. It is so swampy and dense that so far no road has penetrated it. The Mogue River is really just a creek with a riverlike estuary. The passengers were transferred to large dugout canoes powered by outboard motors and taken twelve miles upriver to the head of tidewater. When the water became too shallow for the canoes, we hiked the last half-mile on a jungle trail to a primitive village where native women wore colorful skirts and the rest of their bodies were painted with geometric designs.

I would have loved to spend a couple of days in this village, but we were only allowed two hours, as the river estuary is only navigable at high tide.

Back in Panama City, we found Bob able to walk, and in two weeks he had completely recovered and returned home.

While I enjoyed taking Bob's place in the Darien Jungle, it is the joy of mountains and wildlife that I love. As I got older my mountaineering became less rugged, and walking slower I grew more aware of the beauty at my feet, the wildlife whose home I shared,

world, he sees only what the tourist sees. Occasionally he has done something I envy, such as photographing seals and birds in the Pribilofs, exploring small islands near Bora Bora, and taking a dugout canoe trip to a remote village in Panama's Darien Jungle, which I did get to do.

In November of 1982, I got a frightening phone call from Panama City. Norma was on the line in a state of shock. She said Bob was unconscious in a Panama hospital with a case of cerebral meningitis and probably would not last the night. The doctor told Norma that she better alert the family, so she called me. I called Bob and Norma's son and daughter, Terry and Tracy.

It was decided that Terry and I would fly to Panama and do what we could to help Norma bring Bob's remains home. Panama City is a long way and it was thirty-six hours after Norma called that we reached the hospital. Much to everyone's relief, by the time we arrived Bob had regained consciousness and the doctor had taken him out of intensive care and off the critical list.

and trails that don't have to end up on a glacier or a mountaintop.

PHOTOGRAPHY CHANGES, TOO

As this is written, in fall of 1998, it is sixty-eight years since Eastman Kodak gave me my first camera, the Box Brownie. I have a lot more pictures I plan to take, and expect to be able to do so because the modern cameras are much lighter than the 4X5 view camera I started hauling around in 1940. The new cameras are not only easier on tired old shoulders but also have so much electronic gadgetry they are easy on tired old heads. Film, too, has changed. The only roll film available sixty-six years ago was black-and-white in the newly developed Verichrome, overly sensitive to blue and hardly recording red. Not until we were in college was there a Panchromatic film sensitive to all colors. One marvels at the beautiful black-and-white photographs achieved by the old masters, such as Stieglitz, Steichen, Weston, and Ansel Adams, with such slow and insensitive film.

In 1930, color transparency film was still being developed and color pictures of that era were taken by a complicated process using three different filters on three different negatives. The results were as beautiful as anything we can do now, but the process was too tedious to be practical. Color film didn't come into use until the late 1930s, and it wasn't until 1940 that I bought a package of six sheets of Kodachrome for a trip in the Olympic Mountains. The color was great, but the film had a speed of only ASA 6. After the war the speed was doubled to ASA 12. That was still slow and the camera had to be set on a tripod for every picture.

Until the 1980s, the heavy, bulky 4X5 view camera was essential for color photography; nine out of the ten leading national magazines and art directors turned up their noses at any smaller color films; and even today many calendar companies ask for 4X5-inch films or larger.

However, *Life* and *National Geographic* pioneered the use of 35mm film and, thanks to their high standards, magazine and textbook photographs are now mostly taken with the small camera. We have always developed our own black-and-white films and prints, but we no longer have to get out the scales and mix ten grams of elon, fifteen grams of hydroquione, and a bit of borax to make our print developer. Now we just open a package of premix. At first we developed our color films but after a couple of years gave up. In the summertime we didn't have time, and in winter we didn't have enough films to warrant mixing the expensive chemicals that spoiled in four days.

Bob switched to a 35mm camera for his travel work early on. I belatedly recognized that the 35mm was best for wildlife and flowers and eventually succumbed completely to the lighter camera and now use it for all my color work.

Black-and-white sheet film always has been impractical for the 4X5 camera and we used the more expensive film packs. Inside a pack, individual films were stacked sixteen deep, each tied to its own pull tab. When the first film is exposed it is pulled around

Ira changing film-holders on Artist Point, Mount Baker ski area.

a sharp corner and the next film is in place. In extreme cold weather the film becomes brittle and can break at the sharp corner, as it did at eighteen below on the Juneau Icefield. Film packs aren't manufactured any more, so I was forced to find an alternative. I never did like making enlargements from 35mm film, and ended up with a 2¼x2¼ Hasselblad for the black-and-white photos in the trail guides.

I've taken thousands of pictures in the last sixty-seven years and made almost as many mistakes. I suspect I have some kind of record for boo-boos. I have loaded cameras wrong. I have had them jam. I've gone on long trips, forgetting the film. Once I dropped my black-and-white film holder off a cliff and had to finish an assignment using color film and then convert it to black and white. Once I left my camera in a shelter at Flapjack Lakes and I never noticed it was missing, my pack was so heavy without it.

The dumbest boo-boo wasn't my fault. When I was in charge of the photo shop at Mount Rainier, I was busy one day with darkroom work and when it was time to go I grabbed the pack with the camera and ran up the trail to take pictures of the horse party and then hike on to the Ice Caves for the hikers. The horses were in sight when I reached the photogenic spot on Panorama Dome; I hastily set up the tripod, screwed on the big 5x7 camera, opened it, put the dark cloth over the camera, and tried to focus. Nothing there. Just a blank. No lens! The other photographer had removed the lens to clean it and had forgotten to put it back.

My greatest heartbreak was after the Juneau Icefield when at home in the darkroom I began in high excitement to develop the spectacular pictures of Devils Paw and our lonesome tent in the mile-wide Taku Glacier. I just about committed hari kari when I found all my negatives blank. The cold of eighteen below zero had made the film so brittle it broke.

Cameras, film, and I have changed. I just knew a zoom lens would never be sharp enough for my work and they were not to begin with, but now, what a time saver not to always need to switch lenses. I just knew a "point-and-shoot" camera was a toy for an amateur. Again, how wrong can I be? It's a miracle tool—although I can turn the miracle off and take a picture as I always did. What I like best is the ability to program the camera to bracket my exposure, although it is usually the middle exposure that is correct; it will take an

Ira and the 2¼ x 2¼ Hasselblad used for black-and-white pictures in guidebooks. Much easier on the back than the old 4x5 Speed Graphic.

exposure both above and below the correct one, guaranteeing I get one perfectly exposed film. In spite of the amazing things the "and shoot" can do, the "point" is still the most important ingredient. Besides the perfect exposure it still takes a person to understand the lighting and create a composition, whether it be with an 8x20 Colorama camera, a 4x5 Graflex, a Hasselblad, a 35mm "point-and-shoot" camera, or one of the digital cameras of the future.

FROM GRUNGY PANTS TO GORE TEX®

Good camera equipment is essential for all photographers, but mountain photography also takes sturdy shoes, ice axes, crampons, tents, sleeping bags, packboards, warm clothing, and much more. On the go, year in and year out, all I was doing was rough on equipment. The best backpack on the market was the wood-framed Trapper Nelson, manufactured in Seattle. My loads were so heavy the wooden joints kept breaking. Fortunately, to protect their reputation, the company manager kept my Trapper Nelson in repair and even replaced it five times with a new one.

I was not so fortunate with hiking boots. I would wear out a store-bought pair in a year. However, we had an excellent bootmaker in Seattle. His boots were expensive but fit well and lasted at least two years. Not counting the hiking shoes my parents paid for during my teenage years, I figured I have gone through thirty-eight pairs.

Sixty years ago there was only one place to shop, Recreational Equipment, Inc. (REI). The Spring family has been involved with REI from almost the beginning. The Co-op (as it was known, and still is to those of us who remember when) was founded by Lloyd Anderson in 1938 to import, direct from Europe, mountaineering equipment previously available in the United States only in a limited selection at exorbitant prices.

In 1940, after two summers at Mount Rainier watching mountain climbers, I wanted my own ice axe. Word of the Co-op having reached Shelton, at the first opportunity I went to Seattle and searched for and found the three shelves in a service station at the corner of Elliott Way and Western Avenue (near Pike Place Market) that "housed" the Co-op. For fifty cents, I was given Co-op membership card No. 184. I bought an ice axe, which, because of its long wooden shaft, I still occasionally use, and a down sleeping bag my grandchild is now using.

REI has had to change with the times. Hikers and hiking have changed since the 1940s. Before the war any ragged clothes would do. Afterward, war surplus pants and jackets were so cheap and so good they took over the backcountry. Before the war most of us slept under the stars and when it rained used a tarp. Food came from the corner store, and the cooking pot was a "black crow," made from a five-pound coffee can with bailing-wire for a handle so it could be hung over a campfire.

As the hiking population grew larger and became "style" conscious in clothing and engineering, ingenuity installed the age of "high-tech" equipment. The wood-framed Trapper Nelson pack gave way to a metal-framed Kelty and then came internal packs with

Top: *Before lightweight tents, which among other faults cost a mint, we had inexpensive tarps, which kept out most bad weather and let in the pleasing breezes and lovely sun, but also the bugs. This family camp was about 1965 at Glacier Basin.* Bottom: *A high-tech tent at Kool-Aid Lake, for a price, will keep one sheltered. In the distance is Mount Daiber, officially known as Mount Formidable.*

intricate parts. From the day of tarps, hikers have turned to tents made of high-tech magic material. Freeze-dried foods have found their way into packs, along with the latest gizmo, whatever that is. Once a cheap sport, cheap enough for a poor boy of the Great Depression, hiking has become so expensive that beginners could easily shell out $1,000 before their first hike.

CHAPTER 24

Green-Bonding for a Green Constituency

or
The Mouse That Learned to Roar

Tiger lily.

In 1959, Supreme Court Justice William O. Douglas wrote the preface to our book, *High Worlds of the Mountain Climber,* as follows:

We have precious little real wilderness left in America. The true roadless areas represent only about two percent of our public lands. And the invasion of that small portion by ever-lengthening roads is a constant threat. The ideal of many is to pave the trails, make alpine meadows accessible to cars, and perhaps put escalators on the peaks. When that is done, the wildness that is part of our great heritage will be gone forever.

We need ridges and basins that can only be reached on foot, cliffs and peaks that can only be conquered by daring. The passion to bring "civilization" to the remnants of our backwoods is one sign that we as Americans are getting soft and flabby. We want everything made easy. We forget that only when success comes through great effort, daring, and

hazardous exertion is it worth having. We need the rest of the wildness of America as a testing ground for unborn generations where they can come to grips with elemental forces and, testing themselves against the mountains, get to know their own strength and weakness. We need the woods not as a place to park a car but as a sanctuary untouched, where nature is in full play, where man finds his place among all the creatures of the earth. No better place for building character can be designed. Not all the steel, concrete and asphalt, no degree of ingenuity with electronics and the atom, no man-made inventions can duplicate the wonders of the wilderness.

We must unite to save the tiny islands of true wildness that we have left. If we destroy them, we will have lost forever some of the true glory that was America.

What Congress gives, Congress can take away. The 1996 session set off alarm bells when serious proposals were advanced to decommission "surplus" park and wilderness land and hand it over to the private sector. Fortunately, in 1996 there were enough green-bonded

Lewis River trail.

people in the country to halt the give-away of public lands. Between population growth that needs more wooden houses, and more space for cities and resorts, a well-organized, industry-funded, profit-driven, anti-environmental campaign continues and we must expect more and more attempts. Will there be enough green-bonded people in the year 2005 or 2010 to protect public lands?

WHAT IS "GREEN-BONDING"?

"Bonding" is the term describing the development of ties of a newborn baby to its mother, a newborn fawn to its doe, or any offspring to its parent. "Green-bonding" comes from the emotional ties a person feels hiking wildland trails while enjoying the flowers, trees, wildlife, and mountain views. Green-bonding generated a green constituency that prompted thousands of people to write their congressmen urging passage of the 1984 Washington Wilderness Act. Their letters gave support to the 6 of our 10 congressional delegates who, while growing up, were green-bonded by hiking in the Cascades and Olympics. Again, during the Forest Management Planning process, 10,000 people wrote the Mount Baker–Snoqualmie National Forest

Green-bonding knows no age. It may come from hugging trees, climbing the tallest peak, resting in an alpine meadow, smelling flowers, or listening to the bees. To assure a sufficient number of green bonded citizens, it is important that everyone has access to mountain trails, easy trails for beginners and challenging trails for the experienced. Top: A cedar tree in the Grove Of The Patriarchs. Bottom: Big Tree Nature Trail near Lake Quinault Ranger Station.

telling the importance of trails.

Though green-bonding is a new term, bonding to wild places is old. Jean Stratton-Porter learned that preservation sermons put people to sleep, but when she incorporated preservation in her novels, *Freckles* and *Girl of the Limberlost,* she touched a million hearts. Teddy Roosevelt, another conservationist, was green-bonded at an early age. John Muir's first bonding came as a teenager walking the virgin forests of Wisconsin.

Among my own acquaintances, U.S. Supreme Court Justice William O. Douglas became one of the most influential conservationists of the 1960s. His green-bonding started early while hiking near his home in Yakima and was reflected in court decisions of his era.

Our parents did a fine job of green-bonding my brother and me when we were still in knee pants, and this carried over into our photography. Bob and I paid our mortgages and fed the kids from the sales of our pictures and mountain stories. There were easier ways to make a living as photographers without lugging thirty to forty pounds of cameras (plus our camping gear) around the mountains. But I think Bob felt as I did that photography was more than bread and butter. Our calendar photograph of Mount Shuksan reflected in an alpine pool was a way of sharing our feelings, as were stories in national magazines depicting the geometric designs of shadows and shapes of a glacier, or an avalanche lily in such a hurry to bloom that it pushes through last winter's snowbank.

I know our pictures had an impact. Fan letters have come from across the country and one from Belgium. We've even had people tell us they moved to the Northwest because of our pictures. This was a Jean Stratton-Porter–type approach to green-bonding.

Two events of the 1950s changed my environmentalism from passive to aggressive. One was accompanying Justice William O. Douglas on his famous Ocean March. I had no great objections to the tourist-industry's proposal for an oceanside highway from Cape Alava to Aberdeen; after all we could still walk the beach. But as Justice Douglas pointed out, the challenge of walking the beach would be lost if we looked up from the surf and saw cars. The other was what happened to trails in the two years after the first printing in 1965 of our *100 Hikes*. When I was growing up I didn't worry when a road was built twenty miles to Spider Lake in the Olympic foothills; after all there were lots of other mountain lakes. What opened my eyes and shocked me to my toes was *8 of the 100 hikes* were lost to roads and clear-cuts— this was when I changed from a passive to an aggressive environmentalist!

BANNED BUT NOT IN BOSTON

Harvey Manning and I have always had a great rapport with backcountry rangers, dating back to when we had to stop at a ranger station to pick up a fire permit on the way to a trail and see if we could get a free large-scale map intended for foresters, not recreationists. When lucky, we'd have a chance to get news about trail conditions and hear tales of the "good old days" from Harold Engalls, Nels Bruseth, Bill Butler, and Nevin McCullough. Once on the trail, more often than not the only people we'd meet were fire lookouts atop a peak or a trail crew.

The 1950s and 1960s were a painful period. The rangers we'd known while growing up were barely aware the government trees were supposed to be logged; they thought their job was to protect them. However, as an act of Congress mandated, "multiple use" became the official philosophy, and the forestry schools indoctrinated students in seeing trees as board feet.

"Multiple use" turned into "single use," as trails became roads and all too many remaining trails were converted to wheelways for machine-powered off-road vehicles (ORVs) and gravity-powered all-terrain bicycles (ATBs)—which is to say, for motorcycles and bicycles, the human feet considered to be as obsolete as the dinosaur.

Once trails appeared in our guidebook, the Forest Service took note of the sudden interest of hikers on the 100 trails and, while road-building continued to ruin trails elsewhere, the remaining 92 trails received a certain degree of protection. The hiking guide had become a powerful tool of conservation.

The *100 Hikes* books cannot take all the glory for stopping road-building and halting the conversion of hiking trails to wheel roads; however, our friends in the Forest Service tell us the books have played a major role.

Credit also is owed The Mountaineers Books. I know of no other publisher that would risk alienating a potential market by permitting us to "tell it like it is" and make the extra pages available to present the facts.

PEOPLE, PEOPLE, PEOPLE

Bob and I were lucky to be young when hikers were few and far between. We enjoyed the comradeship of a Scout troop and sharing the day's adventures around roaring campfires. Better yet was hitting the trail with a friend or two, camping wherever and whenever we wanted, building wood fires as big as we liked, drinking from any and every stream, and being out in the wilds for days without meeting another soul; and if by chance we did meet

This 1946 party of 100 on the Winthrop Glacier was a bit short on solitude, but nobody accused them of damaging the ecosystem.

another hiker, it was probably someone we knew.

Prior to World War II the White Chuck River country had many trails but few hikers—too few to prevent a postwar logging road up the valley nearly to Kennedy Hot Springs, converting a long backpack of days or more into an afternoon stroll. We had the Golden Horn all to ourselves, but because there was no trail, there was no constituency large enough to obtain the area for the North Cascades National Park. There are no trails in the Ragged Ridge, Eagle Rock, and Jackman Creek roadless areas, so again they had

insufficient constituency for 1984 designation as wilderness. As there are still no trails, these superb areas may not make the next go-around either. There are trails, but not enough people have braved the motorcycles to hike in the Dark Divide, Mad River, or Golden Lakes areas to speak of the lakes, forests, and flower fields of these former hiking trails to be included in the Washington Wilderness Act of that year.

On my first visit to Snow Lake in 1957 I was impressed when told 800 people a year hiked that trail; now there are 20,000. When I worked at Mount Rainier in 1937 I doubt that 300 a day walked the Paradise flower trails; now there are 3,000. In the 1960s, 300 climbers a year reached the summit of Rainier. Now it's often 300 a day! Granted, the backcountry was uncrowded, and that was the good news; the bad news was that there wasn't enough public support (green-bonding) to prevent logging roads from gobbling up trails or to stop motorcycles from running us out of some of our favorite hikes.

Since I roamed the Olympics as a teenager, the population of the state of Washington has doubled and doubled again, and the number of hikers in our mountains has multiplied. Where once I could hike for weeks without seeing anyone, now I may pass a hundred or more a day. In the 1930s I would have found it impossible to think of 500 people hiking to Lena Lake in one year; however, in 1995 there were 10,000, and if predictions are right by 2015 there will be 20,000. The same is true of Snow Lake: In 1960 there were 500 visitors, and that sounded like a lot of people, but in 1994 there were 15,000! Impossible as it sounds, by the year 2015 there could be 30,000 people starting the green-bonding process by hiking the three and a half miles to the lake. Is there enough green for that many boots, boots, and more boots hiking up and down again? Yes, there is. So far we have been able to accommodate every one, and Lena Lake and Snow Lake are in better shape than when I first saw them. Fortunately, those are not the only trails; even now there are many lonesome paths where there is just me and the chipmunks and sometimes a deer, a mountain goat, or a marmot.

I was unhappy when they paved the trails around Paradise, but now 3,000 to 4,000 a day walk those trails, and yet I can still have the primitive glacier moraine trail and its flower fields to myself.

The number of people is greater, much greater. Yet bit by bit, hiking trails are being compromised away. For the sake of jobs, loggers have obliterated thousands of miles of trails. So motorcyclists could have the same experience as a hiker, more trails were lost. The National Park Service and National Forest Service are allowing bicyclists on more and more trails. On top of all this, hundreds of miles are being abandoned for lack of maintenance and some land managers are restricting trail use in the name of solitude.

From my parent's time in the early 1900s, exploring the wilderness waterways, and my first backpack in 1929, until now, I have watched the huge increase of people enjoying wild places and the shrinking opportunities to accommodate them. The easy, close-to-home day hikes of our youth, so important to green-bonding families with young children, have been lost to clear-cuts or housing developments, to be substituted by former backpacks that roads have shortened to easy day hikes.

Without the wider picture that age has given me, today's hikers are apt to accept the present state of trails as if it had been that way forever. While roads could be converted back to trails, the thrill of winding through 200- to 500-year-old trees that made the long approach so special cannot be duplicated in their grandchildren's lifetime.

Trail users are different. Mountain trails are no longer just the realm of treehuggers, birdwatchers, or those wanting to enjoy the peace and quiet. Now there are joggers who want hikers out of the way and bicyclists who must have wheels on trails so they won't be

Congressman Rod Chandler and I viewing motorcycle-overrun trails in the Teanaway River area.

bored, silently speeding around blind corners on a collision course with frightened hikers. Then there are motorcyclists with their racket and smell turning trails into miniature roads and turning away 98 percent of the hikers. I even encountered eighty marathon runners doing the Wonderland Trail in two days! How lucky I was to grow up before people put layers, whether it be rubber tires, motors, or running shoes, between themselves and the nature they came to enjoy. Are these people being green-bonded? I doubt it. Will these people write their congressman when needed? I doubt it. It will be the manufacturers and distributors of these toys their congressmen will hear from.

Our wild places should be treated like temples, not gymnasiums. If nature is not what attracts athletes to trails, if it's exercise they want, they should go to a health club or build their own trails that do not conflict with other users. A trail is a way to appreciate a temple. A temple is a place where people are green-bonded.

Can we learn how to accommodate so many people and still maintain that sense of adventure, the freedom, and feeling of exploration that we had when young? We must find a better way than having a ranger herding people and yelling to stay on the trail, as is done at Mount Rainier, or the Forest Service limiting the people in wilderness to give a few a sense of solitude.

The importance of hundreds of thousands of green-bonded people should be topmost on every hiker's and environmentalist's mind. The wake-up call came when our most popular modern president and self-claimed "great environmentalist" turned his cabinet members loose to gut environmental laws and ravage the forests. (Was our "environmental president" cleverly in cahoots with the Sierra Club? His action tripled the club's membership.) However, the big warning came in 1996 when his followers actually got a bill on the floor that would start turning our national parks and wilderness areas over to private industry.

Under the guise of giving handicapped and older people (is that me?) an opportunity to have a wilderness experience, a number of congressmen, supported by industry, presented a bill that would open up the Boundary Canoe Waters to airplane landings and power boats, our wilderness areas to "salvage" logging and mechanized travel, depriving the challenge the spastic man was experiencing with a heavy pack and two crutches nine miles from the nearest road, or the blind man enjoying the sound and smells at Cascade Pass. We have talked to people in their eighties on Panicle Saddle every bit as thrilled to reach Panicle Saddle as a younger person the top of Mount Rainier.

Public outrage stopped that bill in 1996. Will there be enough green-bonded people to do so in the year 2006, or 2016?

We may be appalled at 3,000 or more people a day walking the Paradise trails at Mount Rainier or 30,000 a year hiking to Snow Lake in the Alpine Lakes Wilderness, but if that is what it takes for the support of trails to the year 2015, so be it. It is up to us to figure out how to accommodate so many people without harming the temple.

Even though we must share it with hundreds, we have wilderness to hike in which otherwise would be stump lands driven past at high speeds. The Wilderness Act scrapped plans for roads that would have crisscrossed the Alpine Lakes, preserved a few valley old-growth forests from the chain saw, and kept dam-threatened rivers free-flowing.

The 1984 Wilderness Act saved vast areas in Washington from roads and chain saws, continues to protect a valuable asset from exploitation, and preserves the resource for future generations. It is an opportunity for adventure, a physical and mental challenge that builds the character, self-sufficiency, and health in our young folks that was so important to Peter Withers, the seventy-year-old warden at the Columbia Icefields, and Justice William O. Douglas of the U.S. Supreme Court, who attributed his health to a boyhood of exploring wilderness. The American Hiking Society has taken the health issue further by documenting the medical savings by those who live an energetic life.

Any degree of public recognition brings an obligation for a person to use whatever fame is generated by giving back something of himself. In the case of Bob's

Grove Of The Patriarchs, an easy trail at Mount Rainier, where many first-time hikers have become "green-bonded." I used a white smoke device to create the mist.

and my mountain stories and my guidebooks, the re-payment has been an involvement in the preservation of our wild places and mountain trails. I have attended an alphabetical soup of countless meetings of WTA, OPA, GPNFTTF, ALWMP, BSATM, and many more (Washington Trails Association [WTA]; Olympic Park Associates [OPA]; Gifford Pinchot National Forest Trails Task Force [GPNFTTF]; Alpine Lakes Wilderness Master Plan [ALWMP]; Mt. Baker-Snoqualmie Access Travel Management [BSATM]); have written countless letters commenting on EA, EIS, RTT (Environmental Assessment [EA]; Environmental Impact Statements [EIS]; Rail-To-Trails [RTT]); joined a dozen or more environmental organizations, and became deeply involved in REI and WTA.

I made six trips to Washington, D.C., to talk with our state's congressional delegation. My reputation as a guidebook author gave me special entree to lobby for trails, and I have become a pest at Forest Service headquarters. My first trip to D.C. was to promote the 1984 Washington Wilderness Bill. In preparation, I drew up a list of all trails in *101 Hikes in the North Cascades* and *102 Hikes in the South Cascades and Olympics,* separating them in two categories: those already protected in national parks and wilderness, and those with no protection and in danger of being destroyed by logging or overrun with motorcycles. When I showed the breakdown to Jo Roberts, chair of The Mountaineers' Conservation Division, she was so excited she assembled a work party to mark, in red, ten sets of the two books showing the trails outside protected wilderness and thus endangered. They crossed off the title of *101 Hikes* and replaced it with *36 Hikes; 102 Hikes* became *49 Hikes.* These two volumes were to play a crucial role. I took the marked books to Washington, D.C., and personally handed marked-up copies to each of the two

Canadian dogwood on a rainy day in the Big Beaver Valley.

senators and eight representatives of our congressional delegation. Most being hikers, the message hit home. More than one told me I was the first person ever to talk to them about trails as a wilderness resource; after the bill was passed, several asked me how many trails *they* had thus saved.

Since then, my lobbying trips to D.C. have been to obtain trail funding. I know I made some impact, for one year the exact wording I used in my briefing papers concerning trails close to population centers appeared in the final legislation. Another year I was able to have $1,000,000 earmarked for nonwilderness trails in this state.

WASHINGTON TRAILS ASSOCIATION

In 1966, the year our first *100 Hikes* book was published, Louise Marshall, coauthor of the first *100 Hikes*, started a mimeographed sheet she called *Signpost*. The sheet grew into a regular newsletter about trails and eventually a monthly magazine. A loyal group of readers who called themselves "Signposters" would, when asked, write letters or testify at hearings.

In 1970, while researching our second edition of *100 Hikes*, I kept finding large sums of money being spent to convert hiking trails to motorcycle paths (roads?) in the Mad River area. I bitterly complained. I was assured by the Entiat District Ranger that the work was being funded with IAC gas tax money, not federal money. How come? What is the "IAC gas tax money"? I knew that IAC stood for the Interagency for Outdoor Recreation, but I had to go to a Washington State legislator to find out what the IAC gas tax was.

Trail-riding motorcyclists had persuaded the state legislature to allocate a portion of the state's gasoline tax money to off-road vehicle (ORV) use. They had enough friends in the legislature (and enough industry-funded cloakroom lobbyists) to push the bill through without public hearings that would have alerted hikers. Since all travel on nonstate-funded roads is considered by the state as off-road travel (including hikers driving to National Forest trailheads and tourists on the National Park highway to Paradise Inn), hikers demanded their share of the off-road gas tax. Signposters

put up a big fuss but got nowhere. Louise saw that hikers, to be effective, needed to be organized and incorporated the Washington Trails Association (WTA).

The Mountaineers are activity-focused—hiking, climbing, skiing to name a few—and always leaders in conservation. However, in the 1970s they "had a full plate" of conservation matters, as did other environmental organizations, and trail issues were sidetracked. The WTA stepped in to fill the gap and quickly became a respected organization, called upon by congressmen for advice and consulted by the Forest Service.

I have been a WTA leader since its inception in 1970. My son, John, has joined me on the board, and on September 22, 1995, I became president. For now, road-building is not a big issue, but ORVs, primarily motorcycles, still have free reign on some prime hiking trails. While the WTA's steady pressure has made some progress, thanks to Karl Forsgaard, a top Seattle lawyer, there have been two major court decisions helping hikers. The first was the North Fork Entiat River Trail case brought to court by motorcyclists. The court said the 3,000 letters received by the Wenatchee National Forest opposing motorcycles was reason enough to close that trail to machines. The second was when the WTA and eleven other environmental organizations won their case in Federal Court, mandating that the Forest Service must file an environmental statement when improving a trail to ORV standards that may ultimately increase ORV use.

If 41,300 ORVers (and their industry's money) can band together for trail improvements detrimental to hikers, why can't a million hikers do the same to protect our rights? The problem we encounter is that of the thousands of green-bonded people in this state, few join hiking-oriented organizations that publish newsletters discussing day-to-day trail situations. Only when a major threat reaches the mass media do they react. On one such occasion 5,000 letters were sent to the Wenatchee National Forest opposing motorcycles on trails and over 10,000 letters to Mount Baker–Snoqualmie.

That's what we need. More letters (write them!). More well-informed hikers (join a group!). More green power (flex your muscles!).

A 1937 picture taken with my free Box Brownie. The Tatoosh Range, Mount Adams, and Mount Hood on one of my many before-breakfast runs to Panorama Point when I was working at Paradise Inn.

Epilogue

or
Time Takes Its Toll

Unlike the 1937 before-breakfast run to Panorama Point by myself, this visit with Pat in 1997 took a bit longer with several rest stops, and we were accompanied by hundreds of people, including our grandchildren.

It used to be that Pat and I were some of the fastest feet in the west, and when we overtook other folks on the trail I'd just shuffle my feet loud enough so they knew I was there; they would stand aside and smile as Pat and I passed. But when Pat was by herself it was different. When young hikers were overtaken by a woman flying along the trail with her gray hair bouncing in the wind, they'd speed up to avoid the humiliation of being passed by an old lady. After a bit they couldn't hold the pace and had to slow down, but still wouldn't admit that an older woman could be in better shape than they were. Pat had to keep right on their heels until, exhausted, they finally would sit down and let her pass.

Time is taking its toll. Pat and I still love hiking and we still have a lot more trails to do. My pace has slowed down from two to three miles an hour to one, or maybe one and a half miles an hour, or maybe only half a mile an hour. I seldom pass anyone and am very happy to stand aside and smile. Pat and I both have old knee injuries. Mine came helping Dad and Mother move furniture. Pat got hers legitimately, on a hike. Most of the time my knee pain can be controlled, but Pat finally had a knee replacement in February 1995.

By August she had recovered to the point that I could hardly keep up with her. Not that she's going all that fast, but someone has to finish first, even in a turtle race.

In 1996, for old times' sake, we returned to Mount Rainier on a busy weekend, sharing the paved trails around Paradise with over a thousand people. Hiking above the inn awoke wonderful memories. I showed Pat the place where in 1937 I had tried to sleep while working night shift at Paradise Inn. We traced the route we had taken in 1948, across the Nisqually Glacier, up the narrow snow gully to the Wilson Glacier, onward to Camp Hazard, where we arose at midnight to chop steps up the Kautz Icefall to the summit ice cap and the Columbia Crest. We laughed at the comedy of our climbing companions getting lost in the fog on the descent. After avoiding all the tricky turns they had missed on high, we got lost on Alta Vista.

We talked about the wonderful nights at the old Paradise Campground, watching The Mountain turn to gold, and then bright red, as the sun set.

We walked the paved trails in the company of all ages and shapes and sizes of other hikers. Despite the steepness of the trails on Alta Vista, even the overweight huffers and puffers were beginning their personal

Pat and a visitor at our camp near Moose Lake, Olympic National Park.

green-bonding in the color of the flowers, delighting in the antics of marmots and the brilliance of The Mountain.

We headed for Panorama Point. Though it was August, a steep snowbank covered the trail. Even so, 300 or more people crossed the snow, some in street shoes. Snow in August! I vividly recalled how the miracle hit me, back in 1929 when Dad took Bob and me on our first backpack to High Divide and we found ice in our cooking pots. We enjoyed the excitement the people expressed atop Panorama Point, probably for the first time there—or any place so high on a mountain. Their feelings were the same as ours the first time we reached the crater rim on Columbia Crest, almost fifty years before. Surely many of the thousands we saw that day will look for more challenges, will venture onto wilderness trails, and will become truly green-bonded—maybe enough of them to protect the future for others to follow—including our grandchildren.

Above: *Skyline Ridge and Mount Baker.* Right: *Pat with three of our four grandchildren, Erik, Logan, and Michael on a backpack in the Mount Baker area. Ruth, our fourth grandchild, had not yet joined the world.*

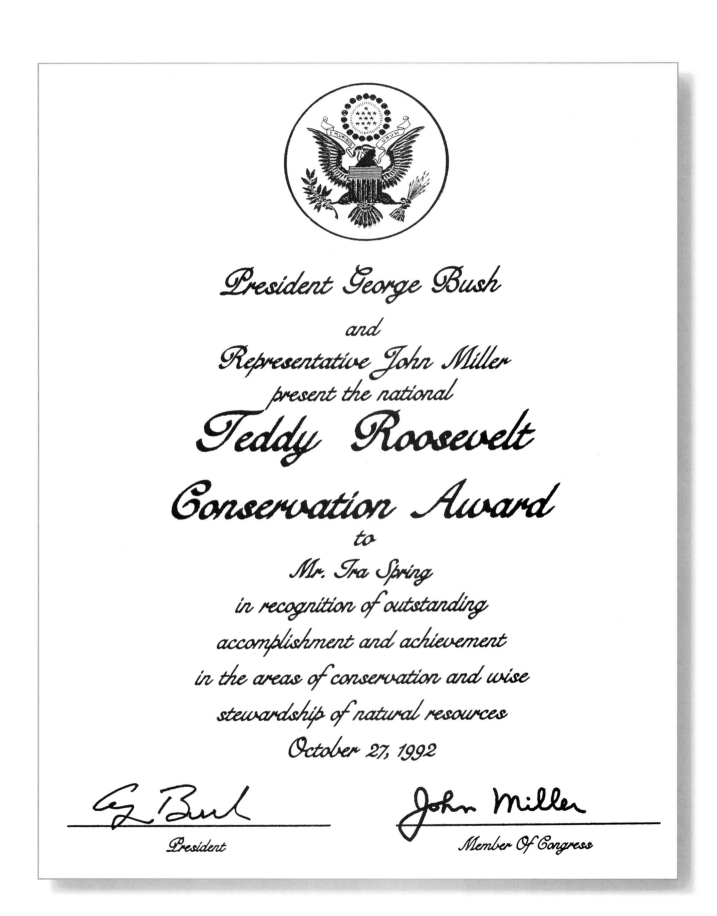

President George Bush
and
Representative John Miller
present the national

Teddy Roosevelt Conservation Award

to

Mr. Ira Spring

in recognition of outstanding
accomplishment and achievement
in the areas of conservation and wise
stewardship of natural resources

October 27, 1992

_____
President

_____
Member Of Congress

Appendix

or
The Shoe Gets on the Other Foot

November 18, to December 1, 1992

Congressman John Miller presented to Edmonds photographer Ira Spring the Theodore Roosevelt Conservation Award during ceremonies on November 5. (Photo by David Angiuli)

Edmonds Photographer one of 25 to receive conservation award
He's more interested in recreational use of forest

When Ira Spring told his father that he had been named as one of 25 persons in the country to receive the Theodore Roosevelt Conservation Award, his father was very excited.

The elder Spring, now 101 years old, once shook hands with Theodore Roosevelt and has been a lifelong admirer of the former President.

Congressman John Miller presented Spring with the award on behalf of President George Bush "in recognition of outstanding accomplishment and achievement in the areas of conservation and wise stewardship of natural resources."

Spring admits that he is a little puzzled by his selection for the honor, for he says he is "more interested in the recreational use of the forest than in saving it."

He quickly adds that he favors neither extremist view regarding natural resources—he obviously does not want to see the forests destroyed, but he also distances himself from those environmentalists he identifies as preservationists.

He strikes the middle ground between these two opposing views, favoring trails and campsites in the forests to enable hikers to get a closeup view of the country's natural resources.

His commitment to this view has led him to spend many volunteer hours lobbying with the Forest Service in Washington, D.C., for more and better maintained trails in the nation's wilderness areas.

Even though Spring may reluctant to admit it, the award appears to come in recognition of a lifetime spent promoting the outdoors.

Ira and his twin brother Bob received Brownie box cameras

when they were youngsters living in Shelton, and the pair began developing what became their lifetime careers.

The brothers have been fulltime professional photographers since 1946. For many years, they jointly produced the photographs appearing in various guidebooks and photo albums of Northwest scenes.

To be closer to the publishing centers in Seattle, the brothers moved to Edmonds more than 30 years ago. They chose Edmonds, Ira says, because at that time the area was sparsely settled. With all the recent growth, he jokes, "I don't know where we'll move next."

Several years ago, Bob Spring began devoting himself to travel photography and has moved to a spot near the SeaTac Airport. Ira, however, continues to hike and produce photographs of scenic

Newspaper release.

B ob and I have been featured in a number of magazines, sometimes the two of us together and sometimes by myself. I don't remember even a third of the occasions. I found in my files *U.S. Camera*, February 1951, *Argosy*, January 1953, *Outdoor Photography and Travel*, March 1991, and a nice plug in *Backpacker*, April 1993. As my concern for saving trails has grown, I have become more insistent that no story be written without telling my concerns for saving trails.

I was profiled in a book, *Cascade Voices Echo*, published in 1993. A number of newspapers have done stories, the *Daily Olympian*, January 29, 1989, *Seattle Post Intelligencer*, November 24, 1993, and *The Seattle Times*, also in 1993. The *Everett Herald* article was reused by *Longview Daily Times*, April 10, 1986, *Gazette Times*, January 22, 1989, *Daily Olympian* (again), January 5, 1994, and the *Saturday Everett Herald*, December 31, 1988.

Over the years Bob and I have received a few awards. In 1961 the Governor's Literary Award was given to Byron Fish, Bob, and me for *This Is Washington*. In 1970 the same award was given to Harvey Manning, Bob, and me for *Cool, Clear Water*, and again in

Teddy Roosevelt Conservation Award.

1986, to Harvey, The Mountaineers Books, and the whole Spring family (including Tom and Vicky) for our hiking guides.

In 1992 I was invited to the White House with twenty-three others to receive the Teddy Roosevelt Conservation Award for "outstanding accomplishment and achievement" in recognition of my work with trails. However, the invitation arrived just two days before the ceremony and I missed it. A month later, the award was presented to me with appropriate handshakes and fanfare by my local congressman.

Books by Bob and Ira Spring

Large Format Photo Books of the Northwest

1951 *High Adventure,* Superior Publishing Company
Photos: Bob and Ira Spring
Text: Norma and Patricia Spring

1959 *High Worlds of the Mountain Climber,* Superior Publishing Company
Photos: Bob and Ira Spring
Text: Harvey Manning

1961 *This Is Washington,* Superior Publishing Company
Photos: Bob and Ira Spring
Text: Byron Fish

1963 *Alaska,* Superior Publishing Company
Photos: Bob and Ira Spring
Text: Byron Fish

1969 *The North Cascades National Park,* Superior Publishing Company
Photos: Bob and Ira Spring
Text: Harvey Manning

1970 *Cool, Clear Water,* Superior Publishing Company
Photos: Bob and Ira Spring
Text: Harvey Manning

1975 *The South Cascades,* The Mountaineers
Photos: Bob and Ira Spring
Text: E. M. Sterling

1975 *Wildlife Encounters,* Superior Publishing Company
Photos: Bob and Ira Spring
Text: Ira Spring

1976 *National Parks of the Northwest,* Superior Publishing Company
Photos: Bob and Ira Spring
Text: Harvey Manning

Small Format Photo Books

1955 *Camera Adventuring on Mount Rainier,* Superior Publishing Company
Photos: Bob and Ira Spring
Text: Norma and Patricia Spring

1955 *Exploring Puget Sound,* Superior Publishing Company
Photos: Bob and Ira Spring
Text: Byron Fish

1956 *Exploring the Columbia River,* Superior Publishing Company
Photos: Bob and Ira Spring
Text: Byron Fish

1957 *Exploring Oregon,* Superior Publishing Company
Photos: Bob and Ira Spring
Text: Byron Fish

1981 *Lookouts: Firewatchers of the Cascades and Olympics,* The Mountaineers
Photos: Bob and Ira Spring
Text: Byron Fish

Travel Books

1970 *Roaming Russia,* Superior Publishing Company
Photos: Bob and Ira Spring
Text: Byron Fish

1970 *Alaska, The Complete Travel Book,* Macmillan Publishing Co.
Photos: Bob and Ira Spring
Text: Byron Fish

Children's School Books

1965 *Sigemi: A Japanese Village Girl,* Harcourt, Brace and World
Photos: Bob and Ira Spring
Text: Ruth Kirk

1966 *Japan,* Thomas Nelson & Sons
Photos: Bob and Ira Spring
Text: Ruth Kirk

1966 *Alaska,* Thomas Nelson & Sons
Photos: Bob and Ira Spring
Text: Norma Spring

1968 *Scandinavia,* Thomas Nelson & Sons
Photos: Bob and Ira Spring
Text: Harvey Edwards

1969 *Lars Olav: A Norwegian Boy,* Harcourt, Brace and World
Photos: Bob and Ira Spring
Text: Harvey Edwards

1970 *Leise: A Danish Girl,* Harcourt, Brace and World
Photos: Bob and Ira Spring
Text: Harvey Edwards

1971 *Eskimo Boy Today,* Alaska Northwest Publishing Company
Photos: Bob and Ira Spring
Text: Byron Fish

Outdoor Guides

1966 *100 Hikes in Western Washington,* The Mountaineers
Photos: Bob and Ira Spring
Text: Louise B. Marshall

1967 *Trips and Trails 1,* The Mountaineers
Photos: Bob and Ira Spring
Text: E. M. Sterling

1968 *Northwest Ski Trails,* The Mountaineers
Photos: Bob and Ira Spring
Text: Ted Mueller

1968 *Trips and Trails 2,* **The Mountaineers**
Photos: Bob and Ira Spring
Text: E. M. Sterling

1969 *50 Hikes in Mount Rainier National Park,* **The Mountaineers**
Photos: Bob and Ira Spring
Text: Ira Spring and Harvey Manning

1969 *Footloose Around Puget Sound,* **The Mountaineers**
Photos: Bob and Ira Spring
Text: Janice Krenmayr

1970 *Wildflowers of Mount Rainier and the Cascades,* **The Mount Rainier Natural History Association and The Mountaineers**
Photos: Bob and Ira Spring
Text: Mary Fries

1970 *101 Hikes in the North Cascades,* **The Mountaineers**
Photos: Bob and Ira Spring
Text: Ira Spring and Harvey Manning

1971 *102 Hikes in the Alpine Lakes, South Cascades and Olympics,* **The Mountaineers**
Photos: Bob and Ira Spring
Text: Ira Spring and Harvey Manning

1972 *Flowers of the Parks: Mount Rainier National Park, North Cascades National Park,* **Mount Rainier Natural History Association**
Photos: Bob and Ira Spring
Text: Jan Henderson

1972 *60 Unbeaten Paths,* **Superior Publishing Company**
Photos: Bob and Ira Spring
Text: Byron Fish

1974 *Wilderness Trails Northwest,* **The Touchstone Press and The Mountaineers**
Photos: Bob and Ira Spring
Text: Ira Spring and Harvey Manning

1976 *Cascade Companion,* **Pacific Search Books**
Photos: Bob and Ira Spring
Text: Susan Schwartz

1976 *Wildlife Areas of Washington,* **Superior Publishing Company**
Photos: Bob and Ira Spring
Text: Susan Schwartz

1977 *Footsore 1,* **The Mountaineers**
 Photos: Bob and Ira Spring
Text: Harvey Manning

1978 *Rocky Mountain Wildflowers,* **The Mountaineers**
Photos: Bob and Ira Spring
Text: Ronald J. Taylor

1978 *Footsore 2,* **The Mountaineers**
Photos: Bob and Ira Spring
Text: Harvey Manning

1978 *Oregon Wildlife Areas,* **Superior Publishing Company**
Photos: Bob and Ira Spring
Text: Ira Spring, edited by Harvey Manning

1979 *100 Hikes in the Alps,* The Mountaineers
Photos: Bob and Ira Spring
Text: Harvey Edwards

1979 *Footsore 3,* The Mountaineers
Photos: Bob and Ira Spring
Text: Harvey Manning

1979 *Footsore 4,* The Mountaineers
Photos: Bob and Ira Spring, Vicky Spring
Text: Harvey Manning

1979 *Mountain Flowers,* The Mountaineers
Photos: Bob and Ira Spring
Text: Harvey Manning

1981 *Northwest Outdoor Guide,* The Writing Works
Photos: Bob and Ira Spring
Text: Harvey Manning

1983 *Nature in the Northwest,* Prentice-Hall, Inc.
Photos: Bob and Ira Spring
Text: Susan Schwartz

1985 *Oregon Coast Hikes,* The Mountaineers
Photos: Bob and Ira Spring
Text: Paul M. Williams

1985 *100 Hikes in the North Cascades,* The Mountaineers
Photos: Bob and Ira Spring
Text: Ira Spring and Harvey Manning

1985 *100 Hikes in the South Cascades and Olympics,* The Mountaineers
Photos: Bob and Ira Spring
Text: Ira Spring and Harvey Manning

1988 *100 Hikes in the Glacier Peak Region,* The Mountaineers
Photos: Bob and Ira Spring
Text: Ira Spring and Harvey Manning

1988 *Best Hikes With Children in Western Washington and the Cascades, Volume 1,* The Mountaineers
Photos: Bob and Ira Spring
Text: Joan Burton

1990 *55 Hikes in Central Washington,* The Mountaineers
Photos: Bob and Ira Spring
Text: Harvey Manning

1991 *Hiking the Great Northwest,* The Mountaineers
Photos: Bob and Ira Spring, Vicky Spring
Text: Ira Spring, Harvey Manning, and Vicky Spring

1992 *Best Hikes With Children in Western Washington and the Cascades, Volume 2,* The Mountaineers
Photos: Bob and Ira Spring
Text: Joan Burton

1993 *Hiking the Mountains to Sound Greenway,* The Mountaineers
Photos: Bob and Ira Spring
Text: Harvey Manning

1995 *Walks and Hikes on the Beaches around Puget Sound,* The Mountaineers
Photos: Bob and Ira Spring
Text: Harvey Manning

1995 *Walks and Hikes in the Foothills and Lowlands around Puget Sound,* The Mountaineers
Photos: Bob and Ira Spring
Text: Harvey Manning

1995 *Washington's South Cascades' Volcanic Landscape,* The Mountaineers
Photos: Bob and Ira Spring
Text: Marge and Ted Mueller

1995 *Best Short Hikes in Washington's South Cascades and Olympics,* The Mountaineers
Photos: Bob and Ira Spring
Text: E. M. Sterling

1995 *Best Short Hikes in Washington's North Cascades and San Juan Islands,* The Mountaineers
Photos: Bob and Ira Spring
Text: E. M. Sterling

KIRKENDALL/SPRING BOOKS

1982 *95 Hikes in the Canadian Rockies,* The Mountaineers
Photos: Vicky Spring
Text: Gordon King

1983 *95 Hikes in the Northern Canadian Rockies,* The Mountaineers
Photos: Vicky Spring
Text: Dee Urbick

1983 *Cross-Country Ski Trails,* The Mountaineers
Photos: Kirkendall/Spring
Text: Kirkendall/Spring

1984 *Bicycling the Pacific Coast,* The Mountaineers
Photos: Kirkendall/Spring
Text: Tom Kirkendall and Vicky Spring

1985 *100 Hikes in the Alpine Lakes,* The Mountaineers
Photos: Ira Spring and Kirkendall/Spring
Text: Vicky Spring, Ira Spring, and Harvey Manning

1988 *Cross-Country Ski Tours 1: Washington's South Cascades and Olympics,* The Mountaineers
Photos: Kirkendall/Spring
Text: Tom Kirkendall and Vicky Spring

1988 *Cross-Country Ski Tours 2: Washington's North Cascades,* The Mountaineers
Photos: Kirkendall/Spring
Text: Tom Kirkendall and Vicky Spring

1989 *Mountain Bike Adventures in Washington's South Cascades and Puget Sound,* The Mountaineers
Photos: Kirkendall/Spring
Text: Tom Kirkendall

1989 *Mountain Bike Adventures in Washington's North Cascades and Olympics,* **The Mountaineers**
Photos: Kirkendall/Spring
Text: Tom Kirkendall

1994 *Glacier National Park and Waterton Lakes National Park,* **The Mountaineers**
Photos: Kirkendall/Spring
Text: Vicky Spring

1994 *Exploring Washington's Wild Areas,* **The Mountaineers**
Photos: Kirkendall/Spring
Text: Marge and Ted Mueller

1995 *100 Hikes in California's Central Sierra and Coast Range,* **The Mountaineers**
Photos: Kirkendall/Spring
Text: Vicky Spring

1998 *An Outdoor Family Guide to Washington's National Parks,* **The Mountaineers**
Photos: Kirkendall/Spring
Text: Vicky Spring and Tom Kirkendall